SPACES IN HER DAY

SPACES IN HER DAY

Australian Women's Diaries of
the 1920s and 1930s

Katie Holmes

ALLEN & UNWIN

Portions of this book have been published in *Australian Feminist Studies; Australian Historical Studies; Lilith; Wallflowers and Witches* (ed.) Maryanne Dever; *The Woman Question* (ed.) Barbara Caine.

First published in 1995 by
Allen & Unwin Australia Pty Ltd
9 Atchison Street, St Leonards, NSW 2065 Australia

National Library of Australia
Cataloguing-in-Publication entry:

Holmes, Katie.
    Spaces in her day: Australian women's diaries of the
    1920s and 1930s.

    Bibliography.
    Includes index.
    ISBN 1 86373 731 6.

    1. Women—Australia—Biography. 2. Women—Australia—
    Socialization. 3. Women—Australia—Diaries. 4. Women—
    Australia—Historiography. I. Title.

305.4092294

Set in 11/12 pt Palatino by DOCUPRO, Sydney
Printed by SRM Production Services Sdn Bhd, Malaysia

10 9 8 7 6 5 4 3 2 1

The cover painting is *Sunlit Interior* (1932) by Vida Lahey, Australia, 1882–1968 and reproduced by permission of the Lahey family, Brisbane.

Index: Geraldine Suter

Contents

For my mother, Bobbie Holmes
the source of my inspiration

Acknowledgments

This book has been made possible by the generous access I was given to a number of diaries and photographs in private collections. In particular I thank Marie Bell, Grace Buchanan, Dulcie Brooke, Frank Duggan, Mandy Gilbert, Dorothy Irving, Dorothy McHardy, Sue Robertson, and Noel Watkins. The staff at the LaTrobe Library, State Library of Victoria, especially manuscripts librarians Tony Marshall, Anne Cahir, and Jock Murphy, have also been very responsive to my search for material, alerting me to diaries I would otherwise have missed and chasing up copyright permissions to read and further biographical details as I required them.

I began this study as a PhD thesis in the History department at the University of Melbourne with the support of an Australian Postgraduate Research Award and completed it during a year of teaching at the Australian National University. In both institutions I benefited from discussions with my colleagues and students. Ian Britain's careful guidance, ready engagement with my project, expert editorial advice and attention to detail and argument, were always accompanied by support and enthusiasm. Donna Merwick also offered invaluable guidance and advice, assisting me to clarify my focus and strengthen my theoretical insights. My thanks to each of them.

My personal debts are many and heartfelt. Joy Damousi has been an unfailing source of inspiration, patience, support, laughter and critique throughout all the phases of this project. She also possesses an extraordinary bibliographical knowledge which she generously shared. My debt to her is deep. David Goodman,

Penny Russell and Julie Wells also read drafts of my chapters, challenged me to sharpen my argument and broaden my analysis, and provided encouragement and humour along the way. I thank them. Patricia Grimshaw fuelled my early interest in feminist history and, with Marilyn Lake and Susan Magarey, continues to challenge me to explore the relationships between history, theory and feminism. My work is richer for their teaching and inspiration. Doug Craig's detailed suggestions proved invaluable as I undertook the task of converting the thesis into a book. The generous counsel and friendship of Pat Boyle and Sue Rickard were equally invaluable during this final process, while Maree Beer's proofreading was a godsend. At Allen & Unwin, Annette Barlow and Elizabeth Weiss remained enthusiastic and patient while I negotiated lengthy copyright problems. Bob Reynolds' final proofreading was characteristically efficient and astute. My thanks. The intellectual and emotional support of other friends and colleagues sustained me throughout: Gaynor Blankley, Paul Collins, Jenny Dawson, Garry Disher, Lucy Healey, Vivien Holmes, Pete Langmead, Barbara Semler, Stephen Ward, Richard White, Wayne Wescott. Gail Jones and Bruce Newport shared with me their wisdom and insights and ensured that this was more than an intellectual journey. My parents, Hal and Bobbie Holmes, remain a constant source of love and support.

Preface

In 1987 I began researching unpublished Australian women's diaries for my PhD thesis. Diaries had long fascinated me, and once absorbed in my research I began to reflect on where such interest had come from. I wrote a few lines by way of introduction:

> She [my mother] used to sit at a desk to write, any desk at first: later she would have her own desk, and eventually her own room. Until then her diary was her room. Its contents were always a mystery to me. They still are. I always felt my mother used her diary to record those things she couldn't tell—couldn't tell anyone, couldn't tell me.
>
> I have long wanted to know what she wrote in it. Sitting at her desk, she would get a look on her face that I interpreted to mean 'Do not disturb'. The time, like the book, was private and not for sharing.

Excluded from my mother's diary, I sought those of other women. I was looking for women's stories. How did women make sense of their lives? What were the metaphors and meanings women constructed through which to articulate their daily experience? Given the model of my mother and my own sporadic periods of diary writing, I assumed that women used their diaries to explore their emotions and how they felt about their lives and daily experiences. It was through women's diaries, I felt, that as an historian I might come closest to understanding the way women of the past negotiated their lives.

I did not find what I had expected. Many women gave no space at all to their emotional lives, and disclosed no secrets about their private thoughts, feelings or actions. Rather, they filled their pages with insistent domestic detail—washing, ironing, cleaning, cooking, childcare—devoid, it seemed to me then, of metaphor or meaning. What I confronted was a tension between what I thought a diary was and what my writers thought it was. I did not find their 'private' worlds waiting for me to analyse. And I realised I was not going to discover my mother, nor myself, by reading other women's diaries! I did realise, however, that these women were writing for a reason: the fact that they were not writing what I had expected suggested that I needed to reframe my questions and rethink my assumptions. What was concealed behind the seemingly petty details of their daily lives? What clues could I find by examining the nature of the genre? As I learned to listen to the silences in their writing, to the rhythms and patterns of the writers' daily lives and all that they revealed through the structure of their words, I began to realise that the material before me was in fact rich and varied and fresh.

I grew to delight in the lists of domestic chores with which Mabel Lincoln filled her day, and to laugh with her over her failed diet attempts: 'I started dieting again this morning. I start every morning and break out every night.' I wept with Una Falkiner at the death of her baby daughter and railed against the treatment she received at the hands of her husband Otway. Fanny Barbour's recording of her life with her alcoholic husband is tinged with sadness, while Kathleen Hughes's sucessful romances bring the joys of love and desire into focus. The failure of Dorothy Kendall's romantic dreams tell a different story. Ida Dawson's diaries offered unimagined riches: her recording of life as a single woman fills volumes. They are packed with insights into family life and the adventures of a woman willing to travel (and forced to do so through economic necessity), and reveal a developing—and frustrated—literary talent.

As I became more absorbed in the diaries I discovered that women did not simply write a record of their days. They could use the diary as a place of resistance to dominant prescriptions on women's lives, or, alternatively, as a place of rapprochement or accommodation, where the conflicting and contradictory demands on women could be integrated. The very process of writing in this form gave women the space in which to define their own lives and to shape their identities.

My main interest in diary writing therefore lies in the very fabric of the text, in the renderings of 'dailiness'. This book explores the connections between what white, middle-class women wrote about in their diaries, and contemporary discussions about sexuality, the body, work, relationships, motherhood, and ageing. It also considers the gendered nature of time and space as an alternative way of exploring women's relationship to their environment, their work and their bodies. In doing so, it places the lives and writings of women not previously regarded as important at the centre of historical analysis. Diary writing, as Virginia Woolf reminds us (Diary, 20 January 1919), was hardly considered to be 'writing', even by most diary writers themselves. Thus Dorothy Kendall noted, 'I would like to try and write but think I would get stuck over the dialogue.' The fact that she, and many others with her, did write, at length and in great detail, is something to be grateful for. Through the drifting material of their lives, we can trace the conflicts, desires and hopes of women for whom the literary world has held no place, and to whom history has offered a marginal, barely recognised existence.

Introduction

In writing a diary a woman shaped her day, her week, her life. From the language and meanings available to her, she constructed her world. This book uses women's diaries to explore the ways women made sense of their lives and the ways they incorporated and lived out—or, in some cases, resisted—social prescriptions for their life and work. It addresses a number of related questions. In what ways were their experiences and the meanings they gave to them historically specific? What guided their self-inscriptions, what 'webs of significance' patterned their daily life? How do we isolate the ways class, age and place shaped the experiences and possibilities available to women? And if we begin to glimpse answers to these questions, how do they change our vision of the past and challenge the historical project? Does understanding women's subjectivity change the ways in which we conceive of the past?

Diaries are a quintessentially personal form of writing. In using them to study the lives of white women in Australia during the 1920s and 1930s I break away from the customary historical approaches to this period, studies which have stressed social, economic and political developments of national and international significance as the keys to understanding the past. Such developments provide an important backdrop to the material studied here, for it was within a specific historical context that these women lived and wrote. Diaries, however, bring into focus the dailiness of life and challenge the usual criteria of historical significance. Many are full of the smallest and largest details of a woman's life. They insist that the individual consciousness matters, thereby inverting traditional hierarchies of importance. To study women's daily life involves giving priority to the seemingly insignificant things that absorbed their time. It also requires rethinking the traditional separation of 'public' and 'private' spheres. The diary is situated at the intersection between women's personal lives and public discourses. It is an expression of their agency and provides us with an insight into the ways women felt, acted, and understood their world. To understand diaries we must look at the connections between what women wrote about, and the language they could use to articulate their experiences. Diaries do not just speak for themselves. We need to place in context the language in which women wrote of their lives, and understand the ways the diary as a genre could itself shape a writer's construction of herself. In the 1920s and 1930s there was a range of possibilities for the meanings of 'woman', depending on age, race and class. All, however, were arranged around relations of gender and power, and it was within this paradigm that women in turn inscribed their sense of self. The diary writing itself was a means of ordering experience and establishing control over one's life.

Genre

Diaries come in many forms and arise from many different motivations. They are full of the daily experiences of life and can move freely between the commonplace and the extraordinary. The diaries in this book are not intensely self-reflective, nor is their stated aim self-knowledge, although this may be an outcome for habitual diary keepers. 'Rough' and 'ungrammatical'[1] are more typical features of the diaries I study than refinement and lucidity. Yet in their stumblings, their timidity, their simplicity and their relentless, even indiscriminate recording of daily life, they capture the art of the everyday.[2] The weather, the shopping, the housework, the mail, are all compressed into entries which reveal the fabric of the writer's daily existence. As Dure Gillikin writes, diary writing 'is the vast world made manageable' through 'fragments that contain the whole'.[3]

The form of diary a writer chooses varies. Some move constantly between seemingly detached observations on world events and notes of more personal reflection. At times the two are indistinguishable. When Ida Dawson wrote in the early years of the Depression, 'there does not seem to be any opening for women in the present depressed state of the country' (19 May 1931), she was commenting on the state of the economy and facing her own limited employment opportunities.

Who wrote diaries and to whom did they address them? Diary writers were generally middle to upper class: women who possessed a sense of themselves and had the time, means and literacy to write.[4] Working-class women have continued to be bound by limitations on their education and leisure time: the double reality of their lives as both women and members of the working class has not, on the whole, been conducive to developing a sense of their life as significant enough to preserve in writing. Their modes of communication have been oral more than literary. Similarly, during a period of genocide, Aboriginal women were more concerned with the survival of their race than with western forms of individual self-preservation. The women in this book shared a literary tradition, and their sense of the future included a belief that their life was important or interesting enough to record.

Diaries communicate their writer's life. It may be that the envisaged reader was the writer at a later date, or members of her immediate family. Others may have perceived a wider field from which to draw their audience. Dorothy Kendall allowed her close friend Sheilagh to read her diary soon after she resumed writing it. It was a move she had some regrets about: 'S.D.P read this diary. I didn't think of a few nasty things I've got about her written in unpleasant moments and I think they hurt' (24 January 1932). Dorothy enjoyed reading her own diaries, and wished, after indulging in the recollection of past days, that she had not stopped writing. She also had some regard for her diary-writing abilities: 'Spent evening going through writing case reading over some old school-days diaries—its marvellous the way you can recapture the old atmosphere from them' (3 August 1935). Una Falkiner was in no doubt that her diary would attract a future readership, and she also read over the numerous volumes, taking notes from them for her memoirs. Next to one entry she put an asterisk with the addition: 'It might be interesting for any concerned who reads this to know that the house boy went mad and was mad!' (8 May 1924). I suspect Una considered her diary writing as an activity suited to her class and station in life. Diary writing was a part of her duty—'I have just sent my self back to my duty by writing my diary till 1st Nov' (12 November 1920)—and she ensured that the family records would be preserved for future historians. Mabel Lincoln's motives in keeping her diary are less immediately apparent. She also considered it in some way a duty, noting on one occasion that writing her diary was to be 'my first duty this morning' (3 September 1930). However, she often struggled to keep her diary up to date and frequently wrote after the date concerned: 'Well here we are again Tuesday 18th I do think I must give up keeping a diary I am always so far behind' (12 October 1932). She continued writing, however, and found a special place in which to hold her yearly books: 'Rise late this morning put a new cover on the old music stool and park my diaries in it' (19 March 1932). Mabel considered her diaries worthy of their own home, and a refurbished one at that. She did not reveal where the music stool was and we may wonder at its accessibility to other prying eyes: nothing is more tantalising to inquisitive minds than a forbidden diary. She may, of course, have stitched the stool up. Yet no matter how 'private' or secret a diary might appear, its writer had hopes for its future: it was an act of faith in herself, a belief that her life may last beyond the given moment. As the writer and critic of diaries, Thomas Mallon, confidently asserts to all diary writers, 'an audience will turn up. In fact you're counting on it. Someone will be reading and you'll be talking. And if you're talking, it means you're alive.'[5]

Women envisaged different audiences for their diaries, and inevitably shaped the accounts of their lives according to their perceived readership. A diarist chose the material from which to create her persona, adjusting, accentuating, defining as she desired. The imagined audience was crucial to this process and could assume different roles: friend, mother, confessor, God.[6] While it may be difficult to guess at the audience the writer imagined for herself, surmising can be important. Una Falkiner was a regular diner at Government House when in either Melbourne or Sydney, and she made a special note of one occasion for wives only: 'we all enjoyed a most delicious dinner & the fun was great & there was no need to keep up a conversation one perhaps felt no interest in' (26 September 1922). On another occasion when she was at home on their property, the men were all away and the women had 'a lovely manless time'. The following day the men returned, and Una wrote, 'so once more we repair to decent legs of mutton & soups & gentil [sic] lady like conversation: attired modestly as becomes our stations' (25 July 1920). In Una's descriptions of herself as the obedient wife, and often even in her recounting of daily events, she created a persona that conformed to the dominant expectations. As Una moved between seeing herself as the subject and as the object of her text, the sex of her imagined audience often also changed.

Women wrote diaries for reasons as numerous as the diaries

themselves, although they rarely disclosed motives. Mary Bicknell (née Clarke) was an exception. She began her diary as a young woman living on a farm near Bendigo in central Victoria, in August 1894:

> My name is Mary Clarke, my age 23. My life has hitherto been rather uneventful, but what I now consider a great event is about to happen. My dear friend and sister Anne is going away to Bendigo, and during her absence I will keep a Diary and Annie will keep one also, so that when she returns we can compare notes and see how we have progressed. We are both hoping for the happiness of one day being able to say we are servants of God. (15 August 1895)

Mary's reader may be forgiven for expecting her diary to chart her religious pilgrimage and to reflect a constant striving to better herself in the eyes of God. Despite her stated purpose, Mary was more interested in recording the daily happenings on the family farm, the visitors who called and occasional comments on the general mood at home: 'Everybody was cross today, scolding and arguing and I have got a cold' (25 August 1894). What remains of this early diary ends four months later. If Mary continued writing her diary, the volumes have not survived, but when we meet her again, at the age of 53, her chronicle of farm life is a well-established form. What began as a specific record for her sister has become a habit. For many diarists, this itch to record provides the necessary incentive to keep a regular diary: details of daily life are jotted down as a record of existence and in a desire for self-expression. Diaries are also a means of making sense of the world, of imposing order on a day and a world which may otherwise seem to be without shape or structure. A diarist translates her experience into words and images, narratives which tell of her way of being.

Interest in women's diaries has grown in recent years as feminist historians have begun reconstructing the lives of women in the past. Despite this growing interest, however, little critical attention has been given to the diary as an artefact or as a genre, or to questions of the relationship between gender and genre. Only very recently have some feminist critics turned their attention to the literary status of women's diaries and begun thematic studies of diary writing. Harriet Blodgett considers the diary an art form, 'literature subjectively interpreting life'.[7] In her study of published diaries across several centuries she discovered striking similarities in sentiment and content. Her emphasis is on the common threads running through the diaries, rather than on the way historical circumstances shaped their content or on the variety of female experience. It is an approach both upheld and questioned by the material she discusses. Diaries of literate women of the middle and upper classes will inevitably reveal common experiences: marriage, maternity, ageing, relationships with family members. Exploring the differences between the diaries, in their language, their form, or their developing sense of self, will, however, suggest and reflect changes in historical circumstances and the range of ways in which women could view and interpret their lives.

Diary writing has long been one of the few forms of writing available to women who sought to articulate their experiences in any enduring way. Some critics have seen it as a form particularly suited to the fragmented, interrupted and cyclical nature of women's lives.[8] But, as Harriet Blodgett rightly points out, the suitability of the diary form to women's lives does not make it an inherently female form, simply a characteristic one.[9] Men also have a significant tradition of diary writing. We cannot explain the abundance of women diary writers in the twentieth century merely by assuming that fragmentary lives are better suited to fragmentary forms of writing. Margo Culley argues that the idea of the diary as a place for private thoughts and feelings developed during the last 100 years. It coincided with the feminisation of the domestic sphere—the allocation of personal reflection and emotion to the 'private' domain and thus the realm of women. The diary became bound up with notions of privacy and the inner life. Given women's general lack of access to other forms of writing, and the pressure on them to be selfsacrificing and to attend constantly to the needs of others, the diary was one of the few places where women were allowed to be self-centred.[10] Whether this makes the diary entirely a 'private' world is another assumption that needs testing.

Diaries do not reveal to us a unified, coherent sense of the writer's self. Just as we see a life in process, so do we also discover a shifting sense of the writer's identity. Diaries are a form of autobiography, for centuries the only autobiographical genre in which women have been allowed to engage. Diaries, of course, do not attempt the retrospective view characteristic of autobiography but, like letters, they are a form of literary self-representation. Letters, however, are generally a form of communication and dialogue with an immediate and known audience. Linda Anderson argues that diaries offer women a place to lay claim to writing. They are potentially a space of defiance, of freedom, validation and acceptance.[11] In writing about their lives, women took the time to record the things that were important to them. They wrote about their work, their children, their relationships, their social activities, and events happening in the world. They asserted the worth of their lives within a culture which rated women's ideas, thoughts and work as peripheral. In an unself-conscious subversion/inversion of masculinist notions of 'great events' in history, the 'great event' which marked the commencement of Mary Clarke's diary was the departure of her sister for the nearby town of Bendigo. Mary continued to record in her diary the significant events of her daily life. Women who wrote diaries claimed a right which had been denied them elsewhere: they named the things that were important to them and they named, gave priority to, and at times even celebrated, the activities of the domestic sphere. They still, however, had no power to influence the public valuing of those activities. Thus the significance of the diary differs for women and men. In women's hands, it becomes a rare space in which to explore identity and self without fear of immediate censorship. Considered in this way, diaries can be read as an attempt by women to empower themselves, albeit within the existing structures of power and gender relations.

As we shall see, the women whose diaries are studied here frequently challenged the prevailing models of gender relations while retaining a conservative political outlook. Their challenges were rarely defiant, yet implicitly, and at times explicitly, they highlighted the dynamics of power operating in heterosexual relations and occasionally attempted to openly subvert them, constructed their lives outside the dominant heterosexual discourses or revealed the conflicts they experienced in attempting to live out the prescriptions for femininity and the 'good woman'. Una Falkiner, for example, recounted the 'wives only' dinner at Government House where women did not have to feign interest in male conversation. While writing a diary did not appear to challenge women's traditional roles as wife, mother, daughter or household manager, in doing so women accorded to these activities a status otherwise denied them. And a few constructed alternative representations of themselves. Diary writers recorded what was essentially transitory and so gave it permanence. Such a use of this seemingly private genre reveals the complex relationship with time and space in which the diary existed. As the private became public, so the transitory achieved prominence. The diary inscribed a present between the past and future.[12]

Time and space

Diaries chart and preserve time. They hold a record of the days, months and years of their writer's existence. Diaries also play with time, sometimes even consciously, in an attempt to create dramatic or literary effect. They capture the moments and fix them in what becomes a continuous present. The writer's relationship to the time she records is ever shifting. As writers return to their previous entries, their understanding of them changes, mediated by intervening events. Diaries become a repository of memory,[13] and for some the temptation to add or change things is often too great to resist.

Attention to the nature of time in diaries, and women's attempts to chart their days, reveals many different aspects of time, and its gendered nature. By virtue of their bodily functions and the nature and place of their work, women have different and at times conflicting expressions and understandings of temporality. How do they cope with these different senses of time? For women living in the twentieth century, the impact of these competing pressures has been complex. As technology and labour-saving devices made inroads into the home, potentially freeing women from hours of drudgery, so the expected standards of domestic management increased and their hours became consumed by more exacting routines. Growing knowledge of birth control paralleled changes in the ideology of motherhood, placing greater significance on the child's psychological and emotional development and thus increasing the burden of responsibility on the mother. Many of these changes had begun before the First World War, but the interwar years in Australia saw a crystallisation of their development and a more widespread implementation of their imperatives.

The modern, western model of time is one of linear progression. Time moves on, as the cliché has it, at an uninterrupted and steady rate. The cause-and-effect model of so much of our historical understanding is premised on this secure fact. Historians have also held to the assumption that industrialisation accompanied and facilitated the ordering of life around clock time: the clock, not the steam engine, held the key to the machine age.[14] With the development of the clock, time became a commodity, it could be saved, should be used gainfully and was the property of individuals. Time imposed its rhythm and its tyranny. This change in perceptions of time affected activity both in and out of the workplace, to the point where, as E.P. Thompson argues, 'mature, industrial societies of all varieties are marked by time-thrift and by a clear demarcation between "work" and "life"'.[15]

In general, historians have perceived time as an objective, progressive and unified reality. Graeme Davison's recent book, *The Unforgiving Minute*, examines this assumption by exploring the way Australians learned to tell the time and the social transformation which accompanied increases in the precision of time measurement.[16] Disciplines other than history have been more alert to different temporal realities, suggesting a multiplicity of ways in which we experience time. Anthropologists and sociologists have considered the ways in which the understanding and experience of time differ not only between societies, but also within social groups. The experience of time is 'necessarily social and subjective'.[17]

The experience of time, like that of space, is gendered. In beginning to explore women's experiences of time, feminists have realised that linear or even plural temporal models which do not allow for differences between men and women obscure large parts of women's experiences.[18] What theoretical and practical difference does women's lived experience make to the way time is articulated and understood? It is too simple to argue that men only experience time as linear and progressive, while women's time is linked to their biological rhythms. Men also share different experiences of emotional and social time, which can be linked to the natural rhythms of the seasons. It is not sufficient, either, to speak simply of women's time as deterministically linked to her reproductive cycle. In affirming women's *difference* from men, particularly biological difference, there is a danger of ignoring the ways in which women have been constructed as different, the ways in which a patriarchal society has used women's biology to determine their destiny. We must see the historical process involved, tracing the ways in which, at any given point, women's bodies are fashioned and their biological possibilities conceived and constrained. And so in exploring the ways in which a woman's capacity for birth and how her cycles of menstruation, motherhood, lactation and menopause affected her daily experience of time, we must be attuned to the historical specificity of her life as well as giving those cycles historical significance.

Different understandings of time impinged upon women's lives in immediate and often contradictory ways. Women's time has had to adjust to the demands of industrial forces and domestic pressures. In Margaret Conrad's words, women's time was usually 'reckoned through the prism of the family'.[19] Women's diaries reveal not only this rich texture of daily life, but also the points at which their time intersects with broader historical forces and the ways in which their daily realities are affected by events such as economic depression, war, drought, fire and so on.

Throughout this book I use three different conceptions of time—industrial, domestic, and biological—as a way of distinguishing between differing demands upon women's use of their days. In doing so I hope to understand common experiences as well as retain the individual life rhythms. By industrial time, I mean time as linear and progressive and governed by the clock—the sense which informs capitalist notions of time management and efficiency. Industrial time is the dominant public time and governs the experience of time outside the home. By virtue of men's participation in capitalist modes of production, it most immediately affected urban men's daily experience of time and was also very significant in the lives of working-class women. Industrial time also had a direct impact on the domestic world. Domestic time is not nearly so easily regulated. By definition, it was determined by the space women occupied—the domestic sphere—and was strongly influenced by contemporary discussions of that environment. It was, of necessity, subject to immediate and conflicting demands and integral to family time. By biological time I mean women's monthly cycle of menstruation, interrupted by periods of pregnancy, childbirth and lactation, as well as the life rhythm of menstruation, menopause, ageing and death. There is a fourth category of time that I touch upon here: that of individual time, used to suggest time as represented by women in their diaries: the time of events, and of daily life. It is not a simple category, but is specific to gender and class, and even more personal than that, subject to an individual's idiosyncrasies. Diary writers, in capturing all these different expressions of time, revealed a further sense of time and indeed challenged the process of separating time into distinct categories. All become linked within the pages of a diary. No particular form of time is privileged in the recording of a day, indeed the moments at which a diarist selects what she will record produce an ever-shifting hierarchy of importance. In this sense the diary contains its own sense of time, what Judy Nolte Lensink calls 'diary time': 'giving a full page to a lover's single sentence, while describing fourteen hours of the day with the single telling phrase, "did usual work"'.[20]

The experience of time cannot be separated from the space in which it is lived. Like time, space is also gendered. Feminist scholars have paid more attention to ideas about women's spatial environments than their temporal ones. The idea of a separate 'sphere' has been treated both metaphorically and descriptively, to denote a separate space in which women lived, but one constructed by a complex ideology and structured by gender, class and race.[21]

To speak of gendered space immediately raises the notions of 'separate spheres', public and private worlds. The image of separate spheres embodies a nineteenth-century view about the separation of the domestic world from the world of industry and commerce. Within the domestic sphere, the bourgeois, private family was enshrined. The home was the refuge from the public world; against the sentiment and femininity of the home stood the reason and masculinity of the public sphere. In the terminology of the nineteenth century, there is an impasse between the public and the private, production and reproduction, morality and market forces, emotion and rationality.

Deconstructing these oppositions is a task to which many feminists have turned their attention. Reconceptualising the meanings of public and private has forced us to be specific in their use. This book draws attention to the spaces women occupy, and the shifting definitions of those spaces. My concern here is to highlight the intersections women encountered between the two supposedly separate spheres. In particular I look at their workplaces, their homes, their gardens, their bodies and their diaries. The variety of 'private' spaces a woman might encounter were experienced, expressed and understood in relation to public constructions of them. Her experience of her body, for example, was influenced by notions of social production, sexuality, power, and bore the inscriptions of class, race, geographical place, and time.

Developments in Australia between the wars provoked considerable discussion about the use of time and space. The sense that the First World War had changed the world forever was pervasive in the early 1920s. Greenwich Mean Time, the aeroplane, the motor car, electricity, the telegraph and the telephone all affected people's perceptions of both space and time. As the artist Anne Dangar wrote in 1929, 'our period stands for life run by machinery, by mathematical accuracy, by scientific law and order'.[22]

This changing perception and experience of time and space can be discerned in the pages of women's diaries, where we can also trace the major social and political events of the interwar years. Charting the historical period during which these diarists lived raises another useful category of time, 'historian's time', which customarily relies on a conventional chronological narrative to sketch specific developments and events. It provides a frame for the specific, individual experiences of the interwar years. This book does not set out to provide a chronological account of those years, although it does allude to many of the developments which affected the lives of the women studied here. Women experienced these events in differing ways and at varying times of their lives. As Drusilla Modjeska notes, '[h]istory does not move in straight lines, it is fractured and runs off at tangents. The temptation is to talk as if the chronology went somewhere, and changes have clear derivations and destinations.'[23] Women did not write their diaries as stories with clear beginnings and endings. Rather, each recorded a life in process: a pattern of repeated events and rhythms with unpredicted and unpredictable disruptions. In the three Life Cycles sections, 'Youth', 'Marriage to motherhood', and 'Ageing and death', which frame discussions of women's work and relationships, I explore the ways in which the stages of women's life cycles were constructed, their experience of such stages and the language they used to describe their lived realities. The sections also draw attention to the changing interpretations of time and their effects on experiences of sexuality, maternity, motherhood and ageing. The focus in 'Youth' is on the changing constructions of femininity and sexuality during the 1920s and 1930s, and their implications for young women's relationships with men, with their bodies and with their leisure time. I also explore some of the tensions between the prescriptive ideals held up for them to emulate, and the daily unfoldings of their lives. In 'Marriage to motherhood' I look at the changes women were expected to undergo in their transformation into wives and mothers. The domestic science movement espoused strict guidelines for the management of home and family, and increasingly sought to regulate women's cycles of birth and lactation to accord with the principles of efficient time management. 'Ageing and death' completes the life cycle and focuses on women's attempts to come to terms with their ageing bodies in a society where youthfulness and maternity were considered the ingredients for successful femininity, and which denied a positive place to the ageing woman. The experience of modernity is a concern that runs throughout these sections, especially in relation to women's struggles to negotiate the meanings of 'the modern woman' in their daily lives. The intervening chapters on work and relationships focus on two of the major themes of the diaries. 'Working lives' looks at women's workplaces, their experiences of time within them, their feelings about their work and, at least for single women in paid employment, their difficulty in finding a language with which to express themselves as working women. The focus in the chapter 'Relating women' is more obviously on the emotional fabric of women's daily lives. I deal with the impact of unequal gender relations on women's emotional lives: as lovers and wives in hierarchical relationships with men, as daughters in a family structure, and as friends in a heterosexual society which was creating ever-narrower boundaries for 'acceptable' levels of friendship between women.

In my accounts of the diarists I aim to elucidate the ways in which women made sense of their lives, and the influences which shaped both their days and their inscribing of them. Diary writing was a significant activity for all these women, a means of valuing their experiences. In their diaries they struggled to integrate competing and conflicting prescriptions of womanhood into their lives. The diary both framed the chronological pattern of a woman's life and provided a place where she could subvert it. It marked a space in her day, a retreat from the pressing demands upon her time. In it, she attempted to make her 'walking shadow' permanent, insisting that her hour upon the stage could last forever, her tale signify something and be of some interest to someone.

Cast

On 31 December 1925, Ida Dawson, aged 46, changed her method of diary writing, a habit she had commenced when only fourteen. It was a decision worthy of reflection:

> Have been keeping a daily diary for 32 years, since Wilf [her brother] was born! Am now going to change the routine and enter only on necessary dates.

On the same day, in different parts of the southern states of eastern Australia, many other women were farewelling their year's diary and preparing to begin again: Dorris Duncan, Fanny Barbour, Mary Bicknell, Una Falkiner, Fanny MacCarthy O'Leary, Margaret Strongman, Winifred Tait. Mabel Lincoln had taken a temporary respite from her daily writing, while Cecil Rowe had ceased the habit altogether. Other women, too young at this stage to be recording, would start diaries at a later date: Dorothy Kendall, Kathleen Hughes and Norma Bull.

These women represent a handful of probably hundreds or thousands who were then keeping diaries around the country. In many cases, their writings have been lost or destroyed, considered not important enough to preserve or perhaps too personal and revealing to disclose. The women examined here reflect an assortment of urban and rural dwellers, married and single, young and old. Many things distinguish them from each other, but of the factors that unite them, the most important (sex apart) are their race, their class, the period in which they lived, and their habit of diary writing.

A brief profile of the main characters who appear throughout these pages quickly reveals this variety. Ida Dawson was born in 1879 and grew up in the small southern NSW town of Bombala. The eldest of nine children in a Catholic family, she learnt early the skills of housekeeping and childcare, to which she later added teaching. Her talents served her well throughout her adult life, years richly recorded in the 36 volumes of her diary which stretch from 1894 to 1955. Her diaries include details of her life as a governess in NSW and Queensland, her travels to Fiji, Java and South America, and the many years she spent in Sydney. Ida remained single throughout her life, supporting herself through teaching, the legacies of relatives and the little she could earn through her writing. Her passion for writing found expression mainly in nature sketches, stories drawn from her overseas experiences, and, of course, her diary. She shared her passion for diary writing with most of the women considered here, while her love of nature and the desire to record it for posterity were shared by a fellow diarist, Una Falkiner.

Una's life differed markedly from Ida's. Born Una Le Souëf in 1883, a daughter of the founder of the Melbourne Zoo, she grew accustomed early to the lifestyle of Melbourne's upper class, and her marriage to the wealthy pastoralist Otway Falkiner in 1910 ensured the continuance of that luxury while introducing her to the challenges of station life in the NSW Riverina district. Una was Otway's second wife and she took over the care of his existing three children before bearing her own. Her second child, John, was eighteen months old when the first available diary opens in 1920. With a retinue of servants and nurses to attend to the housework and the children, Una maintained her diary writing throughout her children's infancy and indeed the rest of her life, penning her final entry two months before her death in December 1948. The joys and vulnerabilities Una found in motherhood are a central feature of her diary, alongside her role as Otway's wife and the mistress of Widgiewa station. She travelled frequently to Melbourne, was a regular diner at Government House in both Sydney and Melbourne and was frequently cited in the social pages of women's magazines. In her spare time, Una loved to paint, especially the land surrounding the Widgiewa homestead, but perhaps her most enduring contribution to the lives of Australian women was her invention of the trolley that women used to wheel their washing to the clothesline.

Washing maintains a constant presence in the three surviving years of Mabel Lincoln's diary: 1930, 1932 and 1935. Mabel was a housewife living in the rural town of Leongatha, in Victoria's

Gippsland region. She was 52 when her diary for 1930 begins. Two of her five children still lived with her, and one grandchild, and her diary charts the constant stream of visitors who passed through her house and ate at her table. The most regular of these was her husband, whom she refers to throughout the diary as 'father' and who lived 8 kilometres out of Leongatha on a farm at Ruby. Her other three children were all married and living in Leongatha, where her daughter Rose ran Lincoln's General Store. Mabel's is a lovely diary, full of wit directed at her own and other people's foibles, and providing regular updates on local gossip. For the most part her days were consumed with domestic work and her diary provides detailed accounts of the hours she filled with washing, cooking and cleaning. We learn of new appliances as they were purchased, and their successes or failures. Even details of the cleaning products she used were recorded, along with the work to which they were put.

Domestic work and childcare are also recurrent motifs in Dorris Duncan's 1926 diary. Dorris moved from Melbourne to the central Victorian town of Shepparton in March 1926, where she and her three-year-old daughter Myra joined her husband, an agricultural engineer. Aged 35, Dorris set about creating a new life for herself, slowly establishing contacts in the local community, while recording in her diary the never-ending rounds of washing and housework. During her second pregnancy her constant battle against fatigue and despair left her without the energy for daily recording and her diary ends in November 1926, three months before her second daughter was born. Despite the brevity of her entries, they build a clear picture of her life in Shepparton. In many ways it is the very ordinariness of her life which makes her diary so interesting, and it provides valuable insight into the daily fabric of domestic life in a country town.

The daily round of domestic labour was of little concern to Fanny Barbour, except during periods when she was without a maid. Born in Queensland in 1865, she kept up her very spasmodic diary for 40 years, the later volumes spanning her life in and around Melbourne with her husband Jeremiah Hutchinson. Neither the social whirl nor the concerns of motherhood feature in Fanny's diary, for she bore no children and appears to have cared little for the social life which claimed much of Una Falkiner's time. Fanny's chief passion in life appears to have been her garden: it provided a space for her creative energy and an escape from the concerns of her marriage. Fanny's relationship with her husband,

and the silence surrounding his alcoholism, provide the underlying focus of her diary.

Relationships with men also provide the *raison d'être* of Kathleen Hughes's diary. Kathleen was 25 when her 1937 diary begins, working as a shop assistant at Paynes department store in Melbourne. Her father had died in her early teens, leaving his wife, Kathleen and her brother in impoverished circumstances. Kathleen left school before she reached fourteen and continued living with her mother and brother, who rarely feature in her diary. Kathleen's was not a daily diary but rather an episodic account of her relationships with men: her dates, the progress of her involvements and the unfolding of her romance with Stuart Robertson, the man she eventually married. Her diary is full of the adventures of a young woman, her active social life, her hopes for her future and her exploration of desire. With a degree of economic independence, Kathleen was in a position to grasp the opportunities life offered her, limited though they were to women in the 1930s. She enjoyed a freedom unknown to women of Ida Dawson's generation: she stayed out at dances until five in the morning, regularly dated different men, worked, and appears to have enjoyed life to the full. Her diary is a delight to read, full of the adventures of a young woman who was obviously very popular and knew how to make the most of her youth. She tells an engaging romantic tale, with all the ingredients of love, jealousy and betrayal to hold one's interest.

Dorothy Kendall was a few years older than Kathleen but not nearly so successful in writing the romance she desired. She was 23 when she commenced her diary for 1932, and working as a typist–clerk and bookkeeper at Employers' Liability Assurance in Queen Street, Melbourne. Dorothy initially lived in the Melbourne suburb of Armadale with her parents, sisters and brother. The death of her mother in 1934 heralded considerable change in the household, and Dorothy took over the domestic and financial management of the family's affairs. Her diary is a detailed account of her family life, her working days, her fantasies about relationships with men, and her intense and at times fraught relationship with her friend Sheilagh.

Long and loving friendships with women are among the riches to be found in the pages of Winifred Tait's diaries, which span the years from 1914 until her death in 1968. Winifred was a prolific diary writer, at times maintaining three separate accounts of her days: an appointment diary in which she later commented on the event concerned, a religious diary in which she recorded her Bible readings, thoughts and prayers and the state of her 'inner life', and a third diary, which has been lost, in which she apparently revealed the feelings and activities relating to her later work at a college for young Anglican women that Winifred helped establish. Winifred was born in 1877, the daughter of two teachers. The most highly educated of the women studied here, she earned a Bachelor of Arts and a Master of Education. Like Ida Dawson, Winifred remained single throughout her life and established for herself a highly successful teaching career. She wrote little of the details of her teaching, however, concentrating instead on the people, ideas and beliefs which provided the meaning and love in her life. Due to restrictions on publication I am unable to quote from Winifred's diary and, as my interpretation differs from that of her family, permission to discuss her friendships with women has been refused. The situation highlights the difficulties of dealing with sensitive material whose meanings can be ambiguous and inter-pretations touch the delicate issues of sexuality and identity. The name Winifred Tait is a pseudonym and details of her identity have been changed.

These are some of the women who appear throughout these pages. Their diaries represent a random collection, some of which were available in libraries and others which came to light through advertising. Many relatives came forth with diaries belonging to their mothers, grandmothers or relatives, most of which had pre-viously been viewed only by family members. Of those diaries housed in libraries, little use has been made of their riches, and the historians who have drawn upon them have generally mined them for specific information, unconcerned with the broader ques-tions they might raise about the nature of diary writing, the writer's construction of herself, or women's experience of their world. My quotations from the diaries retain original punctuation and spelling.

In reconstructing the lives of the women who feature here, I looked for the patterns they created through the daily recording of their lives, the webs of significance which entwined their words. The shape I have given to their lives is necessarily subjective in itself, just one performance of the drama of their lives.

1

Life cycles I: Youth

Sparkle and romance . . . 'I fell in love with his teeth'

Ida Dawson completed her schooling in 1897 and returned home
to the small township of Bombala at the age of seventeen. She
discovered, regretfully, that the period of her adolescence was
drawing to a close:

> Apparently, I am already regarded as 'grown up'. Mother is going to
> take me to the Tennis dance on Monday night! She is a member of
> the club, and today has been very busy cooking for the supper. It is
> to be a select affair, but I don't see why my hair should be put up so
> soon after my leaving school. (18 June 1897)

Assuming the trappings of womanhood—symbolised here by her
hair—also meant taking on increased responsibility in the household: 'Our fowls have commenced to lay, so my cooking will
progress famously. I am very fond of this branch of housework,
and arranged tonight's dinner for which I actually gained praise
from Father.' (5 July 1897)

Ida continued to live at home until March 1898. While she did
not appear to resent this, nor the expectations placed upon her,
her diary reveals conflicting sentiments about her work. She
seemed to regard the period as almost a training time: 'We had
such a busy day. Ellen [her sister] and I did the washing and I also
baked. We were finished at dinner time, and I am sure shall be
quite housewives in time.' Ida's training in domestic work had
begun at an early age, and her family was now reaping the benefits
of her labour. She regarded her housekeeping skills, however, as

1

secondary to her other ambitions. What was really preoccupying her thoughts was the hope of a job away:

> For some time I have been trying to get an engagement in Sydney as a governess, and have received some very nice letters from Mrs Garvin and Mrs Wolstenholme re the matter. Today I got a postcard from Ailanthus College, Darlinghurst saying that the principal would like to see my friends, so I am asking Annie [and] Mabel to call for me. I do hope it will come to something, for I am very anxious to be independent, and a helper besides. (16 February 1898)

Ida's desire to pursue independence yet be of service to others was to create persistent conflicts throughout her life: she would struggle to be financially independent and free to pursue her own interests and work, only to be frequently called upon to care for and nurture her family. But at the age of nineteen the direction her life was to take was only just becoming apparent: it would be influenced as much by Ida's family situation and her own interests as by the economic and professional possibilities open to women in Australia in the early years of the century.

Significant changes occurred between the years of Ida's youth, around the turn of the century, and the interwar years. Young middle-class women of Ida's generation had limited career opportunities: marriage was their expected path and most chose it. The end of the First World War heralded considerable change for young white women: the expansion of industry and the growth of consumer culture offered them increased work opportunities, greater economic freedom and extended fields of leisure. It was a period when much public discussion was directed at determining appropriate forms of behaviour for 'the modern girl'. It was also a time when understandings of youth were being redefined, when the path from girlhood to womanhood became encapsulated in the stage of 'youth': the period from the age of about 19 to about 25. 'Youth' was both a stage of life and a construct. It marked the years between school and marriage, and it became, during the interwar years, a stage of life identified with romance, desire, freedom and adventure. In the language of advertisements, it symbolised freshness, vigour and sensuality. '*Live* Your Romance,' pronounced Palmolive, '*Keep* That Schoolgirl Complexion . . . To *live* one's romances today, one stays young as long as she can, makes herself as *naturally attractive* as she can and trusts the rest to her womanly intelligence.'[1] The ideal woman became the youthful woman: despite her years, a woman was to retain the allure of her youth. Through the construction of the ideal woman as youthful, there emerged a clear image of the ways young women were to live. They were to engage in the adventure of romance, cultivate their (hetero)sexual desirability, and enjoy their freedom. The young women of the interwar period were promised rewards unavailable to their mothers. The increased opportunities for work, greater knowledge of birth control and a more open discussion of women's sexual pleasure placed them in unique circumstances.

How did women respond to these new opportunities? How did they represent their experiences of courtship, sexuality, clothes, and leisure? Did they express a tension between their own experiences of these things and the prescriptive ideals held up for them to emulate? For the young women examined here, youth was a period of adventure and discovery, as well as of considerable self-doubt. Through their diaries we can read their romantic fantasies and trace the conflicts, desires and hopes which characterised their experience of modernity.

Ida Dawson's youthful diary provides a suitable starting point for exploring the lives of young women, as well as a contrast to the diaries of Kathleen Hughes and Dorothy Kendall. Romance and desire in Ida's diary emerge in more muted tones than we find in the diaries of women in the interwar years, changes which reflect the new language of sexuality, the body and relationships.

Ida Dawson's return home from school marked the beginning of her search for employment and her quest for independence. As she continued to apply for jobs she was kept busy at home and with social engagements. She wrote frequently of the men she met and her thoughts on them. Jack Santelle, an old and close friend with whom she seemed to share a strong affection but a fluctuating relationship, featured regularly, but when she eventually moved to Sydney to teach in a school and he failed to contact her, he (temporarily) fell from grace: 'Jack is just the same as other men, I think, and I—I thought he was different' (17 May 1898). Ida articulated an early sense that relationships with men brought disappointment. Her affection for him remained, however. At the end of the school year she returned to Bombala, and held a dance in January 1899 which she recorded this way:

> Jack Santelle arrived a little before eight,—to help. Others did not come till about 8.45 . . . I think the dance was very successful; everyone seemed to enjoy it. Paty and Jack S. flirted most shockingly, with bangles & bella donna flowers. I felt quite out in the cold, till he squeezed my hand in the dark, & I knew it was alright. (10 January 1899)

3

Ida's concern over Paty and Jack's flirtation suggests both coyness and perhaps a degree of envy at their brazenness. Her own experience of reassuring seduction was concealed by the dark and thus was more legitimate than public display. Ida's diary is very circumspect about the nature of the relationship between herself and Jack. When gossip spread around Bombala that she was engaged, there was little doubt about who she was meant to be engaged to, but she had doubts about Jack: 'I cannot understand Jack; in private I seem to be the only girl he has any regard for, and yet if people are around he is merely very polite' (2 February 1900). Ida resisted this division between public and private: personal behaviour should be consistent, whether in public view or not. Ida did not reveal to her diary any details of her feelings for Jack. Perhaps conventional Victorian taboos were operating or maybe activities too private to be revealed were underway: Mabel Ross, another young diarist during this period, who lived on a farm near Hamilton, in Victoria's Western District, made only a brief reference to her marriage, and the preceding courtship did not even rate a mention. The knowledge that Mabel in fact eloped suggests that there were some things with which even her diary could not be trusted. If Ida and Mabel possessed a language for desire their diaries were not the places for its expression. Public discussion of courtship and marriage in late nineteenth-century Australia focused on the need to find a companion in a husband, someone whom you not only loved, but who shared a similar background, intellect and religious sympathies.[2] At its best, marriage was a holy and exalted state, but it could also involve domestic trial, ordeals and grave responsibilities. Some feminists, writing at the turn of the century, believed marrriage had become degraded by men's sexual exploitation of women.[3] Ida Dawson did not reveal to her diary her thoughts on the institution of marriage, nor her feelings about the desirability, or otherwise, of being married herself. She certainly expressed no aversion to the idea, although she could be very cynical about men and their intentions, commenting at one point, 'I do not think there is more than superficial sincerity in any man' (8 August 1899). Ida privileged personal integrity over outward display.

Ida never married. Throughout her twenties, she alternated between working as a governess and living at home. She established herself as a source of local information and colour for the *Stock and Station Journal*, an activity which seemed to give her much pleasure and held the promise of greater things to come. As a single woman, Ida was free to find work where she pleased. She

4

perceived her first duty, however, as being to her family: 'Mother is looking ill . . . and I wrote to Mʳˢ Jasper telling her I cannot possibly think of going back. As things are, my place is at home for a time, at any rate' (3 November 1902). It was a priority which was to inform her life, perhaps leading it to evolve in ways other than those she had intended. Maybe she was already aware of this when she quoted from J.M. Barrie's *The Little Minister* on the inside cover of her 1903–1905 diary: 'The life of every man (or woman) is a diary in which he means to write one story, and writes another.' Ida used her diary to reflect upon her life, and occasionally to protest against popular assumptions about women's lives and activities. Women too, she insisted, wrote diaries.

Women beginning their adult lives during the 1920s and 1930s had more options open to them than those of Ida's generation. Most obvious to contemporary commentators and historians alike was the opening up of white-collar work to women, but other significant changes were taking place as well. The search for a husband moved from the search for a companion, with woman as helpmate, to a romantic quest during which a woman would search for her true lover. The end result, however, was still marriage. Femininity was equated with heterosexual desirability, whose central component was youth. The symbol of this was 'the flapper', who flouted convention, forgot the strains of the war period, and enjoyed herself. Around her raged a debate about the suitability of her behaviour, and increasing discussion on the practicalities and ethics of birth control. Young white women of the interwar period were able to be more self-consciously sexual, in fact were encouraged to be so, because the consequences of their sexuality were more readily controlled. These ideas did not go uncontested and for a while the activities of young women were hotly debated in the pages of women's magazines and newspapers.

One of the influences shaping the new understanding of femininity was the cinema. The girl of the 1920s was 'modern', self-consciously so, and film stars were her model. Youth was central to the new femininity, and beauty products all promised to hold the key to the youthful appearance. 'To-day is the day of youth prolonged, with freshness and charm at every side,' pronounced Palmolive in 1925. '*No woman can afford* to neglect herself.'[4] A woman's reward for a youthful complexion was 'Sparkle and life, admiration and romance!'[5] So noticeable was this shift in the image of beauty and women's pursuit of physical charm that Palmolive felt moved to comment: 'People have changed, and ideals have changed. The "middle-aged" woman is conspicuously absent in the modern scheme of things. In her place we have the woman who values the social importance of youth—and keeps it.'[6] Of course it was part of the role of advertisements to induce the very changes they claimed to reflect. The romance makers, those who constructed femininity in terms of youth and desirability, were creating markets for products. There were economic motives for the images they created. Many young women now had a small disposable income, and the whole portrayal of youth was integrally related to the developing consumer society. By equating 'youth' with desirability, advertisers hoped to create a lifelong dependence on their products.

Women's magazines played an important part in the dissemination of ideas and images about femininity. Before the First World War, and through the early 1920s, advertisements pictured women as the judges of their skin and of the soap they were using. Women looked to the mirror for the answer, and saw themselves. By the late 1920s, men had become the authority on how women looked, smelt and felt. Men were portrayed as being interested in, and thus in some way sharing, women's daily concerns. Significantly, the men in advertisements were husbands, and women were cautioned to work at retaining their sex appeal within marriage. Not until the 1930s, perhaps reflecting the growing influence of Hollywood, did men enter the picture as lovers, inciting women to be alluring and seductive, tempting men with their 'ripe', 'charmingly daring', 'Savage red' lips.[7] Women were to cultivate heterosexual desire. As Marilyn Lake argues, they became 'objects to men's positioning as subjects.'[8]

If women were sexualised objects in advertisements and movies, their diaries allowed them to be subjects, and we find in them diarists' expressions of their own subjectivity. The diaries of Dorothy Kendall and Kathleen Hughes suggest that changes in attitudes to sexuality were having an impact on their fantasies and in their lives. They portrayed themselves as both the object of men's desires and the subject of their own. Men, and what they offered as lovers, were integrated into the daily story.

Dorothy Kendall was 23 and working as a typist and clerk for a Melbourne insurance firm when her diary for 1932 opens. She enjoyed her work, and met there some of the men on whom she focused her romantic fantasies. Some attractions were fleeting, as in the case of a man she met at work: 'Mr Keysell from the London office arrived. I fell in love with his teeth. He's only young and they say unmarried' (29 August 1932). Another man from work became the focus of more sustained interest. She faced, however, competition from another woman:

> I can't make Beau out. He falls all over Maudie yet goes out of his way to talk to me too. Maudie is very nice but I'm not keen on being in the same category. She is easy to get on with though and I always find it hard to think of something to say. (19 February 1935)

In Dorothy's mind at least, issues of class—the 'category' Dorothy identifies—were not negated by feminine charm. Several months later she was to confess, 'I think she'll get him—she's easier to talk to than me. Oh well—I don't know that I want *him* especially, but I'd like to have someone' (21 June 1935). Maudie was evidently more adept at charm than Dorothy, but it was Beau's prerogative to indicate interest. Significantly, Dorothy expressed concern about her quiet nature, anxious that she did not meet the ideal of a vivacious, outgoing woman. Dorothy's desire for 'someone' led her to dream up all sort of things about people she often saw only from a distance. Every man was a potential lover. Her morning bus ride to work from her home in Armadale to the city allowed her ample opportunity to indulge her fantasies. She even chastised herself for this tendency:

> I'm a bit weak the way I get fancies for people I see on the bus. There's one awfully nice chap—I wish I could meet him—I suppose I'd be disappointed if I did, but he's nice looking and seems interested in me. Probably only imagination on my part. Ain't life grand! (22 November 1935)

Dorothy's dreaming served many purposes. She could admire from a distance without risking the possibility that anything might actually happen, and she could also believe that her feelings were reciprocated without having to test the truth of that belief. She was both desired and desirable. In her fantasy world, life could indeed be grand. Dorothy was not the only woman tempted to commuter fancies, and the conduct of such attractions prompted a *New Idea* reader to write in 1933 for guidance to 'Margaret's Problem Club':

> On my journeys to and from work I often see a very nice boy get on the tram as I do. The other night he sat down beside me in the tram, opened his paper and commenced reading. I opened the 'New Idea' and commenced reading. I am sure he was not even aware of my existence . . . What I would like to know is, would it be a very grave breach of etiquette if I were casually to open a conversation next time it happens we sit together in the tram? I might manage to drop something and so bring it about that way. (16 June 1933)

'Margaret' had very definite ideas about the subject, strongly advising against making 'the first move': 'If this young man is not aware of your presence, then he is not interested in you.' She did encourage the writer to take her opportunity if it came along, but etiquette forbade any 'attempt to precipitate matters'. Indeed it would not be romantic for women to take any action to bring about the fulfilment of a fantasy. In the story of romance, men were the pursuers, women the pursued. Women's magazines and advertisements promised that romantic dreams could become a reality, but strict rules of play applied. As the letter suggests, however, women were trying to negotiate the conflicting messages, testing behavioural boundaries that were otherwise left unspoken.

Dorothy experienced both the pleasures and frustrations of romantic fantasies when she changed jobs and began working at Kraft as a senior typist and stenographer. It was not long before Geoff caught her eye and she began to divulge to her diary the agonies and ecstasies of his charm:

> Geoff was hovering round during the morning—he was talking to Mr Brenner when I took a job out to him. Gosh he gives me palpitations. On my way back at lunchtime I think he was crossing the road as I turned into the gardens—but I was too goofy to look . . . I wish all sort of silly things—but oh I do like him. (26 April 1937)

Dorothy's reaction to Geoff was a physical and emotional one. There is a hint of an uncontrollable sexual response which his presence provoked. When she unexpectedly met him at a dance, she recorded the encounter: 'He saw me—and thrill of thrills he stopped near me in the Jolly Miller. It was the last turn and extra long' (11 May 1937). The moment of closeness seemed prolonged, and Dorothy relished every second of their chanced intimacy, his presence delighting and arousing her. Dorothy became extra-sensitive to all of Geoff's movements. A word from him could lift her spirits, its absence plunge her into despair: 'And still he keeps out of the way—this is heartbreaking after all my fond dreams. As long as he came in once a day, even with Betty there it was something, but I didn't even see him in the passage' (30 April 1937). Despite the lack of any indication of interest from Geoff, Dorothy's infatuation with him continued for over a year. Her diary is filled with his movements, the snippets of conversation on which she based her hopes and dreams, and her gradual sense that perhaps she was 'on the wrong track altogether' (24 January 1938). She was forced to confront the difference between her fantasy and possible realities. Amongst other things, it was an experience of loss. Only once, when she realised how dramatically her thoughts about Beau had changed, did she pause to consider whether her attraction to Geoff might pass: 'Beau is growing a moustache—wonder how I ever kidded myself I liked him—he's such a weed. Will I ever think that of Geoff?' (16 June 1937). One of the frustrations Dorothy felt most keenly during the course of her infatuation with Geoff was her inability to act: 'It really does seem heartbreaking sometimes, and such a waste if he really is interested, but I don't know what to do' (4 August 1937). A friend cautioned her not to show her attraction: 'A man doesn't like a girl to show she's conscious of him like that' (14 April 1938). Such was the structure of sexual difference.[9] Dorothy had shown herself ready to take up the possibilities change had brought. She readily incorporated the promises of romance into her fantasies and desires for the future, but her life story was unfolding differently. The point at which she began to question the promises she had embraced marked the point at which her diary writing declined. Perhaps she failed to find alternative narrative structures suitable for her life story.

Despite restrictions on their behaviour, women in the 1930s were able to express their attractions to men in language unavailable to Ida Dawson's generation. They could express their desire and the physical responses it invoked. The extent of the change is reflected in the debates about what was appropriate behaviour for young women in the 1920s and 1930s. Contemporary observers of Ida's generation commented on the changed social habits of the young modern woman and considerable space was given to discussing the faults and virtues of the 'rising generation'. Opinion was divided. One writer to *New Idea* in 1930 believed that a 'third sex' was evolving, 'a sort of semi-woman who craves masculinity, and succeeds in being neither one thing nor the other'. The force of her argument was again women's heterosexual desirability: 'the drinking, smoking type is not in harmony with a true man's idea of womanhood'.[10] Another writer drew attention to the discrepancy between the attention given to modern girls and that given to boys: 'it is remarkable how the modern boy escapes criticism. No interest apparently is taken in his mode of dress . . . His words are not quoted, nor his actions noted as is the case of his sister.'[11] The nature of masculinity, it seems, was not being nearly so fiercely disputed.[12] Young women were the harbingers of modernity, or its more worrying manifestations.

One of the most frequent attacks made on young women concerned their social behaviour. Women were seen to be exercising a 'new freedom', enjoying the stimulation of alcohol, staying out late at dances, using 'powder and paint' until they were 'practically one hundred per cent artificial',[13] a comment which implicitly recognised the changed notions of femininity and viewed previous understandings of it as 'natural'. It also suggests the degree to which women had become more visible, not only in the workplace, but socially as well. In 1933 *New Idea* ran a competition for the best letter answering the question: 'Should They Kiss Good-night?' The winning letter argued that only through a kiss would a woman know her true *'lover'* [sic]: Mr Right was immediately identifiable 'by the thrilling sweet security of his KISS!' Romance promised both sexual passion and physical security. Another letter believed kisses to be 'the small goods in the bargain basement of love, and a girl's got to be a wise shopper these days'.[14] For other contestants, kissing had to be a carefully monitored activity: 'There can be no harm whatever in kissing on the brow or cheek, for it provokes no rising tide of thrilling passion to upset hot-blooded youth'.[15] As this writer made clear, kissing involved a degree of sexual awakening and engagement which, once unleashed, could be uncontrollable. A tight line was being negotiated between the growing acknowledgment of young women's sexuality and the dangers of exploring it too far.

If the debate over the behaviour of young women impinged on the consciousness of Kathleen Hughes, she gave no indication of it in her diary. Kathleen was 24 when her diary begins in 1937, and working at Paynes in Melbourne. Her diary is not at all concerned with her working life but with her romantic liaisons. She never mentioned her rate of pay, the journey to and from work, or staff dynamics, and referred to work only when it related to another more significant event: an admirer rang her at work, overtime restricted her social activities, or she met workmates outside the store. She only made entries in the diary on days when she had been out, during holidays, or when there had been a development with a man she was seeing. If Dorothy Kendall's predicament seems to have been lack of response from the men she was interested in, Kathleen was constantly turning away would-be suitors. At the start of her diary she was going out with Edgar, but the rather tempestuous nature of their relationship led her frequently to date other men. Kathleen had very definite ideas about the way she wanted to feel about someone she dated. Leslie was one of her most persistent admirers, who asked her to marry him several times. 'Les . . . asked me once again to marry him— told me he had a lot more money in the bank & how much money he'd need to get before I said 'yes'—told him it wasn't a question of money' (24 March 1937). Kathleen was not to be wooed by the promise of financial security. Leslie was not easily put off, however. A few weeks later he was again trying to win her affections, but this time he tried a different tack:

> When we got home Les told me he was still crazy about me . . . told me he loves my brown skin, the way I speak & how I enjoy all the same things as he does—in fact says he can't make out why I don't feel the same about him as he has the same attitudes too but I just don't. He stood at the gate & wouldn't go—told him not to be that way, he thinks I'm hard but its just that I can't feel the way he wants me to—don't mind going out with him but nothing more than that. (13 April 1937)

Leslie appears struck by Kathleen's sensuality—her brown skin, the tone of her voice—and confident enough that these were desirable qualities to flatter her on them. Kathleen, in recounting the conversation, conveyed herself as the object of his gaze, and thus constructed herself as desirable. She took pleasure in her own sensuality, if not in his desire. Other men Kathleen dated were equally clear about the way they felt, but much less prepared to compromise:

> As Jack was driving me home he told me that he liked me & that he wasn't coming over any more unless he could be my boyfriend—wasn't going to be one of the many—told him I went with Edgar. (1 April 1937)

Jack obviously saw it as his right to set the rules for Kathleen's behaviour in any possible relationship. Kathleen, for her part, could be very clear in her messages to men. A later date with Jack again left him thwarted in his attempts to win her affections.

> I was snappy with Jack & when he walked to the front door with me to wish me good night he started to get sentimental & said that he hadn't known many girls etc, & that he wasn't used to running around, I told him he had been drinking, he just turned on his heel & banged the gate shut with such force it is a wonder it didn't fall down. I was feeling tired & fed up—25 past one when I got to bed. (23 April 1937)

Jack's 'sentimentality'—a euphemism for physical intimacy perhaps?—transgressed a line Kathleen was not prepared to cross, and she was confident enough of herself to assert her wishes, much to Jack's disgust. In another incident, she was quite happy to exploit a man's interest in her to her own advantage: 'Doug told me that he had fallen for me—got romantic but I wasn't keen, he was quite a decent boy but the car was my interest' (19 July 1937). Kathleen had no time for unwanted attention, especially the sort that demanded from her a more engaged response. The next evening she dismissed Doug's declarations of love as 'silly' and summed up their dates quite candidly: 'I got some nice drives and suppers for nothing' (20 July 1937).

Through the recitation of each of these incidents, Kathleen positioned herself as the object of male desire. The lists of men interested in her convey the significance she placed upon their attention, even if she did not return their feelings. Hers was not simply a passive position, however, for she held the prerogative to reject advances made and to take what she could get from her admirers.

Throughout the period of these interactions with men, Kathleen was ostensibly dating Edgar. When she began her diary there seems to have been a slight cooling in their relationship, but by late April they were seeing each other regularly, although their time together was not devoid of tensions. Edgar did not drink and disapproved of Kathleen drinking, an activity she enjoyed and engaged in at the dances she regularly attended. During one of their 'straightening things out' talks, she promised him she would 'never touch another drop of liquor in my life' (26 April 1937). However, it was not only liquor Edgar disapproved of: he wanted Kathleen to date only him. It was again the man's prerogative to set the rules, and Edgar sought to tame her. She agreed: 'I have made up my mind not to go out on the razzle any more—from now on Edgar is to be the only one—no more dates & no more drink' (27 April 1937). A few days later she turned down two dates because she 'wanted to be true' (3 May 1937). Their relationship, however, was infused with a jealousy which allowed neither of them room to show 'interest' in anybody else. When, at a ball one evening, Edgar asked another woman to dance, Kathleen retaliated:

> Keith . . . held me too close and whispered sweet nothings in my ear, I flirted with him—saw Ed watching me so did it all the more, then Ed asked the nurse for a dance & she made me feel furious the way she laughed & looked so thrilled with Ed & he kept smiling down at her, I knew he was only doing it to pay me out. (5 July 1937)

Both Keith and the nurse had crossed recognised boundaries: they were flirting with another's lover, Keith reinforcing the transgression with physical intimacy—a fact Kathleen obviously realised and seems to have enjoyed. The incident was the cause of an argument, Edgar blaming Kathleen for spoiling his night. 'I stood on the verandah & Ed stood on the path we faced each other both feeling miserable. Ed asked me why it was we couldn't get along.'

Kathleen's position on the verandah subverted the normal power dynamic in their relationship. From a more humble position, Edgar questioned their constant bickering. Yet this seeming subversion was also the very stuff of romance: it was the one time in a woman's life when it was her prerogative to set or reject the terms set by men. As she had done previously with Leslie, Jack and Doug, she was able to set her own terms through the power of her sexual attractiveness. The incident with Edgar precipitated a break-up and Kathleen declared: 'made up my mind never to be that way about anyone again—hurts too much when you part' (11 July 1937). Kathleen was engaging in a style of story-telling, canvassing the actors, developing the themes and the language: 'the way I speak', 'the only one', 'wanted to be true', 'sweet nothings', 'smiling down at her'. The language of these incidents formed part of the language of romance. Kathleen engaged in it, perhaps, as a guide for her own behaviour, perhaps to counter or conceal her ambivalent feelings, but also to place herself within the romantic quest. The writing of her life engaged her in the story of romance.

Throughout this period of Kathleen's life, her diary provided an outlet for her anger towards Edgar and a place to record the mixture of emotions she experienced. She seemed to take some delight in recounting the different men she dated and her experiences with them, and her feelings over her break-up with Edgar were given ample room and elaborated in some detail. The sexual undercurrents hinted at by Dorothy are much more explicit in Kathleen's diary. When she saw Edgar again after their break-up, she noted his response: he 'kissed me like mad when Doris and Bill were out of the room. I was thrilled to have him that way again but didn't let him see it' (16 August 1937). She delighted in his ardour, and the knowledge that she was the object of it, but she kept her own desire a secret, allowing him to be the one driven by passion. The detail Kathleen divulged in her diary was part of its raison d'être. She was the heroine of her romances, and she told her story with all the ingredients of love, jealousy, betrayal and passion. By writing her life as a story of romance rather than of her own desire, she chose an appropriately feminine and socially acceptable form for it. She wrote the story Dorothy longed to write, but was not able to. Kathleen concluded 1937, the year during which she met her future husband, Stuart, with a summary of the year's most important events:

> And so ends the year 1937—it has been a wonderful year for me—went to plenty of shows, dances, balls, picnics etc,—went out with 14

> different boys—went with Edgar Peters from January to July & with Stuart Robertson from August to December, also went out with these boys thru the year . . . [lists names of boys]—also could have gone out with several others but after meeting Stuart in August I gave up all the other boys & haven't been out with another boy since I started going with Stuart—falling in love with Stuart was the most marvellous thing to happen to me—found myself at last & feel contented with life—Stuart told me on Wed Oct 6ᵗʰ he loved me & on Thur Oct 7ᵗʰ I told Stuart I loved him. (31 December 1937)

Her love affair with Stuart confirmed herself as the heroine of her own life. In the years until her engagement, her diary reads as a perfect love story, with enough minor fluctuations to keep the plot interesting, but no major threats to its rhythm. The story served to confirm her belief that all previous dissatisfaction with Edgar and her double-dating was legitimised because she had not yet found the *right* man. Her life was following a public model, well established in fiction, and yet deemed real enough to be emulated. In the early 1930s *New Idea* printed three romance stories a week, a number which increased as the decade progressed. They tell tales of true love which knows itself on first meeting, of love fulfilled or unrequited, of women as wives and mothers devoted to their husbands and children. The stories may have borne little relationship to reality, but they came at a time when the discourses surrounding femininity focused on womanhood being discovered in romantic relationships with men. As Kathleen says: 'found myself at last'.

To understand women such as Dorothy and Kathleen more fully, and to avoid a formula which keeps women still bound and manipulated by social and political forces, we need to tease out what prevailing attitudes to sexuality and romance offered women, and why the interwar years saw such change in ideas about sexuality and relationships. There are two ways of approaching this. First, we can see how the aftermath of the war, class tensions, economic depression and the forces of modernity created a climate in which the ideology of romance provided individual solutions to larger sociocultural problems. Second, we can look at what romance offered women: how did it speak to their fears and desires, and how did it offer a means of control over their lives and their possibilities for pleasure? As Jill Matthews suggests, we need 'a balancing of the social and the personal, of politics and pleasure, of structure and subjectivity.'[16]

The First World War had left Australia not only bereft of 60,000 men—husbands and potential husbands—but had also laid bare bitter class and gender divisions within Australian society. These divisions appeared as early as 1915, with returned soldiers causing street riots, assaulting police officers, and, in one case, murdering a former lover. The antagonism between ex-servicemen and civilian men continued well into the 1920s, and was exacerbated by the difficulties many veterans had in finding and keeping work. Women involved with or married to ex-servicemen, whether the victims of domestic abuse or not, had to deal with the physical and psychological scarring of the war. To this scenario, one of conflict within and between genders, the ideology of romance spoke of harmony and equality. At the same time it revealed the sexual power relations of Australian society. When social tensions became even more pronounced during the Depression, a period when the popular love affair with heterosexual romance reached a new intensity, romance spoke of personal security, of love as a panacea to the problems of unemployment and poverty: couples might have to delay marriage until their financial position was a little more secure, but they would pull through the hard times together.

Romance was supposedly an adventure available to all, irrespective of class: in the modern scheme of things, love was particularly available to the young. Class divisions in Australia had been deepened by the war and would be further highlighted during the strikes of the early 1920s and later the Depression. The new constructions of femininity, however, emphasised age rather than class as the prerequisite for entry into the romantic adventure. Class was not, of course, irrelevant, for it determined the particular style of adventure you could enjoy, but when femininity became associated with overt sexual appeal rather than with such attributes as daintiness, and when the reward for (hetero)sexual appeal was romance, class of origin was less important. At least so it may have seemed. In fact, femininity was not just an elusive gift which one either possessed or did not, it was dependent on all sorts of consumer goods, and thus presupposed a disposable income. The message of the romance, however, was that all could enjoy the delights of love and therefore true happiness. What did economic hardship matter when lifelong happiness was available, free?

But aside from its broader social function, what did, and does, romance do for women themselves? It offers them not just an escape from the current realities of their lives but also an alternative future, one in which they are promised fulfilment and lasting satisfaction. For women such as Dorothy Kendall, living in a home fraught with conflicts between her parents, among her siblings, and across generations, the dream of a romantic liaison provided not only a distraction but the hope of a happier, more peaceful existence. Romance is one adventure women have always been allowed to embark upon, and in the 1920s and 1930s, it was a way of confirming that a woman was successfully feminine. For young women, heterosexual romance was seen as *the* path to fulfilment. The only alternative was a life of implicitly unfulfilling work or caring for parents. That path held no *life* at all.

Romance offered more than the promise of security and the chance for adventure, however. It spoke to desires and fears at once common to generations of women and specific to women in the interwar period: the desire to find a husband and to live happily, when young men had been slaughtered *en masse* during the war; the fear of poverty when so many were without work; the fear of loneliness and the desire for friendship and companionship, at a time when the mechanisation of the workplace was depersonalising relationships; the hope of love and the promise of sex and fun.[17] As Kathleen Hughes wrote: 'falling in love with Stuart was the most marvellous thing to happen to me—found myself at last & feel contented with life'. For the first time women were being offered both an acknowledgment of their sexual desires, and the possibility of sexual relations with the knowledge of birth control. As Alison Light has argued, the fantasy of romance has offered generations of women 'relations impossibly harmonised; it uses unequal heterosexuality as a dream of equality and gives women uncomplicated access to a subjectivity which is unified and coherent *and* still operating within the field of pleasure.'[18] For women such as Dorothy Kendall, however, for whom the fantasy did not translate into daily life, the consciousness of the contradictions between the image and reality could be stark and painful.

While heterosexual desire was offered to women in terms of romance, there were other, related, ideas defining what femininity looked like, and to whom it was available. How was a woman's sexuality identifiable? If romance was the only socially appropriate way for the 'good woman' to discover and experience her sexuality, her expression of it was carried upon her body. Inscribed there were understandings of femininity, of fashion, and modernity.

If styles of courtship had changed since Ida Dawson was in her twenties, so too had attitudes to women's bodies. The prewar emphasis on reproductive health and fitness shifted to a concern with appearance. Women's bodies were to be created, sculpted according to certain ideas about beauty and fitness. The new body image was 'young, slender, tanned, fit but not muscular, attractive but not sensual'.[19] We can see this shift in advertisements for weight loss products and programs. Those of 1919 emphasised health and happiness, with appearance as a corollary. By 1924, 'reducing' had become the key word. Women were to take up less space. Diets proliferated. By 1930, magazines were running feature stories about weight loss programs. In 1935 advertisements began to draw attention to specific parts of the body: busts were to be full and firm but not too large, hips were to be slim. Women working in offices became a particular target for ideas about the shape of the modern body: 'Are you getting an office spread?' asked *New Idea's* beauty page, which suggested exercises to 'counteract a spread caused by sitting too much'.[20] Female office workers, somehow symbolic of the changes occurring in the workforce and the economy at large—changes inseparable from ideas about modernity, efficiency and the increasing bureaucratisation of society—were to have those ideas projected onto their bodies. Their public visibility, both in and outside the workplace, added to their objectification. Once women were visible, the space they were allowed to occupy had to be minimised and the way they fitted into it strictly regulated.

At the same time, sexologists such as Marie Stopes were propounding the view that women were sexual beings, as capable of sexual desire as men and with as much right as men to sexual pleasure.[21] Thus the female body became the repository of ideas not only about modernity but about sexual pleasure. Women were simultaneously objectified and rendered subjects of their own desire. The growing focus on exercise as a means of creating the modern body held this objectification and subjectivity in tension, for exercise was meant to be an enjoyable activity, performed as much for the pleasure it brought as for its cosmetic effects.

The emphasis on 'reducing' in the interwar years also reflects psychocultural anxieties. This was a time of disruption and change, when the prewar order was being challenged, the position of women shifting, and gender relations being renegotiated. Concern began to develop about the excesses of women's bodies just at the moment when their personal and political horizons were expanding. We can see this, in Susan Bordo's terms, 'as a metaphor for anxiety about internal processes out of control—uncontained desire, unrestrained hunger, uncontrolled impulse'. For the women themselves, however, slender bodies could also express freedom and 'the liberation from a domestic, reproductive destiny'.[22] It is not surprising, then, that heterosexual romance, marriage and motherhood were so relentlessly advocated, lest women take their

17

new-found freedom too seriously and reject altogether a future of domesticity and reproduction.

The ideal feminine body denied the effects of time and bore no signs of maternity, menstruation or ageing. Advertisements and beauty directives addressed to women during the 1920s and 1930s reflected and promoted this ideal. Advertisements for sanitary napkins advocated that women should not be affected by their monthly periods. Kotex even declared—in a striking example of the way the language of modernity and industrial time was applied to women's most personal experiences—that its napkins could *'be worn on either side with equal efficiency'*.[23] Life's rhythms were neither to show on women's bodies nor impede their ability to meet the demands of the office or factory and keep up with the unrelenting progression of industrial time.

Just as we can see the influence of ideas about romance and sexuality in the diaries of Dorothy Kendall and Kathleen Hughes, so modern notions of health and fitness are also evident in their diaries. Dorothy Kendall's sister was a gym teacher, and Dorothy attended her classes regularly, taking her friend Sheilagh along with her. She also participated in yearly gym concerts. Gym had become a popular way for young women to achieve the balance between fitness and health without developing 'unsightly' (unfeminine) muscles. Dorothy was also conscious of her weight, although she did not put herself on diets, noting, 'I weighed myself. I'm down to 8.9½. A long time since I've been as low as that' (2 March 1933). She was also conscious of the figure she cut and the difference between herself and the ideal. After a fitting for a new outfit, she wrote that her dressmaker, 'recognised me as a Kendall, and while she was measuring me remarked on my lack of curves in the upper regions' (11 March 1932). Dorothy was not quite so accepting of other people's flaws: of her cousin she wrote, 'I'm sure she's self conscious about her figure and she should wear tighter corsets' (6 May 1932). Dorothy's sisters were also figure conscious, with one of them writing home during holidays that she was getting fat on food and lack of exercise. Dorothy considered it a development worth recording.

Contemporary ideas about the cycles of menstruation and pregnancy are far less easy to deduce from women's diaries than more explicit—and visible—ideas about the body. While the manufacturers of sanitary napkins and pain relief tablets claimed that 'Nature no longer punishes the modern woman',[24] and that menstruation need not affect sexual desirability, Dorothy Kendall's experience was different. Her comments on her menstrual cycle were always allusive: 'Felt pretty rotten all day. I know what that means . . . I am worse than usual when I'm "off"' (31 January 1932). Menstruation restricted women's physical activity, and at times they had to give excuses for their sedateness: 'Sheilagh rang up to ask me to go for a swim but I told her my circumstances so she went with Marnie, Joan being in the same straights as I' (21 January 1933). Presumably Dorothy was able to inform Sheilagh of her 'straights' much more explicitly than she cared to inform her diary. Her most lucid reference to what menstruation actually involved came on a holiday: 'Made rather a mess of the hotel bed, but I couldn't help it' (26 March 1937). The image here is quite graphic, although there is no mention of blood. Dorothy, who could write very candidly of her emotions and the other preoccupations of her life, did not find the words to commit to paper something as intimate and integral to her life as her monthly period. It may be that her difficulty in doing this was not just a vestige of shyness about menstruation and by association sex and reproduction (she could reveal her 'circumstances' to her friends, even if she did use elliptical phraseology), but because the prevailing language of modernity, sexual desirability and efficiency did not accord with her own experience of menstruation. There was an inherent disjunction between her perception of her body and its biological rhythms, and the public discourse infusing ideas of regulation and management into this intensely personal and uncontrollable experience.

Clothes were another integral ingredient in the creation of the public image of beauty, and a woman's style of wearing them transmitted information about herself and her sexuality. In 1919 *Everylady's Journal* stressed the importance of dressing for success at work. 'The girl of today must not only be efficient but effective. Right clothes worn in the right place will make you fifty percent more capable.'[25] By 1926 *Home* complimented the new season's fashion on its utility, an attribute particularly suited to 'modern femininity': the simple addition of a jacket could transform an afternoon frock into suitable evening dress. The modern woman could go from work to an evening function without having to change beforehand.[26] Dorothy Kendall always commented on a new addition to her wardrobe and on any responses she drew: 'Wore my new hat and coat and caused a sensation' (25 April 1932). She also recorded her impressions of other people's clothes, and not always favourably: 'its kindest to say nothing about Auntie Alma's and Wynne's dresses, but I do feel sorry for Wynne' (6 May 1932). Dorothy had very strong ideas about what was appropriate clothing for different occasions, and kept a sharp eye on fashions. When her friend Sheilagh bought a new frock, Dorothy observed, 'It's a lovely colour but besides clinging to her figure it is a bit tight, and I don't think its flared enough, too much like a night dress' (10 October 1932). Dorothy cared about the line she cut and her clothes often boosted her confidence: 'Wore my glad rags and did I cause a sensation. They were so nice about it too except Miss Nichols who didn't care to look' (8 May 1933). Kathleen Hughes was also attuned to the reaction she received when wearing new clothes, especially from Stuart. 'I wore my blue floral satin, it is the first time Stuart has seen this frock & he fell for it' (25 December 1938). Clothes were worn for the pleasure of the wearer and to enhance her appeal to men. Stuart's appreciation of Kathleen's dress, and herself in it, gave her a space for taking pleasure in herself.

Public images of beauty provided women with an ideal, and beauty creams and corsets promised to help them achieve it. Dorothy Kendall 'bought some Kathleen Court vanishing cream for a trial' (1 February 1933) and a month later noted, 'bought myself some cold cream. I'm trying Kathleen Court as I like her Vanishing Cream' (9 March 1933). Kathleen Court promised a 'Fine, Smooth Skin' to replace those ugly 'Coarse Pores', considered to be 'A Grave Social Error'.[27] Hair was also a central part of the image: 'Blondes, remember! Ravishingly gold blond hair fascinates almost any man—few can resist its attraction. But love and romance are often spoiled through carelessly letting light blond hair darken'.[28] Hair care was not easy: 'Mary is queer in a lot of ways but she's one of the few girls I know who knows how to look after her permanent wave' (29 July 1933), wrote Dorothy. Perhaps she was inspired by Mary's example, for a few months later she took the plunge and, much to her father's disgust, had her own hair cut. Short hair opened up a whole new range of possible 'looks' and a new feeling of dependency: 'Had a haircut . . . My ladyfriend broke the news that she may be going elsewhere—that would be a blow, I like her and she seems to understand my hair' (6 May 1938). As a consumer, Dorothy had developed a personal relationship with her hairdresser, the 'producer' of her look. Similarly, she wrote of Kathleen Court as both a product and a person. Not all women attempted to follow the latest fashion in clothes or hairdos. Margaret Strongman learnt about the base used in face powders at a botany lecture, adding 'not that it means very much to me' (6 June 1938).

Margaret Strongman represented her youth in a very different way from either Kathleen Hughes or Dorothy Kendall. She was an English immigrant, arriving in Australia in 1937, at the age of 27, to work in a bank. The first year of her diary gives far more detail about her walking weekends, botany classes on Australian flora and fauna, Quaker meetings and work life than it does about her relationships. The youthful adventure which Margaret embarked upon was the discovery of a completely new country, a task she took very seriously. After about a year in Melbourne, it becomes apparent through the increasing regularity of references to a man by the name of Ernest that she was conducting a relationship with this fellow Quaker. When a work transfer took her to Sydney, she travelled to Melbourne for the occasional weekend to see him, and they eventually married in 1942. Margaret did not divulge any details about their relationship, and the frame of reference for her diary is far broader than that of Dorothy or Kathleen. We need to see much of Margaret's diary in the context of her Quaker beliefs. She regularly attended meetings at which topics such as the political situation in Europe were discussed, and her diary suggests a degree of political awareness absent from many of the other diaries, especially those of younger women. The framework within which Margaret understood this stage of her life, or at least constructed it in her diary, was not the dominant one of romantic adventure found in magazines and advertisements. Rather, she often criticised this view, preferring to see herself not as a consumer but as a social and political agent and a seeker after 'truth'. She found tennis, for example, 'too full of emptiness to satisfy me for long' (9 January 1938), and observed after listening to a performance of Bach's Mass in B Minor:

> Bach's music reveals all the joy of living, but for me it gives no glimpses, as do Rachmaninov and Cesar Franck, of the mysteries beyond the horizon of man's conceptions. It is good to be alive and revel in that joy with Bach, but sometimes I need to go searching to find where that joy comes from. (11 November 1938)

We do not find in Margaret Strongman's diary much evidence of the modern view of femininity, nor echoes of ideas about romance and relationships. But her diary forces us to recognise the existence of a much more muted language, and of alternative frameworks within which women could make sense of their lives. This is not to suggest that there was no intersection between these and the mainstream. While the religious framework within which Margaret Strongman situated herself may have provided alternative understandings of femininity, her ideas about motherhood and domesticity were much more similar to the prevailing ones. Margaret selected, probably unconsciously, the language which best expressed her experience at different points in her life, and which did not appear to contradict her other understandings of herself. To understand more fully women's experience of subjectivity, we need to be able to see the range of possibilities which, at any one time, women acted within and against. The contradictions which we might discern there do not necessarily emerge in women's diaries; the act of diary writing can function as a means of ordering and making sense of events and feelings, and thus suggest a level of coherence not always felt or experienced by the writer herself.

The extent to which women embraced the popular image of modern femininity depended on their own circumstances, and the degree to which the image addressed their specific desires and fears. Through their diaries women constructed their own self-images, selecting the events and recording the feelings that they wished to reveal and for which they could find echoes and meanings in the language available to them. Diary writing was a means of valuing their experiences, of making sense of them, and of asserting control over feelings which may otherwise have seemed too powerful, alien or strange to understand.

Women also used their diaries to record their progress, their 'successes' and 'failures' in becoming modern women. In the process of writing they revealed their hopes, doubts and fears, as Dorothy Kendall did when planning for marriage, competing with girlfriends for the attentions of men, dreaming of a relationship with Geoff, and facing the knowledge that he was not interested. For Kathleen Hughes, the hopes seemed to outweigh the fears and the story of romance was a fulfilling one: 'Stuart and I became engaged—most important event in our lives to date . . . we both feel that our engagement is the first of the many wonderful events we expect to fulfil together throughout our lives' (10 January 1941). The entry marks the end of her diary: her story of romance had reached its obvious conclusion and, in the way of all romances, the details of their life together are left to the reader's imagination. For other women, work and the fabric of their married lives were the very basis of their diaries: the story of youth and romance became lost in the daily round of domestic and paid labour.

2
Working lives I: Paid work

'The conveniences for a girl are not very great'

Dorothy Kendall had been working for many years as a typist and clerk at Employers' Liability Assurance in Queen Street, Melbourne, when she got a job at Kraft, a short walk across the Yarra from Employers'. The position offered her increased pay and responsibility and she soon came to terms with the vagaries of her new typewriter. The awkwardness of a strange office environment was a less technical problem, and more daunting. Dorothy recorded her first day at work, where she shared an office with Betty, the friend who had told her of the vacancy:

> Talk about palpitations—felt terrible going into Kraft—being eyed up and down by everyone. Betty introduced me to a few girls but I'll never be able to remember them. I'm in Betty's room behind the door so I can feel fairly safe during the day. (4 February 1937)

The following day she still 'felt very strange', but was 'getting used to the new typewriter', and managed to complete her first 'job' for her boss.

Dorothy had been with her previous employer for at least five years before she had plucked up the courage to leave. Having made the decision to apply for another job, she anxiously awaited the results of the Kraft interview:

> I've never put in such a day for years. Immediately after lunchtime I started listening for the telephone and my heart sank lower and lower as it got later and still no word. At last it came at 4.45 and I feared the worst when I heard Mr Mason's voice, as Betty had said she would

> make him do his own dirty work if my application was unsuccessful. However it is all right—cheers—I still can't believe it's true.
>
> Plucked up my courage and went and told Stevie—he was flabbergasted. So was everyone else when they heard. (27 January 1937)

Dorothy's news was greeted with such astonishment at Employers' that they offered her an immediate pay rise and 'prospects' in an attempt to keep her. She was unimpressed, although flattered by the upheaval her announcement had caused, commenting, 'I never felt so important in my life before' (28 January 1937).

Dorothy's record of her working days at Employers' Assurance and Kraft gives us considerable insight into the conditions of her employment and her experiences in the paid workforce. The borders between her public and personal life merged in her diary. At Employers' she shared an office with several people. It appears to have been a friendly working climate, if at times a little stressed during the monthly rush to get work completed on time. But Dorothy obviously felt it was time for a change, and it certainly appears she was worth more than she received acknowledgment, or payment, for. Her move to Kraft began a new phase in her working life. As senior typist/stenographer, she felt keenly the pressure on her to perform well and to be consistently up to standard. She shared an office with Betty, who was also a typist/stenographer. Their bosses, significantly, worked upstairs. Dorothy beat a constant path up and down the stairs, returning and collecting work from 'Doc', a man for whom she felt some fear and whose praise was priceless. It was during the interwar period that clerical work became a female domain. Dorothy was one of a large number of young women who entered white-collar employment after the First World War.

The movement of women into the office marked a change in the structure of the labour force: single white middle-class women were working in greater numbers than before, and many of the areas in which they were employed became designated as specifically feminine. This trend had begun before the war, and as women workers proved themselves to be equally efficient but cheaper than men, the mechanisation and female staffing of office work was bound to continue. Notions of efficiency, progress and rationality began to inform workplace management, and with the organisation of the workforce around the sexual division of labour, the allocation of work on the basis of sex took shape.

In the optimistic climate and economic boom of the 1920s, women were encouraged to consider a variety of career options, including advertising, accountancy and architecture. In 1923

Woman's World listed office work as the first answer to its problem, 'What to do with our girls':

> This is the beginning of the commercial age for women. They are invading the business world in thousands and little by little are working their way to the higher positions once deemed inaccessible to any but the lords of creation. (1 September 1923)

Such optimism was not borne out by women's experience. Instead they remained in low-paid jobs and, rather than being encouraged to pursue a successful career in their chosen profession, were usually counselled to view their working lives as a temporary state which would cease on their marriage. Young women were rarely discussed as paid workers. More often, they were represented as pursuing other interests, notably romance. Without positive representations to draw on, diarists involved in paid work had little to say about their working days. Work is mentioned, but often in passing, and only Dorothy Kendall provided expansive detail about her working environment. Dorothy constructed herself as a working woman against a background of concerted attacks on women in the paid workforce. She portrayed her work as important and necessary in itself, and her wage as essential to her family's survival. This challenged traditional hierarchies of importance. In the later years of her diary writing, her work assumed less significance and she focused more on conventional female pursuits, notably romance.

Dorothy took considerable pride in her work and did not take lightly the responsibility with which she was entrusted. When her diary of 1932 opens, she was working as a clerk and typist: she had the duty of balancing the books each week and the 'returns' each month. This entailed, among other things, checking the calculations of the other staff members and making sure that they all tallied and were ready for the beginning of the next month. 'The usual rush round after the end of the month. The auditor is in—worse than ever—if he doesn't get more sense about vouchers soon I'll do something serious' (2 May 1935). As information from interstate was often late in arriving, and Dorothy was dependent on other people to complete their work before she could complete hers, she was often held up and forced to work back late, hours for which she was not initially paid. 'Work is a hell of a mess. Managed to finish the Accident Returns, which balanced but Mr Kelsell is still holding me up on the fire returns and I must balance with Miss Crellin before she goes away' (9 March 1933). Dorothy's co-workers did not share her skill in efficient time management. Dorothy was not paid for overtime work until 1935, a development which considerably shortened her working week. Some days she had worked as late as 11.30 pm, diligently trying to get things finished in time for deadlines. The very notion of overtime work highlights the relationship between time and money, and the impact of industrial time on the structure and management of the workplace. When the rumour concerning overtime was in the air, Dorothy noted a distinct change in the company attitude: 'Worked back to try and get the accounts out all right. There really must be something in the rumour about overtime—they make such a fuss about working back' (11 November 1935).

Dorothy's income made a significant contribution to the comfort and well-being of her family. The Kendall family may have been middle class in their status and aspirations, but they were not spared the hardships of the Depression, although doubtless they were not as severely affected as working-class families with no income. The financial position of Dorothy's father is unclear from her diary, but his veterinary business seems to have suffered considerably, leaving the children of the family as the main bread-winners. Dorothy pawned her mother's jewellery to help make ends meet, and faced the disappointment of a smaller-than-hoped-for pay packet: 'We were all on tenderhooks [sic] anticipating our 10 *op* [or 10%] but when we were paid before lunch we only got our bare pay, not even a rise. . . . Bought a new suspender belt and broke the sad news re my pay to Jack [her brother]' (29 January 1932). The suspicion of more bad news prompted feelings of despair: 'Rumour going round that instead of getting back our 10/*op* we are to have another cut. How do they expect us to manage. Felt miserable all day on that account. Just my luck' (12 February 1932). Dorothy, of course, was not alone in her despair and in less anxious moments was conscious of her comparative good fortune in having a job at all, and of its respectable status. Not all her friends were so lucky. One of them worked in a shoe store: 'She's very sensitive about people thinking her in a low position but after all a job's a job' (6 April 1932). And when those around her were getting retrenched, Dorothy was able to sympa-thise: 'I know what it feels like to wonder how safe you are' (16 January 1932). Four years later, when the severity of the Depres-sion had eased for the Kendall family, Dorothy was anxious to change employers but felt her time had passed: 'when I was young enough to get out the depression was on and we were so grateful for any kind of job that we put up with things. The firm does not realise that and cannot understand why the junior girls are dissatisfied' (13 February 1932).

Dorothy's hours at work were often long and pressured. While at Employers' she worked every Saturday morning and often overtime during the week. She rarely mentioned receiving any praise for a job well done. Instead she was often given other people's tasks to complete: 'Typed R/I proposals for Bo. He's an ungrateful wretch. He doesn't realise its not my job' (23 February 1932). Undoubtedly Dorothy had a sense of her central role in the smooth running of the company, but the strongest indication the firm gave her of how valued she was came on her decision to leave, making her wish she'd threatened to do so earlier. Even then she was generous enough to continue to help them with the books after she had joined Kraft, commenting after one return visit, 'The books would break your heart' (8 February 1937).

Dorothy's work not only provided her with an income and thus a means of contributing to the family finances, but also gave a sense of purpose and structure to her day. She generally enjoyed her work, and appeared to like the people with whom she worked. And the social activities of the company and the office staff, though limited, added another dimension to her world. When Dorothy joined Kraft and her infatuation with Geoff began, work assumed another meaning as well, and the job itself became secondary to the opportunity it provided to fantasise about her future and her romances. At Kraft Dorothy was engaged mainly in typing and shorthand work. Her boss was a hard task-master and it took her some months to gain confidence in the quality of her work for him. 'Did Doc's Air Mail letter all right and for once did not have to retype it. He really seemed pleased with it. Dictated another one—harder, feel dubious about it' (19 July 1937). Praise from Doc was rare and thus appreciated all the more when it did come. She had been working at Kraft a year before she really felt she had pleased him:

> Doc back—sent for me early and dictated pages and pages of report. However, for once I got a good go at it and was almost finished by lunchtime—took it up immediately afterwards. Later in the afternoon he rang for me again—remarked that the report was a good effort, not a single mistake. That is high praise from him—I was thrilled. (24 March 1938)

Whereas at Employers' Dorothy's sense of her work had derived from measurable factors such as whether the books balanced or were finished on time, at Kraft she looked to her male employer for a sense of the worth of her work. Her comments on Doc's reactions to her work reveal the vulnerability she felt in relation to him, and her unarticulated sense of the power imbalance in the office. This was played out in an even more dramatic way in her infatuation with Geoff. The gender roles were as defined as with Doc, but now the arenas of work, romance, and fantasy overlapped in complicated ways: 'Geoff came in for a chat while Betty was absent . . . later on he came in about Miss Barnes having a week's holiday. Wouldn't it be a thrill if I had to do his letters' (29 July 1937).

The routines and time demands of the paid workforce were quite different from those of the home and kitchen, despite reformers' attempts to suggest otherwise. Office and factory workers had set hours for the commencement and conclusion of their day's work, and a set time for lunch. They were paid according to the hours worked. Thus a degree of regimentation imbued each working day, and it could be closely monitored. Dorothy recorded the lack of flexibility at her office: 'There was a bit of a rumpus on Monday on account of Miss Clarke getting out in her wrong lunch hour. I'll have to watch my step' (5 May 1932). Dorothy was very conscious of time, and of the need for punctuality at work. She usually caught the train to work, although if she was running late, buses provided a more expensive but quicker means of transport: 'An awful job dragging myself out of bed. Went in by bus again. I am getting extravagant' (7 January 1932). Her trip to work took her from the suburban spaces of Melbourne's tree-lined eastern suburbs to the heart of the city's business district. Employers' Assurance was situated at 9 Queen Street, just down from the corner of Flinders Street, in the Fenton Building. Dorothy's train would have taken her to Flinders Street Station. From there she had only a short two blocks to walk to Queen Street. The firm shared the building with a number of other companies, including four other insurance firms, two commission agents, an auctioneer, a sign writer and a grain merchant. The surrounding buildings would have shared similar work cultures: the south end of Queen Street housed many insurance firms, as well as solicitors, merchants, and timber and shipping agents. It was a business part of town, away from the shopping areas, small factories and State Parliament.

At lunchtime, Dorothy frequently went down to Bourke Street, the commercial centre of town and home of Melbourne's main department stores: Myer, Buckley and Nunn, Coles, and, further up the street, Paynes department store, where Kathleen Hughes worked. Dorothy would regularly meet a friend for lunch, concluding the hour with some mandatory window shopping. At other times she shopped, replenishing her supplies of items such as underwear, or selecting a gift for a friend. Dorothy's main shopping time, however, was after work on Fridays, when she became a consumer in her city rather than a worker with an hour to spare. On other evenings, she enjoyed the leisure activities the city had to offer: she often went to a show or a film with a friend, her brother, or occasionally her father. Dorothy's experience of the city changed according to where she was, her purpose, the day of the week, and the time of day. Her experience of the office could also vary: 'Worked back until 7.30, on my own from 6 onward, and had a scare when a drunk man came in. Then had a yarn on drunk men and their funny ways with the caretaker while she was sweeping the floor' (7 January 1932).

When Dorothy went to work at Kraft, her relationship to the city changed. Kraft was situated in Riverside Avenue, a few blocks walk across the Yarra River from Employers'. She still may have caught the train to work, or after moving house to Dandenong Road, Prahran, a tram or bus might have provided the quickest route. Riverside Avenue was on the banks of the river, a short street containing just a few buildings. There would have been fewer people working in the immediate vicinity, and the area would have had a very different atmosphere from that of Queen Street. Bourke Street was too far to walk for the lunchtime break, and Dorothy ceased meeting friends during her lunch hour. As an alternative, the gardens a few blocks away on St Kilda Road provided a pleasant and calm place to spend an hour. The city was now a place Dorothy went only for shopping or for entertainment, but at this point in her life her diary became so absorbed with Geoff, his movements and her fantasies, that she ceased recording the usual details that had filled its pages in the past. Romance was a far more acceptable pursuit for a young woman than paid work.

Margaret Strongman also had a paid job, but in a bank rather than an office. Margaret arrived in Australia with her friend Lexie from Britain in December 1937. They had both worked for the National Bank in England and started work in Melbourne the day after their arrival: 'We were glad it was taken for granted that we were starting work on the morrow. A more purposeful life will be very welcome after so much lazing' (6 December 1937). Margaret had obviously been used to structured time. On her first day of employment, she discovered difficulties similar to those Dorothy Kendall encountered when faced with a new typewriter. Office machines may all have looked the same to the uninitiated, but for

Spaces in her day

Margaret and Dorothy, their machines affected the quality of their work.

> A typewriter felt a strange thing after 6 weeks holiday from it, and as it was an Underwood with a large carriage, fingers were worse than thumbs. If a knob pushes down on a Royal, it pulls up on an Underwood. If it goes up on a Royal it goes down on an Underwood, and everything that should be on the right is on the left.
>
> I have been stationed in Staff Office (apparently Mr McLeod, Staff manager intends to keep an eye on me), and Lexie has been put downstairs on Securities in Branch Department. There is plenty of room everywhere, and after the cramped conditions of London Office, everything is luxurious. I have been given a pile of statistics to copy, which is going to take me several days—weeks if I continue to have the interruptions at the same rate as to-day, but it is nice to see the old faces again. (7 December 1937)

As Margaret settled into her new workplace and new country, machines and work routines were not all she had to adjust to. Bank staff were required to wear uniforms: 'I received my uniform today; Lexie's had to go back to be altered. They are quite smart, navy blue with white collar. They will save our clothes but it is going to be a great fag changing in and out' (15 December 1937). Margaret did not say so, but uniforms were probably restricted to female employees: the suits and ties of men were no doubt uniform enough. Uniforms presented a clean, neat exterior to the public, streamlining the look of a company's employees.

The sexual division of labour was very marked in banks, and Margaret already felt the watchful eyes of her superior. At Christmas she discovered another side to this when all the female staff received a box of chocolates from the men. Some branches, however, were still getting used to the presence of women, and made the most of their services. In March 1938 Margaret was transferred to the Stock Exchange branch, and commented, 'The conveniences for a girl are not very great, especially when it comes to tea making, but the staff are very pleasant working companions' (28 April 1938). The introduction of women into the workplace required the rearrangement and clear demarcation of space. Margaret was not always treated with great consideration. Over one three-day period she was moved four times between departments and branches, and on another morning she was told she was needed in Ballarat by the afternoon:

> Asked at 11 o'clock if I would be prepared to go that afternoon to Ballarat for sick relief. Accepted, although it rather upset plans for the week lunch with Ernest. Dashed around, cancelled arrangements and

packed in time to catch half-past two express which got me into Ballarat by 4.45. (17 January 1939)

There were also days when Margaret did not relish the work she was allocated to do: 'Sent up to Western Branch for a week. Changing from ledger to machines and I have the tedious and monotonous job of heading up cards and addressing envelopes etc. in preparation for the change over' (28 November 1938). With 1000 to be done, it is no wonder she harboured misgivings about the task. New technology may have been designed to save time and money, but its implementation could mean weeks of repetitive, boring work, which often fell to women.

The scant references to paid work in most of these women's diaries may reflect the lack of positive public representations of working women. Women's work was usually equated with domestic work. Magazine articles that did discuss women in the workforce tended to focus on the appearance and attitudes required by employers, but even these articles—never numerous— all but disappeared during the 1930s. Margaret wrote at great length about her leisure activities, her walking and travel, Quaker meetings, and about the self-improvement lectures she regularly attended. Diary writing could thus be a leisure activity in itself, providing a break in the day and a retreat from other demands. But the demands of domestic work receive far greater attention in these women's diaries than those of paid employment. Margaret usually mentioned work only when there had been a significant disruption to the normal routine, or a development, such as her transfer to Sydney, which would have a great impact on her daily life. And at these times, she was concerned not with details about the daily round of work, but with how the changes would affect her life as a whole.

Both Dorothy and Margaret worked in a formal work environment and work structure. They lived within easy travelling distance from their workplaces—Dorothy in Armadale and later Prahran, and Margaret in Hawthorn—their hours were set for them, and their pay was governed by industrial awards. Both were single and ceased working soon after marriage. They worked in highly segregated work environments, where the tasks of male and female employees were classified differently and paid accordingly.

Ida Dawson's conditions of employment were radically different. She took her first position as a teacher in Sydney at the age of nineteen in 1898, and in 1900 got a job as a governess at Bullagreen, south-west of Goulburn, NSW. Ida was acutely aware of the restrictions placed on women. Her recognition of this extended from her inability to vote to the occupations she was prevented from pursuing: 'I love the sea, and sometimes I wish I were a man, so that I could be a sailor' (31 July 1899). Instead, as had so many women before her, she pursued her fantasy in fiction, posing as a sailor and telling of 'A shred of life'. Ida wrote this short story for a group she attended during her stay in Sydney. She disguised her identity and the story received very favourable comments.

Ida worked as a governess or 'companion' for almost 40 years, with a few years of school teaching in between. For the most part, she appears to have enjoyed her work, and as she was a great traveller with a keen sense of adventure, governessing provided her with a perfect opportunity to travel widely throughout NSW as well as overseas, to Fiji, South America and Java. Yet the flexibility of the work was also one of its major drawbacks: appointments were never guaranteed from one year to the next, working conditions could vary enormously and were very difficult to establish until you were committed to a task, and the hospitality of the employing family could determine whether the job was an enjoyable experience or a difficult and lonely one. Predictably, Ida had her share of both ups and downs. As insecure as governessing could be for a younger woman, it was even less reliable as a source of income as one grew older. As Ida became increasingly restricted by ill health, so the positions she could apply for diminished and she was forced to support herself through short-term jobs which provided little satisfaction and often proved emotionally and physically taxing.

In theory, governesses were employed to teach standard subjects such as English, History, Mathematics, and so on as well as 'accomplishments' such as music, sewing and fine needlework. Many found themselves called upon to perform tasks more akin to those of a domestic servant than of a teacher. While they struggled, as Ida Dawson did, to maintain their independence, in many ways they merely replaced their dependence on their own family, subjecting themselves to the routines, disciplines and eccentricities of another family. Ida, when she worked as governess to her brother's children, felt keenly the ambiguity of her position. As a teacher, she performed all the tasks required of her, but as a family member, she also found herself taking charge of the kitchen in the absence of her brother and sister-in-law, and supervising the running of the household and staff. She was not rewarded for her efforts with the companionship of her brother, but instead felt excluded from the family and suffered bouts of extreme loneliness, noting on one occasion, 'Wish something out of the way would happen—something nice for me. Have the blues lately—too much loneliness—in the house' (24 November 1921). Ida left her brother's house in 1923 and went to work for another family in Argentina. Used to a degree of disorder and undefined roles, initially she found the structure of her new job a welcome relief:

> The house is very well ordered, & my hours are fixed & regular, thank goodness. I have a very nice schoolroom; & bedroom: the maid brings me tea in the morning, & arranges my bed, etc. We all eat & sit together, but the nursery & our rooms & bathroom, etc are in a sort of separate wing. Electric light hot & cold water. The children have 'nursery tea' at 4.30, when we have afternoon tea, the babies go to bed at 6.30; the bigger children at 6.45. About 6, we all play some sort of game with them—poker is the rage at present. (11 June 1923)

Ida, however, had too active a mind and spirit to find such an environment satisfying for long, and the lack of alternative stimulation weighed her down:

> Read, knitted, etc. after school hours. I find time hang [sic] rather heavily at most times, when I am not teaching. The place is too—civilised. The grown-ups had their dinner in bed the last 2 nights. The fog did not lift all day. (9 August 1923)

The fog, like the time, hung heavily in the air, dampening Ida's spirit: the order and structure imposed upon the house and the day left no room for spontaneity. Unlike Dorothy or Margaret, Ida could not leave her place of work at the end of the day and find comfort or entertainment elsewhere. The times of her work were set by her employers, and their routines, plus the location of individual jobs, also determined the possibilities and scope of her leisure activities. To a large degree, Ida's environment was constructed for her: she had no place of her own to retreat to, while set, unspoken limits constrained the degree to which she could imprint her personality on the space around her. In this situation, Ida's diary became the only space that was her own, a place where she could divulge her feelings and express her own sense of the people and places that were important to her.

The ambiguity of Ida's position as a governess is further highlighted by an experience she had while in Java. She had initially hoped that the climate and the people would make up for her lack of interest in a job she had recently commenced, but she was disappointed:

Several to lunch & dinner. Not much for me, as I feel an outsider, & my chief occupation consisted of going for miles—long walks with the children both morning & afternoon. Unfortunately things are not always what they seem & this job isn't going to last. It is merely a nurse-girl's billet. (15 August 1927)

Ida had more respect for her talents than to stay with a job for which she was overqualified and which offered her nothing. She left two weeks later, commenting, 'it is purgatory to remain here' (27 August 1927). When she returned to Australia in 1929 she was faced with the prospect of again finding work. Teaching was not her first option: 'Have been answering ads. all this week, but have not had replies; suppose I will have to go to the country again, & teach' (10 May 1929). She duly took a job in Murrumbateman, near Yass, in NSW. Plagued by rheumatoid arthritis, she stayed only five months and left, by 'mutual agreement'. The following year she took up another position in Goodooga, near Brewarrina on the Queensland/NSW border. This was sheep farming country, whose flat plains extended seemingly forever and were subject to long droughts and bad floods. Ida seems to have been happier here than she had been for a long time. The homestead she described as a 'real old fashioned, rambling station homestead', boasting a wonderful garden—quite an unexpected bonus given the general shortage of water (11 April 1930). She got on well with the family, participated in local events such as dances and races, and joined the local branch of the Country Women's Association. And as the station was large enough to employ a manager, an overseer and bookkeeper, not to mention jackaroos and station hands who would also have been around, Ida was not dependent on the family alone for her social activities.

As a single woman struggling to support herself, Ida felt keenly the insecurity of her financial position and the diminishing openings for a woman with her talents and skills. When resident in Sydney, which she usually was between country or overseas positions, she appears to have sought temporary jobs as a companion or live-in help: 'Yesterday morning I came here (Hurlstone Park): to look after house & 3 kiddies while the mother is in hospital. Busy time, & much tired, but not so bad, I think' (3 June 1929). Ida resigned herself to some jobs, accepting the money if not enjoying the work: 'My job is all right as far as it goes: serves the purpose of keeping the pot boiling; & they are nice to me' (3 August 1929). Again, neither Ida's time nor space were her own. She appears almost grateful for her employers' kindness, knowing that they had the ability to make her time unhappy and difficult. Not all employers were so satisfactory:

> Yesterday I left my billet at Darlinghurst,—the lady was 'incapable' every day . . . Came out here to Hunters Hill. Oh, how glad I shall be to get settled once more—this work is only a stop-gap, as I need the money, so badly, until I can sell the cottage.' (22 December 1926)

Ida had bought the cottage she referred to with money left to her by a cousin. Owning it seems to have caused her more trouble than she felt it was worth, and she wrote of it as a millstone round her neck, limiting her options for work and travel.

Ida managed to survive on the money she earned from governessing and teaching, although it is clear from her reaction to news of any inheritances that she felt the limits of her financial situation very keenly. A cousin left £3000 to be divided among four of the Dawson sisters: 'It is too wonderful to be true, almost. I have had a headache ever since & couldn't sleep all night' (3 March 1926). Two days later she was still dreaming of the money: 'Can't help thinking a lot about the wonderful legacy, & am building "castles"' (5 March 1926). She did not elaborate on what happened to this money, although she and her sisters put some together to help their brothers buy land in Queensland. Unaccustomed to such sums, she may have had an exaggerated sense of what might be done with £750. By the end of the year Ida was lamenting her lack of income and clearly not living in luxury. She may have invested the windfall for later use: in 1947 she comments that her sister Margy bought a cottage in Hornsby 'with C. Harry's legacy' (18 July 1947).

Whatever the finer details of Ida's financial arrangements, it is clear she was assisted in her later years by the generous legacies of relatives. Before this, however, she supported herself through teaching. Teaching was not Ida's first love: it was a means of making ends meet. With the money she earned this way, she pursued a far more rewarding interest: writing. She began writing stories and poetry while still at school, and continued after she left. She showed a collection to an older male friend, who advised her to 'keep writing & so perfect myself in the technique of the art' (6 July 1898). In 1900 she submitted her first contribution to a magazine and a year later was accepted by the *Stock and Station Journal* to write notes on her district for its 'gossip' column. The male editor of the column told her she could succeed if she had 'grit'. To succeed, Ida was required to adopt the attitudes and values of a male-dominated world. By 1919 she had pieces appearing fairly regularly in the *Bulletin*, some of which brought her considerable satisfaction: 'Am in the Literary Page of the Bulletin this week. Quite stuck up about it' (17 November 1919). She referred to a letter written in reply to another on the reading tastes of the Australian public, and whether the compulsory education system developed them. Ida believed that a taste for good literature began at home.[1] On her departure for Argentina, the *Bulletin* hailed her as knowing 'as much about the wattle and the wallaby as any Australian woman-writer'.[2] It was fine praise, although qualified: she was being compared to women writers, not writers in general. She may also have questioned the timing of such praise, coming as it did on the eve of her departure. She wryly noted in her diary while in Argentina, 'I seem to have more recognition of my nature writing & work since I left Australia than when I was there' (19 October 1920). This lack of appreciation was common to most Australian women writers. Drusilla Modjeska observes that to 'be a woman and a writer in Australia during the twenties was an isolated and often desolate existence . . . Women's intellectual and literary endeavour was simply not taken seriously and often . . . not even recognised.'[3] No doubt living and teaching in the country, as Ida did before her departure, exacerbated her isolation. But it was not only isolation that made women writers' lives desolate, it was the persistent under-valuation of their work.

Ida used her time away from Australia both to write and to create a reserve of ideas for future articles and stories. She lived her present with a constant eye to her future and similarly viewed her environment through eyes set on distant horizons. Ida did receive some recognition of her work when she returned, and for a while her pieces on life in the Argentine seem to have been in demand. Her return was noted in the *Bulletin*, along with claims that she was the first white woman to have crossed the Andes.[4] It was the printing of her own articles which really pleased Ida, however: 'The [Australian Woman's] Mirror has printed my article on Argentine cooking—with photographs. Very proud I am!' (24 November 1925). She was even more delighted when she was paid for her labours: 'Recd. £1.15.0 for my Mirror article! Must write another' (12 January 1926). Ida continued to write articles, an occupation which both brought some remuneration and, more importantly, gave her great satisfaction. The public acknowledgment she received confirmed her sense of herself as a writer. The early years of her diary suggest that she would have liked to pursue writing as a profession. Unable to make a living that way, she was forced to write in her spare time. Ida was not a complete stranger in literary circles. She mentioned dropping in on the writer Mary Gilmore, and was among Nettie Palmer's many correspondents. These women do not feature prominently in her diary, however, although their presence there at all suggests a link with a wider network of Australian women writers, a sense of her identity as a writer, and the existence of a source of support and intellectual engagement:

> Returned to C'wood [Chatswood] this evening: on the way called on Mrs Mary Gilmore, & we had a long afternoon together: very interesting talk, & she took me to tea at one of her clubs,—an 'art' place with an extraordinary 'colour scheme'. (15 July 1929)

The year of Ida's return from Argentina, she noted in her diary, in large, well-spaced letters, 'Began *The* Book' (26 October 1925). Unfortunately, she did not elaborate. But at that time she was publishing regular articles in a variety of magazines and newspapers. My guess is that 'the book' was Ida's own writing, drawn from stories of her travels. An entry nine years later suggests that she did not abandon her project: 'Will Lawson came out one day to look at my "book" & manuscripts, & had an idea of "ghosting" it, but his price—£10,—is too high' (15 August 1934). Not given to disclosing her emotions in her diary, Ida revealed nothing more about how she had received such an offer. 'Ghosting' was not an uncommon practice at the time. Writers could assist one another by ghosting articles if time or money was short: the ghost writer received a sum from the original writer, who made up the money on sales. It is unclear from Ida's diary what she thought about the idea. She may have thought her book would sell better under a different name, or, at 55 and no longer a young woman, she may have felt unequal to the task of finishing it. However, as one who had all her life aspired to be a writer, she is unlikely to have embraced the idea of publishing under someone else's name. Whatever her feelings, Ida recorded only her rejection of the offer. Hidden behind her excuse of financial excess, perhaps lay a sense of considerable disappointment.

That women's creative urges have been silenced, the record of their talents hidden from public view or lost altogether, is by now a truism. Virginia Woolf's well-known question, 'what would have happened had Shakespeare had a wonderfully gifted sister . . .?' throws into relief the obstacles women have had to overcome before they could approach the point from which many men begin their creative life.[5] Ida Dawson did not have the financial security, nor therefore the leisure, to turn her writing into a profession. Forced to move around the country in search of work or to care for her family—travel which admittedly provided her with interesting subject matter for articles—she was often deprived of the stability she needed to write consistently, and of the support of other women writers. And even when she was living in Sydney, she invariably worked in temporary live-in situations which were a far cry from Woolf's 'room of one's own' and £500 a year. Ida's has been the fate of many women writers, tied as they invariably have been to family responsibilities or to earning a living, and thus with only limited control over their time or their space. When Ida next mentioned writing a book it was in 1947: this one was to be a collection of her articles previously published by the *Bulletin* and the *Mirror* (12 July 1947).

In contrast to Ida, Una Falkiner had both the leisure and the money to pursue her interest in painting and drawing. She even had the money to finance the publication of her illustrations in *The Spider's Telephone Wire*, a religious children's book with a text by Rev. David Millar.[6]

Winifred Tait also enjoyed writing although regarded it as an addition to her teaching rather than as a substitute. Unlike Ida, Winifred loved teaching. For her it was not merely a matter of making ends meet; it provided her with constant stimulation and enjoyment. She took a keen interest in different methods of teaching and explored their effectiveness on her pupils. But Winifred wrote little in any of her diaries about these aspects of her life. She recorded problems with staff, and students' results, but rarely wrote of her feelings during the daily round of classes and instruction. In the years for which Winifred wrote more than one diary, any details about her working life would be kept in one book, while a much fuller record of her emotions, and in particular her spiritual life, would be kept in another. This diary itself was a space of leisure and an escape from the demands of her working life. The two came together at points when Winifred felt herself in need of divine guidance on certain issues relating to the school, or sought forgiveness, for example, for her sharp handling of a staff member.

In many ways, Winifred was in an unusual position for a teacher. Most female teachers were concentrated in primary education, which the Victorian chief inspector of education in 1928 said 'should be regarded as women's rather than men's work': men were to be entrusted with the higher responsibility of secondary education, which boys were more likely to continue with than girls.[7] Very few female or male teachers would have been as well educated as Winifred, and few would have had the opportunity to open their own school, which Winifred did along with other members of her family. But there were other unusual features about Winifred's position: as the principal of the school she often had greater control over her teaching hours than would most members of staff, and a degree of flexibility in structuring her day. The other side of this, however, was her position of responsibility, which in most of her appointments required her to be in permanent residence at the school and thus always wearing the principal's cap. No doubt this contributed to her anticipation of and delight in the Monday afternoons she spent with her friend Jean, a time when she could escape the school grounds and her role of authority. As for Ida Dawson, the personal and private spaces available to her were very limited, but while Ida was aware of the effect this had on her, Winifred did not reflect on the tensions it may have caused in her life. Nor did she draw links in her diary between her state of mind and her teaching, except when bad end-of-year results brought on feelings of despondency. Only in the later years of her working life did Winifred write relatively frequently of her work. Before she took up her position as principal of St Anne's College, late in her career, she gave weekly lectures and classes on literature to adult students, an occupation which gave her a small income, a structure to her week and a sense of satisfaction. She commented on her happiness and love of teaching. However, when Winifred assumed her responsibilities in another residential position, she ceased to write about her teaching, if indeed she was doing any. Her diary carries many rather cryptic comments about the politics of the school and conflict between herself and members of the male hierarchy who oversaw the administration of the college, but it is apparent from the little she did write that she recorded considerably more detail in a third diary she was keeping at the time but which no longer survives. Winifred may have had a passion to record, but she also had a keen eye for material she believed too sensitive for the gaze of others.

If Winifred's living arrangements blurred the distinction between her public and her personal life, she reasserted that division through the use of different diaries. Those which related to her professional life held no comment on her emotions. They served as memoranda, chronicling her teaching activities or occasions such as a prefects' meeting or a gathering of 'old girls'. As an intelligent and ambitious single woman, Winifred was able to pursue a career far more like those open to men most women of her generation could. That career model insisted on a clear distinction between a person's professional and personal life.

Winifred's numerous consecutive diaries reveal how tenuous this division was for her, but they nevertheless served to reinforce it.

Winifred's diaries raise other issues about work, notably the relationship between paid work and writing. All the diaries draw attention to this dynamic, and the ways in which the diarists perceived their work and shaped their time. For women such as Dorothy Kendall and Margaret Strongman, who travelled to work each day and had set times for arrival, lunch and departure, working hours were clearly delineated. Dorothy and Margaret would write about events which transpired at work alongside other happenings which occurred before or after work, at different times, and in different places. For Ida Dawson and Winifred Tait, it was not nearly as easy to make such distinctions. And for Ida in particular, there was a close relationship between diary writing and work. The diary entries she made while away in Argentina served as references when she came to write articles for publication, thus blurring the distinction between the so-called 'public' and 'private' aspects of her life. So while Ida's governessing work features little in the diaries, and her diary while she was 'on location' became one of the few personal spaces available to her, at the same time she used it with an eye to the future for more professional and public reasons. Winifred Tait reinforced in her diary the distinctions between her professional and personal life, but in Ida's diary the two become collapsed.

What is perhaps most notable from the diaries of women who were paid for their labour is their general silence about their jobs. Aside from Dorothy, they provided scant detail about work, much less than they accorded other activities, thoughts or feelings. The advocacy of maternity as women's natural occupation meant that for women who were not mothers, their paid work received little or no social endorsement. While women themselves may not have worried about whether their work was being socially endorsed or not, especially if they needed money to survive, they did not have the language with which to write about, or even conceive of, their work in positive and expansive terms. Women's main concern, as represented in magazines, in advertisements and in newspapers, was to pursue the romantic quest, or, having done so, to be absorbed in homemaking and childrearing. It is not surprising, therefore, that Kathleen Hughes, who was working as a shop assistant at Paynes, rarely mentioned her work: the focus of her diary was the side of her life which received public acknowledgment as a worthwhile pursuit. For her, diary writing could be a means of self-validation, and did not need to be one of defiance.

Similarly, Dorothy Kendall's more detailed accounting of her working day all but ceased when she became absorbed in her romantic hopes and dreams of a future with Geoff. By contrast, married women engaged in the unending round of domestic labour had considerable material to draw upon for their constructions of themselves as working women.

3
Working lives II: Domestic work

'I get but little done'

Mabel Lincoln lived at number 10 Peart Street, Leongatha, in a neat, weatherboard house just ten minutes walk from the town's main street. She had moved there in 1923 from Ruby, a small village only 8 kilometres out of Leongatha, where her husband ran a dairy farm. The move marked a significant change for Mabel: at 45, her years of farm labour had come to an end, only to be replaced with the equally taxing task of assisting her daughter Rosie in establishing and running Lincoln's General Store. Mabel's domestic labour, however, probably remained constant. She worked hard in her house, as most homemakers had always done. The work was heavy and constant, with few reprieves and few labour-saving devices to ease the burden. The combination of maintaining wood or coal fires, coppers for washing, and heavy irons, and a sizeable household to cook for, left little room for other activities. Added to her daily tasks was the regular and detailed recording of them in her diary:

> Rise 7.30 Light fire dress scramble eggs for breakfast, do out front of house & front verandah, tidy dining room & make meat pies & apricot pies for dinner make Mabel [her granddaughter] a little meat pie & a tiny apricot pie all for herself, after dinner get cleaned up by 3.30 bake Apricot milk pudding for tea, get on to the back rooms until 6 oclock, do out broom cupboard, clean seven pairs of shoes & slippers clean bath, mirror & Bon Ami the kitchen windows, clean radiator, do the floors, try out Trio Bright on kitchen floor, do not have a brush, use

a tiny bit of rag, & rub it in like floor polish, seems to be alright does not stick. (20 May 1930)

This entry conveys a sense of Mabel's day as filled with domestic chores. It was organised according to the time taken for each task as well as the spatial arrangements of her house. In the account of her cleaning we can see the influence of advertising and prescriptive literature, but also shrewd scepticism (and the possibility of resistance): '*try out* Trio Bright'. Having laboured over her floors with a 'tiny bit of rag' (how long *did* it take her?), Mabel pronounced the new product 'alright'.

Interspersed with Mabel's cleaning was her cooking. Food and housework are two of the organising principles of her diary, both firmly grounded in the temporal and spatial patterns of her day. The centre of her landscape was her kitchen, a site of both work and entertainment. Ten Peart Street was a popular stopping place for many of Leongatha's residents, and Mabel was generous with her hospitality. To some of these visitors she would read out sections of her diary,[1] presumably entertaining them with her accounts of local kitchen dramas as well as asserting the high standard of her housekeeping. She was making public the nature of her domestic work at a time when public prescriptions for women on the efficient management of their homes—the so called 'private' sphere—were reaching new heights: the divisions between public and private were being dismantled from both sides of the front fence.

The spaces people inhabit and the 'things' with which they fill those spaces tell us a great deal about people's individual psyches and their relationship with their environment. Similarly, the architecture and internal design of a house can tell us not only about women's domestic labour but about gender and labour relations within the home, and the social values placed on factors such as cleanliness, hygiene and efficiency. Studying the physical shape and space of houses in conjunction with contemporary discussions about domestic labour suggests many avenues for understanding the constraints within which women performed their work and lived much of their lives. It does not, however, tell us how they experienced their space, how they knew it and how they lived in it. Nor does it convey the conflicts women experienced in attempting to structure their day around concepts of time not designed to accommodate human demands and individual life rhythms. Women's diaries do not offer us such ready-made clues either. Diarists did not sit down and describe their house, taking us through its rooms and drawing our attention to specific items of furniture or ornaments. Perhaps their lack of self-consciousness in this regard is an advantage: their houses are unconscious allegories, not deliberately constructed ones. We learn of a diarist's house and garden almost exclusively through her account of the work she performed in it. Mabel Lincoln referred to cleaning the front or back of her house, itemising the windows she cleaned and the floors she polished. She knew her home through the work she performed there, as we know our environment through our activities within it. Una Falkiner's experience of her home, in which she did little physical labour, would have been radically different from that of her servants, for example. By looking at the home, the garden and the place, we can trace women's representations, and their experiences, of domestic work.

The home

The type of house most commonly built in the interwar years was the 'bungalow'. This differed from the prewar house in many ways, most noticeably in its lack of accommodation for servants and its implicit enshrinement of the nuclear family. Typically it included two or three bedrooms, a lounge room and a kitchen, and while it had been extended to incorporate the bathroom, the toilet remained outside. A veranda, which could also be used as a sleep-out, provided extra accommodation if necessary. At the front of the house was the main bedroom, alternatively called the 'master bedroom', and a lounge room. The laundry was moving closer to the house, although it remained outside, attached to the main structure: the heaviest and dirtiest of women's work was separated from the interior.[2]

Not only the structure of the house was changing. Definitions of women's labour within it were also undergoing a transformation in keeping with ideas about efficiency and rational management. Through the influence of the domestic science movement, domestic labour became defined as *work*, and to this work women were encouraged to apply scientific knowledge. The principles of scientific management, efficiency and rationality which had come to dominate the organisation of paid work were applied to the domestic sphere. Hygiene was a key value, reflecting as much a practical concern with reducing the prevalence of disease as it did voguish scientific ideas about cleanliness and efficient home management. Women were urged to adopt capitalist notions of time management and perform their domestic tasks in accordance with the linear, progressive time of industry. These values were informed by asumptions about the supremacy of white culture: 'modernity' was coded white. The cleanliness, whiteness, hygiene and efficiency of the modern home were values against which was counterposed the perceived degradation of the Aboriginal race.

The decline in numbers of domestic servants following the First World War prompted unprecedented discussion about women's work in the home. Domestic labour comprised several different tasks: cleaning, washing, cooking, childcare, budgeting and shopping and, for those still able to employ help, the management of domestic servants. The categories were subject to extensive 'expert' advice. In place of domestic servants, technological developments were to aid women in the organisation and administration of their work. 'How to make housework simpler and easier is a question that is becoming increasingly important in these days when labour is scarce and the cost of all materials high,' stated an article on 'halving housework'.[3] Appliances were to be the new servants, 'Do away with household drudgery . . . let us show you how Electricity can be your servant.'[4] In 1920 *Home* ran an article entitled 'The conquest of housework: A practical study of mechanical substitutes for Mary Jane (deceased)'.[5] If life was to be tolerable without servants, the article argued, ways had to be found to reduce the drudgery of housework wherever possible. Electrical appliances provided the answer, but their cost was prohibitive. Release from the oppression of housework remained the privilege of the wealthy, who had never had to suffer under it anyway! As the decade progressed, however, electrical appliances—mainly in the form of vacuum cleaners, jugs and irons—found their way into an increasing number of homes.

Women were the target of a sustained advertising campaign by appliance manufacturers and electricity producers to promote the use of electrical appliances in the home. Electricity was to relieve women forever from housework *drudgery*. Women's work in the home suddenly became publicly acknowledged for what it was: 'Snap the Fetters of Drudgery—do it Electrically', ran the slogan. No longer was it woman's role to endure the hardship of the domestic round, rather it became her duty to her family to use electricity. Electrical devices, however, could not always be relied upon, as Mabel Lincoln, a keen introducer of change into her home, discovered, noting, in a self-conscious reciting of domestic woe: 'our immerser is out of action & our jug has konked out & both radiators are useless, what a list' (12 June 1932). While Mabel used the new technology, she also resisted the idea that it would lift women's domestic burden. Not only was it unreliable, but it did nothing to change the unrelenting nature of women's domestic work nor challenge the division of labour.

In magazines and advertisements, the site of women's labour was depicted as the home. According to the ideology of separate spheres, the home was also to be a retreat, a place for the male breadwinner to escape to after a day of paid work. In women's diaries we see the home as much more than this, and different areas of it assume different functions. It was a site of women's work, but equally a location for friendship and socialisation. Definitions of the space were not constant. In Mabel Lincoln's diary, we see the kitchen as a place of work as well as entertainment and the negotiation of labour relations. Perhaps most significant for Mabel, it was the place where food was prepared:

> Lorna Buller goes up the street & gets me a cauliflower, so we have roast beef, potatoes & cauliflower for dinner & it is very nice, I am a clever girl I took my roast into three pieces before cooking, undercut to grill & chunk end to stew or make pies so that is three meals from one roast. (19 September 1930)

Mabel wrote at great length about food. Here she represented herself as the creative and economical cook, able to stretch a piece of meat over three meals and not repeat the dish. In other entries we see her fitting in her cooking around other tasks, and visitors.

> Rise 7 oclock get washing up & sweeping done before dinner, Kornies & toast for breakfast for dinner we have another Middle Rib Roast (ordered Loin of lamb but could not get it) Roast potatoes & turnips (boiled in water I cooked corn Mutton in last Wednesday) baked tapioca Milk Pudding after dinner Dad comes along helps me with the clean clothes & the dishes do a couple of hours of ironing & just get scones baked for tea, have cold meat as well after tea Ruby & father clear up I have bath & do my nails then we play cards & West arrives as we finish supper. Clara White called in afternoon with her little girl. (24 May 1930)

Mabel recounted her cooking in considerable detail, occasionally pausing to note down the details of a recipe. Reading through her diary we are confronted with the range of dishes she cooked and the constancy of food preparation. Meals divided the day into three parts: morning fell between breakfast and dinner, afternoon between dinner and tea, and the evening between tea and supper. Tasks had to be organised around these times, or interrupted. In constructing herself as a competent cook, Mabel was not just bringing notice to her culinary skills, she was asserting herself as an adequate mother and provider, attending to the needs and desires of her child.

> Rise 7.30 Kornies & toast, no eggs to be procurred in the town, tidy up generally get to washing 11 oclock, for dinner we have Puree made from Rice & beans I have in the meat safe & Mutton stock, boiled potatoes (in skins) tin kippered herrings, Tapioca warmed up (left from Yesterday) do three coppers full of white washing, finish at 5 PM cook scones & jam tarts for tea (pastry scraps left from yesterday makes 15 tarts) cook corn beef for tomorrow (Harolds favourite dish) after tea clean up & wash my face, Mabel Maureen & Lorna go up to the train to greet [son] Harold, Rosie goes too, I stay home & have hot soup ready for him, balance of Puree 1 small tin of tomato soup, 1 tin of water, this makes a delicious meal for him, says he knew I would have soup or something so we talk & read until bedtime . . . get to bed 12 PM. (16 May 1930)

Mabel portrayed herself as a woman who wasted nothing. She prepared a balanced midday meal of rice, beans, potatoes, meat and fish, finished off by tapioca pudding. Around this meal she completed three loads of washing, and she had the evening meal finished, and something put aside for her son, Harold, in time for the others to go and meet him at the station. We can find echoes of this sort of efficiency in the language of the domestic science movement. Menu planning was one of the aspects of housework to which domestic science 'experts' paid detailed attention. Experts were called upon to advise women on how best to plan their meals and feed their families. Too much was left to chance when it came to feeding the nation, it seems: women needed to be trained in this all-important task, which could not be left to those who would

> undertake the duty of buying and preparing the food for a family, without the slightest knowledge of food values or the necessity of balanced diets to preserve health. It is for this reason that social reformers are now advocating a scheme of domestic training for girls during the final two years of school life . . . this training lies at the root of national health, child welfare, safe maternity, national efficiency and happy home life.[6]

Women were encouraged to view their cooking as a skill which required intelligence and creativity. 'Australian women are too fond of having dishes which appear on every daily table made from recipes that seldom carry either originality or novelty,' complained one writer for *Home*. 'It encourages an atmosphere of grooviness and dullness that shows a lack of intelligence and brain effort' (1 September 1920).

For women such as Mabel, cooking consumed much time, effort, and creative energy. It restricted the extent to which she could go out during the day, and necessitated considerable forward planning to ensure there would be food enough, and of the right sort, to feed her family and any others who happened to be dining with them. She considered a well-stocked pantry a reflection on her housekeeping, and would chide herself when she slipped: 'no eggs these days, it is dreadful housekeeping [a] house without eggs' (26 May 1930). Una Falkiner knew her kitchen more as a site of labour relations than as a workplace. She employed a cook, as well as a maid (at least one), a housekeeper and a laundress. The cook appeared to be at the top of the domestic hierarchy, or at least able to provoke the most disturbance. If Mabel's diary reflects prevailing views on the necessity for culinary expertise, this excerpt from Una's diary shows the distressed mistress having trouble with the servants:

> How one woman can be the cause of such upheavals as our house has presented this morning can scarcely be imagined! Mary O'Brian! our new cook! Old Peter calls her 'Clever Mary! or the O'Brian girl!' Every maid in the place came & in a trembling & tight pitched voice as the excess of rage gripped them & gave me notice! . . . Of course I am not taking them seriously as she will go tomorrow herself. We will pay her fare gladly to get rid of her. I wish she would go to Ireland. (16 April 1923)

Una's frequent problems with her servants taxed her skills as a negotiator and consoler to the limit. The worst crises always occurred upon her return after days or weeks of absence, a pattern she recognised herself: 'There is always chaos at home when I am away. This time things were terrific. Annie has left in tears & old Nurse is crying & the whole household is upset' (9 October 1922). Una believed her presence necessary to the smooth running of her household, and she acted as the mediator in many domestic disputes. She entered the kitchen not as a fellow worker but as the employer, issuing instructions and asserting control. Unlike Mabel, she did not see the kitchen as the centre of her house, although there were times when, without a cook, it did become her workplace:

> I cooked a delectable mina & poached eggs for our lunch, & cold beef & salad & delicious scones & tonight oyster soup. Baked meat & vegetables, prune shape & hot bread & butter pudding & kidney in bacon, so lets hope they will be hungry. (1 August 1922)

The entry carries echoes of Mabel Lincoln's recitations of her menus, and in another a few days later, Una similarly asserted herself as a good cook: 'Still cook! & remarkable good meals they are getting too!' (3 August 1922). The ingredients Una used, however, were more expensive than Mabel's, and Una's emphasis on 'delectable' and 'good' meals, contrasts with Mabel's pride in providing ample nutrition in the face of frugality. Similarly, the nomenclature each used reflected their different class positions: Mabel cooked dinner and tea, Una dined at lunch and dinner.

Una portrayed herself as an adept household manager, able to handle the tensions of dealing with servants or to fill in for them in their absence. By 1920, women such as Una were increasingly rare. It was the scarcity of servants which caused the domestic science movement to focus attention on the layout and design of the kitchen. With more mistresses working in their own kitchens, they needed to be attractive places: the comfort of the servants had not been worthy of consideration. *Woman's World* believed the kitchen should be an attractive place, but even more importantly, a clean one: 'in the first place, one must decorate one's kitchen on strictly hygienic lines. There must be no unnecessary dust collectors, such as ornaments and pictures.' A colour scheme must be decided on: 'White or cream are very much the prettiest for a kitchen and, in addition, they lend that air of freshness and cleanliness to this part of the house'(1 January 1923). Somehow, bright kitchens were magically to produce better housewives who would be cheered by the colourful hues and set about their work with added vigour and enthusiasm. It was a private, female space, yet women's labour within it was to reflect public ideas of progress, rationality and efficiency. Attitudes to the kitchen's space were thus integrally related to the use of time within it.

The modern housewife would have needed renewed vigour. While the introduction of technology to the home was theoretically designed to ease the burden of women's labour, the new, higher standards of cleanliness merely added to it. Clean, sparkling surfaces had to be maintained in all their glory, and efficiency had little to do with it. As a correspondent of the Melbourne eugenicist Dr Wallace noted, 'the modern home, with good lighting, light paintwork, polished floors, large windows etc, shows every fleck of dust, every fingermark and calls for a high degree of housework cleaning [sic]'.[7]

The kitchen Mabel represented in her diary was primarily a place of work. We know it through her cooking, her dishes, her floor cleaning. It was also a site of constant family interaction and could, on occasion, be a place for guests. The degree to which the kitchen also functioned as a place for hospitality depended on the number of other rooms in the house and the social class of the occupants. Una Falkiner did not usher her guests into the kitchen for a cup of tea: they were waited on by maids especially trained in the art of tea rituals. When Mabel welcomed visitors to her kitchen, it became a public space, her housekeeping on view for all inquiring eyes. It was perhaps from this centre that Mabel entertained her guests by reading portions of her diary, reasserting the nature and value of her domestic labour for those who had failed to notice.

The laundry was another section of the house which was characteristically a female space, the site of considerable hard work. Before the introduction of washing machines, washing involved setting a fire under the copper, filling it with water—which could entail carrying the water to the copper (if the washhouse had no running water)—heating the water, washing the clothes, rinsing them, and wringing them either by hand or with a hand-operated wringer. In warm weather it was hot work and women might begin it at night in the hope that the temperature would have cooled a little. A friend visited Mabel Lincoln on one such occasion:

> I start washing at 7 oclock in the evening, it is hot work, West comes down about 10.30, brings a bottle of firy, I am pleased (the perspiration is pouring into the tub), so we have a drink I work till midnight Rose [daughter] hangs out some of the washing for me, light up jug & have a cup of tea. (6 February 1930)

It had been a long day for Mabel, who had risen at 6 am and spent an hour working on the front garden before getting breakfast. Until 1932 Mabel seemed to spend almost as much time washing as she did cooking. During that year she employed someone whose main task appears to have been the washing. Even this did not relieve her altogether. There were days when she still performed the work, commenting on one occasion, 'What do I do Tuesday more washing, what came down from the shop, I am pretty sick of washing' (23 July 1935).

The washhouse, and women's work in it, was the focus of almost as much prescriptive literature as the kitchen. Washing day was frequently selected as an example of how to order time and use it efficiently, perhaps because the tasks involved in washing were easily identified. Monday was wash day, noted for hard physical work. But even this could be eased through good management. *Woman's World* advised its readers: 'Don't Make a Drudge of Washing-day: How to systematise meals, housework

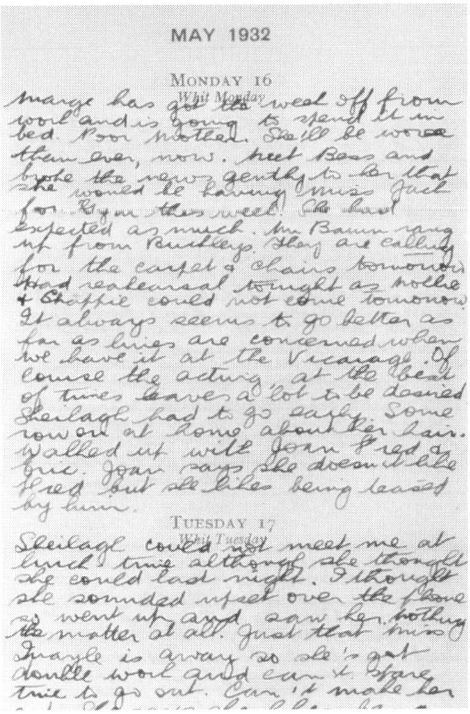
MAY 1932

MONDAY 16
Whit Monday

Marge has got the week off from work and is going to spend it in bed. Poor Mother. She'll be worse than ever, now. Met Bess and broke the news gently to her that she would be having Miss Jack for Gym this week. She had expected as much. Mr Baum rang up from Buckleys. They are calling for the carpet & chairs tomorrow. Had rehearsal tonight as Mollie & Chappie could not come tomorrow. It always seems to go better as far as lines are concerned when we have it at the Vicarage. Of course the acting at the best of times leaves a lot to be desired. Sheilagh had to go early. Some row on at home about her hair. Walked up with Joan Fred & Eric. Joan says she doesn't like Fred but she likes being teased by him.

TUESDAY 17
Whit Tuesday

Sheilagh could not meet me at lunch time although she thought she could last night. I thought she sounded upset over the phone so went up and saw her. Nothing the matter at all. Just that Miss Quayle is away so she's got double work and can't spare time to go out. Can't make her

Dorothy Kendall's 1932 diary.

Dorothy Kendall, c. 1934.

Dorothy Kendall with her good
friend Sheilagh, c. 1934.

Kathleen Hughes, c. 1930s.

Kathleen and her future husband, Stuart
Robertson, 1937.

Una Falkiner, c. 1912. Mitchell Library
Collection, State Library of NSW.

Ida Dawson, 1925.

Norma Bull, n.d.
La Trobe Library
Collection, State
Library of Victoria.

and the family laundry routine'. Order and preparation were the keys for the mother who was 'cook, housewife, laundress and hostess all in one'. The organised housewife cleaned the house, attended to the flowers, and organised her washing on Sunday. Wash day could no longer be an excuse for neglecting other chores. Instead, wash day and its preparation now consumed nearly two days. Meals on the day were to be simple. A tray lunch was recommended: 'sit on an easy chair with your feet up, if you like. Eat slowly and completely relax; you'll find you can get on with the work much better if you spoil yourself a little at lunch time. And see that you *do* get your lunch uninterrupted.' Children too were to be amused with a tray lunch, and the possibility that they might not be so obliging does not seem to have occurred to the writer. Finally, removing clothes from the line was also to be routinised: 'Use system when bringing the clothes in from the line . . . Do the sprinkling and rolling up straight away and, if you have time, have the handkerchiefs ironed while damp from the line.'[8]

Directives such as these were based on the assumption that women's tasks could be divided up into neat time allotments, determined by a rational assessment of how long a specific task should take. Such things as the vagaries of climate and weather were omitted from the calculation: nothing was to get in the way of a woman's domestic routine. But domestic time was not nearly so easily regulated. One writer to *Woman's World* objected to the notion of the 'perfect housewife': routines were easy to plan, but carrying them out was 'an entirely different matter': there were visits from hawkers, the canvassers, insurance agents, until it seemed 'sometimes as if everything conspires to prevent the accomplishment of the daily tasks'. In particular, children were guaranteed to upset any routine a woman might devise for herself: they did not understand concepts such as efficiency and time management.[9] Most of all, in the language of domestic management, women were not to be defeated by exhaustion. Mabel Lincoln, now aged 54, knew well the mental battle this could involve:

> Rise six AM, have a big wash up to start the day, it is an awful day, I do the washing & I am so late getting the clothes out, & I am so tired that I almost reneg. make up my mind twice to leave the last basketful, but I am awfully glad when I do get them in the tub, because they are mostly pyjamas & not hard to wash besides Rosie is home in time to put them through the last water & we get most of them hung out. (13 December 1932)

There was no room, in the language of time management and efficiency, for other kinds of time: the time of women's bodies, for example, their changing levels of energy and the rhythms of pregnancy and menstruation, not to mention the differences in their ages. The leaders of the domestic science movement may have believed they were equipping women to cope with the demands of housework, but in fact they were adding new burdens to an already oppressive load.

Mabel was not alone in her struggle against time and exhaustion. Few women seemed to find domestic work an enthralling task: they complained about its repetitiveness, the quantity of it, and the heavy physical nature of much of the work. Dorris Duncan, a housewife living in Shepparton with her husband, Tom, and daughter, Myra, usually gave a brief account of her day's work and often a comment on the effects it had on her energy levels. Like many diary writers, she began most entries with an account of the weather, a particularly important factor on wash day:

6/4/26. Tuesday
Very wet morning. Start on a huge white wash—hang clothes out about 4 p.m. & leave out all night. Children from next door in to play with Myra.

8/4/26. Thursday
Pleasantly warm day. Ironing with flat irons on gas stove in morning. Tom brings home car at dinner time—Take Myra to have her hair trimmed & shop on way home.

9/4/26. Friday
Busy morning finishing rest of ironing. Gas man calls—£1.40 to pay. Take Myra for walk—call at Tom's for money . . . Pay Grocer's Bill. Little sewing in evening. Very tired.

It had taken Dorris at least two mornings to finish the ironing from one wash. She fitted it in around the demands of her three-year-old, callers, meal preparation, messages to attend to and accounts to pay. Balancing the demands exhausted her. Routines were meant to help women organise their day, but human demands and individual time could not be so easily rationalised. Biological rhythms and maternal demands did not fit the industrial, scientific model of time. Dorris always noted the onset of menstruation by writing 'P-l-y', meaning 'poorly'. It added another strain to her day: 'P-l-y. Wash flannels—make grape jam—strain it. Good. Indoors all day. Slow & tired' (29 April 1926). Dorris, aged 35, found domestic work stressful, exhausting and laborious. 'Very fed up with domestic duties,' she wrote. Soon after this she discovered she was pregnant, knowledge she did not relish (she actually tried to induce a miscarriage). 'Have to be extremely careful of what I eat. Very unhappy all day. Wash flannels. Keep going' (23 July 1926). The 'options'—menstruation or pregnancy—appear equally painful for her and, it seems, a continuous reminder of bodily imprisonment. Here we see the maternal body firmly placed within the domestic sphere, having to cope with the emotional conflicts pregnancy raised, the physical discomfort it induced, and the demands of housework. We have the example of different temporal frames of reference—industrial, domestic and biological—and the conflicts between them, and we can see an implicit challenge to the ideology of the domestic science movement, and motherhood.

Mabel Lincoln's diary often appears to endorse contemporary notions of efficiency and time management, but she too could testify to times when the negotiation of her work load over-whelmed such principles:

> Start work 8 oclock finish 11. PM, feel awfully fed up, this life is much worse than the farm was even if I didnt have any clothes, here I do not have time to wear them, so it is worse, dont know what to do about it, but I am fed up. (21 January 1930)

Mabel resisted the dominant idea that women's time could adjust to models of scientific precision. Yet her regular chronological recording of her day suggests both an attempt to give order and structure to her time, a desire to reflect a sense of purpose and organisation, and an acknowledgment of the practical difficulties in her way. Order and disorder are, like the public and the private, not opposed but at once competing and complementary forces. Diaries show, in their form as much as their content, the blurred boundaries between these forces: they were a way of ordering the disorder as well as recording order and disorder alike.

Diaries were also a means of resistance, defiance or protest. Mabel declared the domestic load an impossible burden and the notion that it could be shoehorned into a routine a fallacy; Dorris Duncan expressed her resentment of domestic work and her rejection of motherhood as the ideal state. Fanny Barbour had equally strong views on the matter. Fanny, a woman used to the luxury of live-in domestic help, found herself responsible for the house-work during the winter of 1920. She was living on a small farm out at Berwick, on the eastern edge of Melbourne, with her hus-band and dogs. She frequently noted in her diary 'Nothing to record'. What she meant, as she made perfectly clear in one entry, was that nothing apart from everyday work had been happening:

> No entries since the middle of August.
> There has been nothing to enter except the rain, & wind—and every day alike—get up in the morning at 7—skim the milk etc. Get breakfast. Wash up—clean out fireplaces—do the rooms etc get dinner—pouring all day—so iron or wash—or do something in the house—most monotonous.

Fanny was troubled not only by the interminable nature of her housework, but by the lack of any recreation to relieve the monotony. Aged 58, having recently moved to Berwick, and living with an alcoholic husband, she was plagued by the isolation, and only work prevented her from feeling completely bored and dispirited. She continued her entry:

> The Barkers had a little birthday party on the 21st of August that is the only amusement for weeks—been trying to get a servant no luck. Just as well in this weather, better to be doing the work—I wish there was a little more amusement though. very dull. (1 October 1920)

The domestic science movement argued that women's work was important and even nationally significant. Fanny Barbour did not appear to view it as such: used to having her time free for social activities and gardening, she may well have thought the work beneath her. This entry suggests that the difference between what she found worthy of recording and what she did not was less a question of significance versus triviality than of the remarkable versus the humdrum. Housework was definitely humdrum. She would much prefer to have been gardening.

The garden

Gardens, like the houses they surround, are a reflection of social and cultural ideas. The size and style of a garden will also reveal much about the social position of the owner, the amount of time they have to work in the garden, or their ability to employ someone to work for the beauty others may then enjoy. Gardens can serve a double function as places of beauty and as providers of sustenance, and act as a reminder of the ever-changing seasons. They are harbingers of life and death yet also offer a sense of permanency to those who watch flowers grow, trees strengthen, and bulbs rejuvenate. The pleasure derived from a garden is based not only on the immediate picture it offers, but also on the knowledge of the labour that has created it and the anticipation and planning still in its making.[10]

A garden is an intermediate space between the domestic hearth and the world outside. It dresses a house, preparing visitors for what they can expect once across the threshold. Overgrown hedges, uncut lawns, scraggy rose bushes suggest a state of abandon and lack of care which may also exist in the interior. A neat, manicured garden promises order and method on the other side of the front door. Like rooms, however, different parts of a garden differ in function. Front gardens are for public display, while back gardens or yards generally share a more utilitarian purpose: vegetable plots, chook runs, woodsheds, clothesline and perhaps, by the interwar period, a special place for children to play. The relationship it shared with rooms in the house itself was integral: produce for the kitchen, a clothesline for the laundry, a wood heap for the fires. The garden was an extension of the house both visually and practically: there was a constant interrelationship between the two. At the intersection between the public and domestic worlds, the garden was one legitimate place of women's entry into public space. For women, it was also seen as part of their domestic sphere, and gardening an appropriate pastime. Raising and tending plants were extensions of women's nurturing skills, and a flourishing garden was regarded as reflective of domestic contentment. Gardens could serve other functions for women: Susan Hosking describes women gardeners as

> often spirited individuals who are not beyond practising a little insubordination in that tiny piece of no man's land between the home and the world outside. Within that space, a woman can freely exercise territorial rights: she can express her feminine values with the approval of society at large, but she can also resort to acts of wilfulness.[11]

Australian gardens of the 1920s and 1930s were subject to a wide variety of influences: 'evolving local traditions, the continuing input from established sources such as English garden books, and the more immediate fashions.'[12] Beds of colourful flowers, curving pathways, ornaments or statues could all be found in gardens of the interwar period. Beyond the domestic garden, city planners designed suburbs complete with parks and recreational areas, rational road systems and service lanes. These 'garden suburb' developments sought to integrate 'public' and 'private' needs.[13] Increasing home ownership meant increasing numbers of gardens to be created and attended to, and the 1920s and 1930s saw an expanding market for gardening books and magazines. Many of these propounded principles similar to those of domestic management. 'Thrift and neatness resumed their sway as the great garden virtues,'[14] while planning and privacy were high on the priority list of the famous Australian gardener Edna Walling.[15]

From a distance of 60 years, it is difficult to re-create the gardens of the diarists. Time and human agency have reshaped the borders and restyled the designs. We can now know this 'no man's land' only through the words of the diarists themselves. As with the house, we find in diaries not so much descriptions of the garden's layout and appearance as comments about the work performed in it, records of the flowers in bloom, and, from those women who had time, a sense of the energy that went into creating this space. For neither the time nor the space to garden were available to all, and the influence of class on women's experience of time and space is nowhere more evident in their diaries than in discussions of the garden.

Una Falkiner spent a considerable amount of time in her garden. Management of the station homestead was Una's responsibility and as the first impression visitors would receive of the homestead was through the glory of the garden, the picture it created was of considerable importance. This was the face of the house, the place of entry into the domain over which Una had control. It served to prepare visitors for the interior of the house and to impress on them both the culture of the station homestead and the skills of the mistress. The garden at Widgiewa was one of Una's great joys. She tended it carefully, pruning and planting as the seasons dictated. In an entry for June 1921, she noted the progression of her day:

> Knowing I am alive. Choosing spots for planting out with the gardener, cutting old wood & trees in the pepper drive. Feeding hot food to fowls with boy, seeing Billy Wilson who is papering the school room, killing fowls & a goose for Sunday, talking to cook & parlour & house maid, arranging for guests, & hanging pictures. writing & talking to sixteen people on the telephone! (3 June 1921)

Una's garden features centrally in this entry, represented for the pleasure it brought—awakening her senses, reminding her of the joys of her life—the sustenance it provided, and the future it offered. She planned a garden whose beauty would be realised in time. Knowing she was alive was integrally linked to her sense of purpose: a purpose that included planting out and feeding chooks, working to maintain a style of life and guarantee an enjoyable future. Her sense of purpose structured her time and informed her whole existence. The sense of space evoked in this entry is also striking: she ranged around the garden, wandered down to the schoolroom, attended to household tasks, planned for visitors and spoke to sixteen different people on the telephone, her voice reaching into homes far away. Her movements were constrained along gender lines—she did not venture down to the shearing sheds or class sheep for sale—but it was extended by virtue of her class. When Mabel Lincoln wrote of her garden, it was very much as she wrote about her housework: as a chore to be done. There is no sense of the pleasure she may have gained from working in the garden, nor of the flowers it produced, rather she seems to have regarded it as she would a room that always needed cleaning:

> do one hour out in the yard, clean the shelves down in the shed & weed the same piece of garden that I always weed, it is perfectly sickening, that piece of garden is like a red rag to me, it is always producing another crop of sturdy fat hen. (4 March 1930)

In a similar vein, Mabel wrote of the difficulty in even getting time to work in the garden: 'I try to do the front garden this afternoon, but I have too many helpers and get but little done' (20 January 1930). Her comment came after a recitation of a morning full of chores preceded by days of constant, tiring work. Writing to maintain control, she used literary artifice and touches of ironic humour to assist her.

Una Falkiner's work in her garden comprised mainly pruning and planting, and no doubt some weeding. For her it was not a site of hard labour which consumed precious hours of her time and prevented her from working on other things. The Falkiners employed gardeners to look after most of the heavy gardening work, and at times seem to have had one gardener for the vegetable garden and another for the less functional and more ornate sections. Although Una was relieved of most physical aspects of gardening, she still worked hard enough in this space to consider it exercise, noting on one occasion, 'Did gardening, am getting quite slim' (16 March 1923). The healthy, life-enhancing aspects of gardening were not lost on the producers of gardening catalogues and advertisements, and tie in with the broader promotion of health and exercise. Una's most frequent references to her garden, however, delighted in its beauty, reflected the glory of the surrounding day and told the tale of seasons:

> Such a wonderful day. Dreamy autumn & golden colours! . . . The garden is full of growing things, brilliant green spikes pushing up through the warm damp earth! bulbs, & chrysanthemum buds bursting! & such zinnias & huge marigolds! . . .
> Such a sunset! The quiet creek mirroring huge cumulous clouds &

golden stalked gum trees! These turn pale & then deep pink. (30 April 1930)

Una's garden was functional as well as beautiful. It provided fruit for eating and preserving, and flowers with which she could decorate her house, thus again asserting the relationship between the interior and exterior of her home:

> Went off down the garden for figs & pears & plums to put on the ice for the day, & picked my flowers & did the roses. Glowing huge karmas, & rock roses & zinnias (17 January 1932)

The plants in Una's garden reflect a variety of influences. She had traditional English plants, roses and bulbs which brought forth great bursts of colour, and fruit trees to add blossom and produce. Alongside these she left some Australian natives: a wattle and gum trees which situated the house and garden in the context of the surrounding landscape. Una's garden had an important relationship to the Falkiner property. Like the great houses of the English gentry, the Falkiner house drew much of its status from the reputation of the station and Otway's status as one of the leading Australian pastoralists. The garden was both part of the house and part of the property: it had a strong connection to the land around it and was to reflect the status not only of the Falkiner stud but also of Otway and the Falkiner family. It is no wonder that the desire for control of the garden and the people who worked in it generated such marital tensions. Una's vision of the garden, both present and future, and the qualities she looked for in those who worked it, were very different from Otway's. She sought to extend the house into the garden, he the station to the homestead. They met head on.

Fanny Barbour was another woman whose financial security enabled her to employ domestic help and freed her to work in her garden. It was one of her favourite occupations and she made regular references to the different plants she was planting, including specimens such as silver holly, violets, roses, tulips, purple petunias and hollyhock. Gardening was not just a matter of planting, however, it also involved removing unwanted trees and reshaping the landscape to suit a certain vision. Fanny's garden had no room for one particular native: 'Jer with help from Ian and self made a bon-fire & burnt up the old wattle that Mr Harnet cut out. A lovely day . . . I am doing a lot in the garden' (22 April 1922). Fanny wrote more about her gardening than she did about any other activity. Frequently she would write 'gardened', followed by a description of what this meant: 'Gardened—getting holes ready for shrubs & roses. Planted some holly-hock seed that Harry Walcott sent me & transplanted a little pink rose' (25 April 1922). Gardening was not just a pleasure, it was a form of communication: Fanny obviously shared her love with others, and exchanged seeds, cuttings and maybe even plants. The system of exchange that gardeners established was based on dialogue, a knowledge of shared values and an exchange of gifts. There were some people though, with whom this communication was not shared. For these, the garden was to be simply an object of beauty; they were not to know how much work went into its creation and maintenance. Fanny wrote on one occasion, '"Gardened" after lunch & Mr Haines caught me in my gardening togs' (9 March 1920). For her the garden was a place of work as much as a place of beauty, but it was not to be seen as a place of work, nor she as a worker, when certain visitors called. Fanny's garden, like Una Falkiner's, spoke of desire and transformation. It anticipated a future which, after years of labouring, she was able to realise: 'Lovely day—The garden looks lovely in the afternoon sun' (31 March 1933). Fanny sought refuge in her garden, solace from the turmoil often present in the house, and a place of her own in the context of a marriage often fraught with tensions.

Ida Dawson was another woman who loved gardening. Her gardens, however, were always temporary, but she embraced the chance to plant a few things, creating a small space which was of her own making and carried a sense of self and roots. When she arrived in Argentina, she helped Prima, Guy's wife, to establish a garden: 'Prima and I had a great morning working in the garden. I dug, & pruned, & she transplanted from the hot house. We shall have a gay garden later on' (30 October 1920). Ida wanted more than a shared space, however: 'Glorious weather all this week. We are gardening in spare time, & all things are growing . . . I have started a little garden near my room' (4 November 1920). Ida could look out on her creation and invest it with any dreams and memories she desired. For Una, the memories her garden evoked were sometimes too painful to be endured. After the death of her 20-month-old daughter, Diana, in January 1922, the garden became a constant reminder of the child's absence. The lawn became a carpet where her feet no longer walked, and while Una sought solace amongst the trees and flowers—'[t]he best place for a lacerated heart', she wrote at the front of her 1923 diary—their perfumes carried other meanings. Similarly, spring and its promise of new life held shadows: 'Too glorious a day with Cookoos singing! How I long for my wee Diana, she loved this so! with her little nose screwed up smelling the flowers' (26 August 1923). The evocation of time—past, present and future—was a constant and complex feature of a garden's life.

Gardens marked the boundaries of women's domestic space, but like homes, they existed in and drew their definitions from their surroundings. Similarly, a woman's domestic work was influenced by the location of her home.

The place

Just as the dimensions of her house and garden bore an intimate relationship to a diarist's experience of her domestic labour, so her sense of place informed her reconstruction of herself and structured her telling. The location of a woman's home in a city, a country town or on the land, determined the meanings and possibilities of her life and shaped the patterns of her domestic labour.

Mabel Lincoln's house and garden were on a corner, bounded by roads on two sides and houses on the other sides. Unlike Una, she did not look across a luxurious garden to the 'lines of wild flowers' scattered on the plains beyond.[16] Mabel's house was a short walk to the main street of Leongatha, past the Mechanics Institute, over to the post office and train station, and along to the Leongatha shops, including Lincoln's General Store. The country surrounding Leongatha, and visible a short walk from Mabel's house, was and is dairy country: gentle rolling hills almost English in their post-invasion appearance. Mabel had all the services she needed at hand and did not need to rely on her garden to produce food for her family. In the location of her house, its proximity to the town and the centre of Leongatha life, we can read much about Mabel and her sense of place. She portrayed herself as integrally involved in Leongatha life, not just through events such as community singing and euchre nights, but through her constant recounting of local events, gossip and dramas. The news Rosie brought home from the shop kept her in touch with the activities—and financial status—of many fellow residents and provided an overview of town life. Thus her relationship to Leongatha was both a geographical and a psychological one, as is any expression of a sense of place.

Other domestic women had very different experiences. Women who lived on the land were not in daily interaction with their local township, nor even its inhabitants. The members of their immediate family often provided the only human contact for days at a time. They needed, therefore, to be far more self-sufficient, both emotionally and practically, than town women. From the surrounding land they drew their sustenance, and they ordered their days and weeks according to the rhythms and demands of the seasons. Nature's impact on their work was immediate and tangible.

The distinction between women who lived in cities or country towns and those who lived on the land is one of the strongest features to emerge from their diaries. It was also a distinction recognised by contemporary magazines and advertisers. *Woman's World* noted in its first editorial that it aimed to be a special help to country women, providing interesting reading to 'while away the lonely hours' and practical suggestions for problems:

> One of the greatest deprivations she suffers from is her inability to personally conduct her own shopping. Generally speaking, she cannot make a pound stretch as far as her city sister. Her showcase is the mail order catalogue.[17]

It seems that women on the land found it easier to organise their time; adherence to routines was built into their way of life. These were not, however, the time management routines of the domestic science movement, but those demanded by seasonal variations in work and daylight hours. The work of rural women was closely interwoven with that of the men who worked on the property. Women were usually required to provide daytime meals and tea breaks and were expected to be on hand in case they were needed. Other factors also influenced the use and allocation of time: wood had to be carted, fire stoves kept burning, vegetables grown, butter churned and hens tended. Stock from the property might provide meat. Shops were therefore relied upon for only a few food items such as sugar, flour and sometimes tinned produce. As shops were always some distance away, this not only kept the rural housewife's dependence on bought goods at a minimum, but considerably reduced the time she needed to spend shopping. Urban women were rarely as self-sufficient as rural women. They may have grown some of their own vegetables, and occasionally had their own poultry, but most of the rest of their food and household requirements came from either the local store or door-to-door salesmen.

Standard domestic chores—washing, ironing, cleaning and cooking—varied little between rural and urban women, although the facilities for doing them could. Electricity took many years to be connected to some country areas, making the promise of time- and labour-saving appliances sound very hollow.[18] Water taps, which by the 1920s had become standard in most urban houses, were still a rarity in some rural areas (and water a precious commodity), meaning women had to carry their water for washing and cleaning. (Some more wealthy farmers, such as the Falkiners, could of course afford to have electricity connected, and windmills and pumps to supply water, again suggesting the ways money could save time and labour.) Wood for fires had to be chopped and the kitchen hearth kept burning, restricting the length of time a woman could be away from her home. Seasonal variations also had greater impact on rural women, linked, as they inevitably were, to the regular rhythm of farm life. The yearly cycles of ploughing, sowing, harvesting, lambing, marking and shearing—work which primarily engaged either the husbands or sons of the diarists—impinged more on their daily routines than did the work of urban women's husbands. Shearing time on a small farm could mean extra mouths to feed, while men could require their midday meal to be taken to where they were ploughing or harvesting. Hence Mary Bicknell, living on a small farm near Bendigo, 150 kilometres north of Melbourne, nearly always recorded the farm work her husband and son did each day, and where they were located, if far away from the house.

> Father & Billy [son-in-law] went to Billy's place & brought lambs, had dinner drafted lambs here, took lunch with them & off to Elmore did not get back until 8.P.M. I felt very lonely. Had a headache. Billy stayed all night. (3 January 1932)

At other times there was more immediate reason for her to know the men's whereabouts:

> Very hot today & in P.M. thunder & a terrible wind storm dust limbs of trees flying one tree fell into the dam, both W.C.s went over ours badly broken hay bags & etc flying everywhere. Jack [her son] was harvesting JG [her husband] & Alf bag sewing. V [Jack's wife] & I scared of the storm & worrying about men but they got home alright. Talk about dust every thing in & out side the house was smothered. (10 December 1935)

The presence of dust connected the men's world of work with her own. In rural areas, the elements of nature also collapsed the boundaries between the public and domestic. For Mary, drought, fires and storms all affected her interaction with her landscape. Both these entries reveal how closely integrated Mary's life was with the farm and its fortunes. Her diary is not the idyllic jottings of a woman with nothing else to do, nor only an account of her own thoughts and activities. She used it to record the farm work and her own work, as well as prices gained for stock, wool and crops. Mary also earned cash by selling eggs. Each Monday she would pack eggs, count them, and send them off to town. Her relationship with her immediate surroundings was quite different from that of Dorris Duncan. Dorris, living in the rural town of Shepparton, did not keep chooks, nor tend a vegetable garden (at least she did not mention it), and although she regularly noted the late hour of her husband's arrival home and the effect it had on his dinner, the routine of his work day did not impinge on her own routine to the same degree as did that of Mary's husband and son. Nor was she required to go and help in his workshop, as women on the farm often were, depending on the time of year or activity at hand. Rural women's adherence to a more regular routine also ensured that other family members would know of their availability and whereabouts. Monday, wash-day, for example, was not a day on which a wife or mother was 'free' to assist.

Roo Cameron, living on a farm near Penshurst in Victoria's Western District, also represented herself as integrally involved in the affairs of her farm. A widow, she ran the farm with her sons. She recorded all details of sales, frequently accompanied by comments on their success:

> Lovely day. Boys sale all busy sheep brought from 33/7 to £20.3.0 each most successful sale the sheep were all in splendid condition My cows (3) [illeg] £8 a head & one old cow 26/ We're all up in the boughs over the Sale. (21 July 1924)

Roo's farm stock seems to have comprised mainly sheep and cattle. Her sons helped her with the heavy work such as dipping, but many of the other farm activities she saw to herself: she milked and churned and sold cream in the local town on a weekly basis, raised chooks, sold fowls and ducks, and maintained an extensive vegetable garden: potatoes, lettuce, peas, beans, cabbage, cauliflowers, as well as a number of fruit trees, making summer a busy time of jam making: 'did nice bit of work made 22 lbs of Jam—G Plum looks good' (12 January 1924). Roo divided her time between outdoor farm and garden work and internal domestic labour. 'Just ordinary work', she occasionally called this, 'just' usually meaning she was at it from morning until night: 'Just busy about the place until night' (5 December 1924). Unlike Mabel, she did not divide up her day according to how long each task took, and we do not find in her diary the same echoes of time management and efficiency so evident in Mabel's. Perhaps the greater sense of relationship between the farm and the home lessened the terror of a domestic routine. The seasonal cycles of the farm determined much of the work routine, adding a broader perspective to the context of domestic labour. Roo did not make a distinction between her indoor work and outdoor work. It was all work, some of it more appealing than others: 'I cleaned the piggery out such a nice job.' Roo's humour conveys her distaste at the task, but there appears nothing so self-conscious in the sights she set on her labour-saving device: it was not electrical appliances Roo looked to to ease her burden of work, but something much more humble: 'Got pot scrub. hope it will save & improve labour conditions' (22 July 1924).

From the diaries of both rural and urban women, a detailed picture emerges of the ways in which they used and divided their space. Rural diaries in particular graphically illustrate the problematic public–private dichotomy which conventionally governed the distinction between men and women's work and lives. The home, the garden and the place all existed in close interrelationship, drawing their meanings from each other, and together and individually conveying much about the class and status of the people who lived in them. In each we can see different understandings and manifestations of time, sometimes in harmony with each other and with human time frames, often in conflict. Women's lives were far more complicated than the domestic science movement would have had them believe. Through the daily recording of their labour, the diarists worked to order each day, hold the shape of it together and convey a sense of tasks achieved and standards maintained. They were keeping their time and making their space, suggesting a hope that their diary might accord their life and work a more prominent and permanent future than its lived reality.

4
Life cycles II: Marriage to motherhood

'I have been married'

On 4 May 1897, at the age of 24, Mabel Ross married Walter Armstrong. The way in which she recorded the event in her diary gives little indication of its significance for her life. Her name changed from Ross to Armstrong, her residence changed, although not her locality (she remained living at Caramut, in Victoria's wealthy Western District), her legal status changed, and she began a period in her life marked by maternity, motherhood and her responsibilities as a wife. None of this, however, was registered in her diary. She drew a line after the entry for 25 April 1897 and noted in the following one:

> *June* Tues 15th. Since April 25th I have been married—the W'bool Races. The Shearer's Dance—went to town stopped at Menzies got a lot of presents—The McAthrlys came to call yesterday. Walter [her husband] went to Geelong. Judy & I drove him—

The entry registers the wedding as one among several events, significant enough to warrant a division in her diary but not worthy of detailed comment. We are almost left wondering if the event took place at the races, while receiving 'a lot of presents' was accorded more detail than the wedding itself. Mabel did write of her marriage in the active, long-term sense, as of something she had done and continued doing, as distinct from a mere passing event such as the races or a dance; but neither her courtship, her feelings for her husband nor the ceremony was accorded any space. The knowledge that Mabel eloped, however, transforms our

65

reading of this entry. The forbidden nature of her relationship with Walter presumably prevented Mabel from disclosing any details in her diary—there are some things too secret to reveal even there—and the paucity of the entry in no way reflects a lack of significance. She was no doubt clearly conscious of the implications of her actions. The break in entries between April and June is perhaps the most telling sign that Mabel did recognise the significance of the change in her life: her separating line distinguished between events before and after and symbolised the invisible threshold she had crossed.

At the turn of the century, marriage was considered a legal, sexual, spiritual and reproductive union. Mabel was bound to her husband, able to divorce him only on proof of repeated acts of infidelity and cruelty, while he needed to prove only one act of infidelity to divorce her.[1] It is unlikely that Mabel spent much time reflecting on these issues, although she could not have helped but notice the change in status the marriage ceremony, however rushed or informal, brought about. Not until her eldest son divorced in 1936 was she forced to confront the legal implications of marriage. Of the diarists, only Margaret Strongman provides any insight into the changes she felt marriage made to her status. She recorded the event simply:

> Married at 2.30 at Friend's Meeting House, Melbourne, after a busy morning preparing for reception at Y.W.C.A. Rooms. E. [Ernest, her husband] moved work centre from Fisherman's Bend to City. Changed at 'Whitehall', caught train to Lilydale. Arrived 'Hermitage', Narbethong, about 8.30. Settled ourselves in one of cottages for three nights stay. (12 December 1942)

Margaret's entry provides some indication of the rituals involved in marriage: the ceremony was followed by a reception, after which the bride and groom left for a short honeymoon. Perhaps more interesting and revealing than her actual description of the day was the subsequent change in her diary writing. From this point on, she referred to Ernest as 'E', and herself in the third person, 'M', almost as though she had disappeared, becoming a character in a novel instead. The diary reads as if either E or M could have been writing it and as Margaret always typed her entries, not even handwriting identifies the author: 'M sunburnt on oneside as a result of lazing in the sun after lunch yesterday' (14 December 1942). Gradually, however, Margaret's imprint and a sense of her character emerge, although the diary remains an account of both partners' activities, if a somewhat abbreviated one: 'E. to committee meeting of Welfare Officers' Association. M.

ironing etc' (1 March 1943). When she mentioned both of them together, E nearly always came before M. Not until after several months of writing in this fashion did Margaret explicitly state who was writing: 'M. started work again. In the evening, E. reading, M. typing diary' (3 May 1943). For Margaret, marriage seemed to entail a dovetailing of lives, a fact she symbolised by writing a joint diary and distancing herself as the writer. Her own identity became subsumed into a joint one in which Ernest was at the fore. The change allowed for little expression of individuality and created a style of writing which forced an understating of emotion, even during periods of extreme stress. Her accounting for two sets of actions and two responses to situations reduced the significance of her own response.

Despite the opening up of work opportunities for young women in the interwar period, careers for women were seen as a short-term substitute for what was still regarded as their true calling: marriage and maternity. Middle-class women were expected to cease paid work when they got married, and magazines of the period—which generally catered for a middle-class audience—assumed that married women were supported by their husbands and did not themselves engage in paid work. The roles of marriage and motherhood were central to the social construction of femininity and the meaning of the 'good woman':[2] a woman expressed her femininity by progressing from youth to marriage and then to motherhood. Although marriage and motherhood received considerable discussion in books and magazines, women themselves rarely reflected on either state. We can learn much from their diaries, however, about what each involved, and also discern the influence of prescriptive literature, especially in relation to childrearing. The diaries of Una Falkiner, Dorris Duncan, Mae Murphy and Margaret Strongman relate different experiences of their mature years, differences brought about by their respective class positions, their places of residence and the years during which they were rearing young children. Popular notions of marriage and maternity were based not only on the presupposition of a gender hierarchy in which men held the ultimate power in a relationship, but also on assumptions about women's biological destiny as mothers. Yet while maternity was supposed to come naturally to women, the interwar years witnessed a flourishing of advice on how to mother. They also saw the introduction of attempts to regulate cycles of parturition and lactation in keeping with the principles of time management and efficiency, principles which made way for the increasing (male) medical control of women's bodies.

Only rarely did the possibility of a woman's not marrying arise, despite the fact that in 1921 16.6 per cent of women in the 45 to 49 age bracket had never married. Several of the diarists were in this group: Ida Dawson, Winifred Tait, Norma Bull, Cecily Rowe. Their lives were full and active, yet their middle years are less easily discussed than those of women who married and bore children. This is a problem both of historians' conceptual tools, and of social expectations. The lives of single women have generally been explained by historians and contemporary observers alike in terms of their failure to marry, without adequate exploration of their experiences of single life.[3] Single women themselves had few standards by which to evaluate their lives: if unmarried and childless, they had no access to the status of the 'good woman', and if they chose to pursue a career, the criteria for success were generally masculine and thus unhelpful to women who could. not compete on equal terms. As Carolyn Heilbrun observes, '[t]he choices and pain of women who did not make a man the centre of their lives' are far more difficult to discuss than the lives of women who married, because there are 'no models of the lives they wanted to live, no exemplars, no stories'.[4] The lives of such women are most easily discussed in relation to their work and their relationships, which are considered in detail in 'Working lives' and 'Relating women'. They feature in this section as points of contrast, a reminder that many women, by virtue of their single status, were excluded from the dominant concerns of married women, reformers and magazines alike.

Marriage was a regular topic of discussion during the interwar period. In the early 1920s, attention was focused on what was expected of women in marriage. *Everylady's Journal* in 1919 offered an article directed at 'wives who think they are neglected'. It urged them to stop complaining and start counting their blessings. Women had to have sympathy for the difficulties of a man's world: 'A man comes home very tired, very weary—often heartsick and sore. Be kind to him, loving. If at home no affection waits, no true rest, no peace—where, oh, where on earth, under God's blue sky, can a man hope to find it?'[5] While home was separated from work on moral, physical and gender grounds, it was to be a refuge for men. Women were invariably held responsible for the breakdown of marriages: 'Women lose their husbands' love, in most cases because they do not make sufficient effort to keep it,' declared *Woman's World*.[6] As the 1920s progressed, the emphasis shifted from the idea of women's having to respond to their husband's every need and demand, to consideration of the different basis upon which men and women married and their different understandings of marriage and love. Implicit in the discussion was the assumption that men and women experienced both love and passion differently. Lady Buckmaster, writing for *Woman's World* in 1929, stated: 'Marriage is often a failure because men, instead of seeking friendship and companionship in a wife, seek only the satisfaction of a fleeting passion.' Marriage should be 'a true union of spirit and purpose and a faithful partnership in weal and woe, [it] should be the source and fountain of the most sublime felicity that life can offer'. Lady Buckmaster conceded that the 'old ideas of family life' involved the domination of the male and 'the subordination, sacrifice and servitude of the female'. Such times had passed, she believed, and modern marriage should be based on ideas of equality and justice.[7] By the 1930s, discussions about marriage were addressing marital problems with one writer urging young couples to give considerably more thought to the decision to marry in the first place:

> [too many] never see past the wedding bells, the joyful throwing of confetti and the splendour of the wedding feast . . . For every man and woman who find themselves bound together for all time by the memories of the romantic past, the welcome ties of the present, and the hopes of the future, there are a hundred or more who find that the inevitable passing of the thrill of physical love leaves them stranded on a desert of dead emotions.[8]

Another writer singled out women's economic dependence as a major cause of marital disharmony.[9] The blame for unhappy marriages had shifted, in public discussions at least, from the woman to the institution and the unrealistic expectations placed upon wives: 'We know that women have progressed more in the last twenty years than throughout the rest of history, yet we still expect wives to be the same.'[10] We can discern in these discussions the influence of feminists who had been discussing the inequality inherent in marriage for at least thirty years in Australia, and who during the interwar period were actively campaigning for equal pay, motherhood endowment and child endowment. Yet despite the recognisable shift of attitudes to women's role in marriage, there was little public critique of the inequality inherent in the institution, and responses to well-publicised divorce cases revealed the prevalence of the belief that women were responsible for maintaining a marriage and thus, inevitably, for its breakdown.

If divorce was seen as the ultimate downfall for women, the

pinnacle of their experience was motherhood. Throughout the interwar period, white middle-class women were exercising considerable control over their reproductive lives. The declining birth rate was a cause of some concern for politicians and doctors, who believed that women were not adequately fulfilling their responsibility to the nation. The concern to build a white nation was uppermost in the minds of many politicians. Only white mothers were nationally endorsed and their childbearing encouraged. Aboriginal mothers were regarded as neither feminine nor acceptable, and, in the terms of white society, incapable of 'mothering'. They could not be 'good mothers' or 'good women', and many of them had their children taken from them, but reproduction remained imperative for the survival of their race.

As white women continued to restrict their childbearing, commentators looked for possible reasons. In a radio broadcast in 1944, Enid Lyons, herself a mother of eleven, blamed the standard of feminine beauty as a reason for the declining birth rate. The women on magazine covers were not mothers but 'those who have kept the extreme slimness and suppleness of early youth'. In her opinion, there was 'no beauty greater than the soft roundness of a young matron . . . I want to see magazines showing happy mothers and happy babies.'[11] The comment highlights the difference between the sexualised body of the young woman and the desexualised one of the mother. The mature woman's sexuality, when it was portrayed at all, was directed solely towards her husband; the figure of the caring, attentive mother was portrayed in advertisements as generating his respect, love and protection. Yet though the maternal body, the body which carried any suggestion of pregnancy, childbirth or lactation, was conspicuously absent from discussions of youth and femininity in the 1920s and 1930s, those on motherhood and domestic management had to recognise women's reproductive lives. The femininity of the mature woman was represented by her status as a mother and wife.

Pregnancy was portrayed by reformers, 'experts' and the press as a special time for women. The pregnant woman, although not portrayed as sexual, was definitely feminine, and indeed pregnancy was a crucial stage on the path to a woman's mature expression of her femininity. Women's magazines ran regular articles on care of the expectant mother: 'at no time in your life do you need more love, care, and sympathy than in the waiting months when you stand, perhaps for the first time, at the gates of motherhood'.[12] Most of these directives, however, instructed the mother on how to care for herself, rather than how other people might care for her. High on the list of recommendations was a consultation with the doctor. The medicalisation of pregnancy and childbirth went hand in hand with the development of gynaecology and obstetrics as specialties, resulting in the expectation that women's most 'natural' function should be supervised by men. One woman doctor, in a striking example of the devaluation of women's knowledge, went so far as to advise first-time mothers not to consult their mothers, neighbours or friends for advice:

> All these kindly ladies cluster round the prospective young mother. They give her idiotic and conflicting advice. If she quotes the doctor they tell her he is wrong . . . The first cardinal rule for all prospective mothers to follow is, therefore, avoid all female relatives, friends and neighbours and never let them know of your condition. The second is, engage your doctor early—at the sixth week if possible. Follow his instructions to the letter, in any trouble go to him, and to him *only*, immediately.[13]

Women who followed this myopic—or tendentious—advice may have found themselves without support not only during their pregnancy but afterwards as well. Women's family and friendship networks offered not only advice but also practical and emotional support before and after childbirth. Dorris Duncan frequently left her three-year-old daughter with her sister-in-law, giving herself time to rest, play golf or shop. When she was pregnant with her second child, this support became even more important. Mae Murphy went to stay with her aunt soon after her daughter's birth, and both Una Falkiner and Margaret Strongman were accommodated and cared for by family members following their deliveries.

Despite the open discussion of pregnancy in the periodical press, very few diarists wrote about their experiences of it, suggesting, again, that there were some things women did not feel free to commit to paper. The seemingly private diary was still too public a place in which to discuss this very intimate and personal experience. Perhaps the appropriation of pregnancy into the domain of medical science also hindered their discussion of it: as the above quotation suggests, women's traditional knowledge of pregnancy was being dismissed. It is possible that women writing diaries during this period felt unable or unwilling to write of their experiences in traditional terms, yet were still unfamiliar with, and lacked confidence engaging in, the medical discussion of their state. The first mention Una Falkiner made of her pregnancy in 1920 was when her child arrived, two months earlier than they had calculated she was due. Errors in calculating the arrival date

71

of a child appear to have been common during this period. The advice page in *Woman's World* carried regular inquiries about the timing of a birth. During their childbearing years, most women, whether married or not, kept a close eye on their menstrual cycle and used their diaries to record their dates: a missed period meant possible pregnancy, a prospect not all women welcomed. The women who noted their periods most regularly were those who used a printed diary with the days and weeks marked in. Some noted the day with a cross, others charted it on the calendar at the front of the diary, and some mentioned the start of their period in the day's entry. Dorris Duncan noted the onset of menstruation with 'P—l—y' [poorly] and occasionally a comment: 'P—l—y (7 days late)' (7 January 1926). On that day she was obviously so relieved at the arrival of her period that she mentioned it twice in the same entry! Five months later she was not so lucky. With 'P—l—y's noticeably absent from her diary, she 'Commenced with xxx' (15 June 1926), her euphemism for an attempt to induce an abortion. Eight days later she noted 'Finished with 1st xxx' (23 June 1926), but it had failed to have the desired effect. After a visit from a woman friend, she tried an alternative remedy, 'Commence with J.P's treatment' (29 June 1926) but that also failed. Three days later she wrote:

> Attack dry reaching [sic].
> Very down. Tom takes me in car in early afternoon to see Dr. Grützner.
> Leave off taking J.P's treatment.
> Letter from Mother. (1 July 1926)

Seven months later, Dorris's second daughter arrived.

Dorris found the twin demands of looking after a child and being pregnant exhausting. In the early stages of her pregnancy she regularly mentioned feeling tired and depressed: 'Feel very tired low spirited' (12 July 1926). Fatigue and a sense of despair permeate her entries. Her diary reveals a woman struggling to meet the demands placed upon her and to balance different time frames: there is no hint of the delight and anticipation women were supposed to experience during pregnancy, a prescription which didn't even allow for morning sickness. Enid Lyons may well have implored magazines to show 'happy mothers and happy babies', but for many women the reality was different.

The first indication Margaret Strongman gave of her pregnancy was an entry in 1944. With her usual eye for detail, she recorded her admission to 'Avonhurst Privat [sic] Hospital, Queen's Road, Melbourne about 3 a.m.' on May 9. Her next entry recorded what transpired there:

Wed., 10/5/44 to Sat 14/5/44
M. in dry labour. Everybody worried. E. not least! E visiting hospital
every night, except Thursday, which M. spent at home, but such a bad
night for both went back to hospital next day.

Monday the 16th brought the birth of her daughter, recorded
simply as 'Faye born 2 p.m.' The trauma of the preceding days
was not elaborated upon: had Margaret felt any inclination to
recount her ordeal, she may well have found words inadequate to
the task. Instead, she satisfied herself with a short account, keeping, however, careful note of the times at which she was admitted
to hospital, and the hour of Faye's birth—the points of intersection
between biological and linear time. She had spent six days in
labour.

After ten days in hospital following Faye's birth, Margaret
recuperated for a week with her brother and sister-in-law at
Brighton. The ordeal of her labour would have taken some time
to recover from and family support was crucial. On returning to
Melbourne she assumed responsibility for her own and Faye's
care. Her diary became dominated by details of trips to the Baby
Health Centre and regular recordings of Faye's weight gain. Faye's
growth was to be regularly and accurately checked, suggesting the
influence of the infant welfare movement on Margaret's mothering. By the end of July, just over two months after her birth, Faye
became fully incorporated into Margaret's life, reduced in the
diary to her initial: 'M & F to Botanic Gardens in afternoon' (23
July 1944). The task of keeping a diary while running a household
and caring for Faye proved too much, however, and Margaret's
last entry was written on 30 July 1944.

Una Falkiner was almost as circumspect as Margaret Strongman
in her account of the actual birth of her daughter Diana. She left
for the hospital at 5 am:

> we drove thro' a wild sun rise to Mount Wise. The only hospital out
> of dozens rung up that had a corner for us.
>
> After arriving in with apps. the undertaker, we were put in the most
> awful little cubicle of a room where I felt I would rather do anything
> than stay. After a weary wait Nan [her sister] came, then Otway & Dr
> Lloyd, poor Otway was distractedly trying for flats, anywhere! Anyway
> dear old Nan said to come to Kilbride, that the girls had the room
> ready & every thing, so after more discussion we shook the dust of
> Mount Wise from our souls & came.
>
> At five minutes to eight in the evening little 'Diana Wales' was here,
> & the rejoicing!!
>
> As we thought the date was July! two months early, but it wasn't!
> (9 May 1920)

The 'great rejoicing' was enhanced by the health of the baby. Una had obviously spent her fifteen-hour labour under the impression that the child would be two months premature and therefore have no chance of survival. Given this, her decision to have the child in the warmth of her sister's home was significant. Una obviously judged her own comfort to be more important during her labour than any facilities the hospital may have had to offer. In 1920, home birth was still a common choice: by the beginning of the Second World War, however, childbirth—especially for women of Una's class, invariably took place in hospital.

The miscalculation of Diana's arrival suggests another issue. Despite the considerable attention given to maternal health, little information about the different stages and physiological changes of pregnancy was available to women. Thus, while a woman might be very focused on the different sensations she was experiencing, conscious of the changing shape of her maternal body and the movements of the baby, and awaiting her 'time' with a mixture of foreboding and excitement, she probably had little idea of what was actually happening to her. The euphemisms for different stages—'time of trouble', 'the difficulty', 'the quickening', 'confinement', and her 'time'—reflect the way women viewed and experienced this uniquely female event.

Although infant mortality rates and the incidence of maternal death during childbirth had declined since the late nineteenth century, childbirth during the 1920s and 1930s was still risky for both mother and child. Mabel Armstrong noted that several of her friends had still-born children, and Ida Dawson's sister-in-law died soon after childbirth. When noting a birth, most diarists reported on the health of the mother, often with relief if all was well. Miscarriage was another danger associated with pregnancy. Una Falkiner noted: 'Something happened that should not have, so I nearly decided to go to town, but far better & did not' (5 August 1927). The fact that Una never spelt out exactly what 'happened' suggests something gynaecological: like most diarists, she wrote freely about other forms of illness, and it was only in reference to 'women's troubles' that silence prevailed. Again, even in the ostensible privacy of the diary, she could not reveal the details of her condition. The possibility that what she wrote might one day become public prevented her from discussing her more intimate experiences. Two days after 'something happened', Una had to go to Melbourne, regretting she had not gone in the first instance, and was admitted to hospital for an operation which kept her bedridden for 20 days. When, just after she left hospital, her period started, her obvious distress prompted her to call the doctor. 'Spent an unhappy night to say the least of it!' (6 September 1927). Four years later Una appears to have had a similar problem:

> Alas! Community singing did it for me & carrying round bucket of milk for fowls!
> At 3.30 things happened, before that I felt alarming, so there was only one thing to be done, to hasten to town to Dr Lloyd which I did, alone. Of course Otway was away! gone to Sydney. (23 March 1931)

Una's distress at having to make the trip to Melbourne alone was thinly veiled. No doubt she still felt 'alarming' on the journey. She was admitted to hospital and underwent an operation for which she did not give details, but commented later, 'What a waste of time to be in here! & to have lost such wonderful material as I have lost!' (28 March 1931). The most likely explanation for both incidents is miscarriage. With this reading, Una's experience of motherhood acquires a different shape: it was marked by loss and grief—two miscarriages and the deaths of two children. Perhaps 'wonderful material' was a reference to a hysterectomy, an operation which would have left her grieving for both her lost child and the impossibility of bearing other children. Una only alluded to this, perhaps trying to let us know in as genteel a way as possible: she fashioned her life for her imagined audience, leaving only a few hints from which we might reconstruct the most private parts of its fabric. The details she omitted were the most personal ones, the incidents and events which challenged her public persona and revealed a more distressing side to her experiences of motherhood and marriage. Thus within the diary, many aspects of Una's personal life remained her own private knowledge. The division between her public and private life assumed a complicated form.

The glowing representation in women's magazines of mothers and motherhood gave little room for alternative images. The typical mother was portrayed as young, white, well groomed, and enjoying her responsibilities. She was also well organised and efficient. The attention to time and its management was a dominant feature of directives to mothers of very young children. This was particularly true of breastfeeding which was supposed to be done every four hours. Strictly scheduled feeds were supposed to inculcate order, regularity and discipline, all essential requirements for the future citizen of a modern, industrial capitalist society. The system was also supposed to give women increased leisure time and allow her to plan her day with greater ease and efficiency. By the 1940s four-hourly feeding become widely practised. For diarist Mae Murphy, it initially seemed a good idea. Mae began her diary when she and four-week-old Marie Anne, her first child, went to 'Avonview', her Aunt's small Gippsland farm. Obviously the previous weeks had been very trying: 'Came to 'Avonview' with Marie Anne. Very weary and troubled with a cross baby but expect it all to be changed now' (7 April 1943). Regulated time, it seems, was to relieve the situation: 'First day & night of our stay a different baby. On to 4 hourly feeds a far better idea. No night feed for first time and a good baby. Lovely verandah for her during the day' (8 April 1943). However, things did not continue to go as planned. She stopped keeping her diary for a year; upon resuming, she wrote of the 'weary and exhausting struggle trying to provide Marie with her natural birthright for sustenance' (30 April 1944). Mae tried for two and a half months to breastfeed Marie, and then put her on cows' milk. No doubt she suffered considerable guilt over failing to fulfil the expectation that mothers should breastfeed. So hard did she try that the struggle left her 'weary and exhausted'. In her short account of the unrecorded year, Mae made several mentions of difficulties with Marie's health and teething, as well as the delight she experienced when Marie began to crawl and walk. With an active and at times ill child, Mae obviously had little spare time for diary writing, despite her desire to keep a record of Marie's growth for her husband, Peter, who was away at war.

Women with young children were frequently too busy to keep regular records of their days. They became absorbed in another's time frame, focused completely on the needs of their child and unable to detachedly contemplate the linear progression of time. The cycle of lactation—despite reformers' attempts to make it fit in to a neat routine—did not rationalise itself so precisely. A young child's cycles of feeding and sleeping hold little respect for the clock. It was probably a combination of the exhaustion so many women faced and the difficulty of finding time to perform anything but the essential tasks, that resulted in shorter or absent entries during this period in the diarists' lives, a time when, like Mae Murphy, they may otherwise have been anxious to record their experiences and the development of their child.

Children not only threw the order of the day into disarray but also increased the volume of work while reducing the time available for it. Nappies meant larger, dirtier washing loads, and extra time to hang them out and fold them. Shopping, cooking, cleaning and tidying took longer and were subject to constant interruptions. A sick child required attentive care, often day and night, and could be the source of considerable anxiety. Una Falkiner did manage to keep up her diary throughout her childrearing years, but with an almost permanent nurse and a retinue of servants, she did not have to attend to the regular domestic chores which consumed so much of the other diarists' time. Thus, Una's diary provides us with greater insight into the experience of motherhood, albeit for a rather privileged minority. Some of her reflections, however, would probably have been shared by most mothers.

Una greeted 1920 with a sick child. John was 18 months old when the year began and Una was on holidays with him in Melbourne while her husband, Otway, remained on their property, Widgiewa. Una began her diary for the year by noting her concern for John, a theme which remained dominant throughout the 24 years of his life. 'So glad to get Sister Templeton for John, she seems so calm & reliable, & takes off tons of responsibility. It is so miserable to see a baby so weak & white' (1 January 1920). As John slowly recovered, Una turned her attention to other matters. When extensions to their house, consisting of a sun veranda and a billiard room, had to be postponed, Una complained 'we have waited for the war & now we hear tales of the drought!' (13 April 1920). By May she had given birth to Diana, and her diary focused on the health of her daughter and her own well-being. The day following the birth of Diana, Una noted, 'In the seventh heaven of delight—& oh! the relief of knowing all is well with little Diana Wales, such a sweet wee pink thing, & the delight to be here' (10 May 1920). Una was assisted by a nurse for a month after the birth, and when she left, noted, 'We took over the wee babe & I could do it entirely' (18 June 1920). Una's meaning here is unclear: perhaps she was changing nappies, feeding and so on without help. She did not disclose whether she breastfed Diana.

Una felt the vulnerability of her young daughter very keenly. She worried over Diana's health and absorbed herself in the progress of her ailments. Her relative freedom from domestic work allowed her more time to do this. Despite numerous servants to oversee all the housework and cooking, however, as mistress of the house she often had her hands full: 'Down on my dumps as Diana's spots have returned on her head, poor wee darling. Very busy filling the house maid's place & showing the new parlour maid round, & doing the house keeper's chores. Up at 7 a.m. Oh! This is the life!' (22 September 1920)

While her children were young, Una represented herself as a mother delighting in their activities and actively involving herself in their education and recreation. Her diary records their early words, their development and their play antics, and points at which she was reluctantly forced to acknowledge their growth: '[John] sat up in the barber's chair at Menzies & had his curls cut for the first time. I hated it as it means he will only grow up now' (20 December 1920). Each of John's advances took him a step closer to the time when he would no longer need Una. Infancy was a time of vulnerability for children and mothers alike. Throughout the 1920s Una's diary is dominated by the well-being of her children and her feelings about them. The death of Diana at 20 months shattered her, and she mourned her loss with intensity. Diana died after a protracted three-month illness. Una took her to Melbourne for expert medical attention, but even that could not save her from a fate which still befell many children. 1922 began with Diana very ill and Una's words: 'What a travesty of a New Year! We have heard all the joy bells ringing & the waifs singing, & our hearts are like lead'(1 January 1922). Two days later there was cause for hope: 'Diana continuing better. We are deliriously happy after the locum puncture.' As Diana's recovery seemed to continue, the details of her health consumed less space in the diary but a subsequent decline prompted Una to write, 'Stayed in bed till 11 a.m. as all my interest in everything seems dried up' (25 January 1922). Time became delayed, its unfolding long-awaited but also dreaded. Diana 'rallied wonderfully' the night before she died but the next day Una wrote simply 'At a quarter to four this morning the angel came. I left for Macedon before seven and Otway came later' (30 January 1922). Grief consumed Una. Her writing became listless, with frequent comments such as 'Another lovely mocking day' (9 February 1922). The future extended eternally, but it was dominated by the past, by memories of Diana which almost obliterated both the present and the future. Over two years after Diana's death, Una wrote 'I am so happy for my blessings, but all day long I miss my sweet Diana' (24 July 1924). Her grief was only overshadowed by a sense of foreboding that something would happen to her son John. It was as if the future held a time bomb and she was waiting for the explosion: 'If anything happened to my precious John I feel it is more than I can bear' (14 February 1923), she wrote after he had fallen when playing tennis and was suspected of having water on the hip. And her fear returned again after a remark he made about her 'being away too much for [his] liking'. Her fear was linked to her sense of incommunicable love, making any loss unintelligible for others: 'I do hope nothing happens to him: if people only knew what I feel for Lauré & John!' (22 January 1925). When John was killed in a flying accident during the war, it was as if all Una's fears had been realised. Her wealth may have sheltered her from many of the hardships less fortunate women endured, but it could not protect her from death. Motherhood could bring moments of considerable sadness, as well as joy.

Una portrayed herself in her diary as a mother whose sense of purpose was integrally linked to her love for her children and to the role they gave her. When John was first sent to school in Melbourne, at the age of nine and a half, she observed, 'I feel like a bachelor maiden with nothing authentic to do' (26 February 1928). The notion that motherhood was the only authentic occupation for women was consistently reinforced by public discussions, not only in women's magazines and in the information booklets distributed by the infant and maternal welfare movement, but also in the short stories carried by newspapers and magazines. 'The Wife They Misunderstood' told of a successful businesswoman, married to a successful man, who was criticised by all the women in her street for not having children and for being selfish in her career. A friend discovered that the woman's only child had died and that she was unlikely to conceive again. Predictably, the story ended on a happy note: she became pregnant and gave birth to a healthy boy (male children being preferred). And the moral of the story: 'Peter's mother was in her element at last, happy, interested—a real wife!'[14] The public idealisation of motherhood not only affected the way in which childless married women perceived their situation or choice, but also cast judgment on single women. Failure to marry or have children was not considered authentic. Women who remained childless were perceived to lack vital elements which would prove their femininity and promise fulfilment throughout their lives. A career was not regarded as a satisfying option for women, yet Winifred Tait, for example, found her work tremendously enriching and rewarding and expressed no desire to marry, commenting late in her life, 'I had no inkling that way ever.'[15]

The idealisation of motherhood and the stress on the science of domestic work did serve to heighten the profile of women and bring their concerns into public debate.[16] There was also another influence pervading the discussion of motherhood: the emphasis on the mother's role in the psychological development of her children. Just as women became able to regulate the number of years they spent bearing children, the time thus freed up became consumed by heightened expectations about maternal performance. Motherhood became a 'nationally controlled, learned activity'.[17] The new emphasis on parenting put the focus on the mother, holding her responsible for the psychological health of her child. In 1935, *Woman's World* offered an article on the need to prepare a first child for the arrival of another. An ill-prepared child might display difficult behaviour, and the mother must take care not to punish unnecessarily: 'the greatest calamity in childhood is injustice—the quite small child who is punished by his parents for something the child is really innocent of, this leaves an effect on his mind which, with many, is retained through life'.[18] Mothers were encouraged to assist their children's development, through the careful choice of toys specially designed to promote learning.[19] The 'modern mother' did not discipline fiercely, she talked openly with her children and befriended them. She was relaxed and calm. The result was happy children, and happy families:

> Quite unreservedly the children tell their mother everything, who listens as a 'cobber' and not as a judge. And like a wise woman, she never rebukes, nor lectures, nor comments . . . And in later years these children will be our most valued citizens.[20]

The language used to denote a modern mother's style of listening, ('as a "cobber"') suggests that through motherhood women could enjoy the female equivalent of mateship. Bearing and rearing children provided white women's only point of entry to a status of national significance.

The impact of child-rearing directives on mothers can be clearly seen in Mae Murphy's diary. She charted all of the significant stages in Marie's growth—the arrival of teeth, her shift from diluted to full milk, her gradual move from sitting to crawling to standing and walking—proudly asserting her to be 'a picture of health and an alert intelligent mind!' (30 April 1944). Once Marie had begun to walk, she was given a 'pullable' horse and cart, designed to help her 'coordinate other movement with her own, as is the swing'. She also had a set of blocks, 'if only so far to handle and appreciate colour and smoothness' (13 May 1944). Her entry reads as if taken from directives promoting the educational benefits of toys for children.

While Mae's diary is about Marie as a growing child, it is also implicitly about Mae as a mother. In keeping an account of Marie's progress, she was proving herself to be attentive and knowledgeable, in touch with the developmental stages of a child's life, and providing her with toys and games to facilitate her progress. Perhaps Mae even recognised this aspect of her diary, commenting, 'Our Daddy sent a sweet little letter for Mother's Day—it shall go into the diary' (8 May 1944). The letter no longer remains in the diary, but it was obviously the correct place for it: her husband's acknowledgment of her careful mothering. Mae conveyed herself as a woman whose life revolved around her child and the memory of her absent husband. Her points of reference were her child's activities—teeth, walking, illness, vaccinations—and her perception of her environment became dominated by Marie's interaction with it:

> The house paddock is spacious and safe from 'traps'—flowers & vegetables well shut off. Her time is divided between a path of gravel and the box of pegs and a space in front of the fowl pens. (13 May 1944)

Mapping out areas safe for Marie inevitably affected the way Mae, too, related to her surroundings. The veranda was a safe and favourite place for Marie to play, but other areas had to be made 'child-proof'.

Mae's assertion of her mothering formed part of her persona as a wife, for being a good wife involved being a good mother. Her husband's 'regular letters put meaning into the lonely days' (13 May 1944), and she left him in no doubt as to her faithfulness: 'Every night we light the little lamp and go through the ritual of kissing Daddy's picture Goodnight—longing always for him to be back with us always' (30 April 1944). Clearly Mae envisioned her husband as the main reader of the diary and included in it evidence of her devotion. News of his unhappiness upset her and cast gloom over the days, and her final entry imagined his return: 'our beginning of Heaven' (13 July 1944). The realities of their later life together are left to the reader's imagination.

As their children grew older, the demands on mothers altered. While exhaustion diminished with the passing of constant feeding and sleepless nights, the amount of physical work required to maintain a house and family changed little. For women not engaged in paid work, the last child's entry into school marked the most obvious change: while children were at school, a mother was free to work uninterrupted by the demands of childcare. Una Falkiner exercised her freedom with more frequent travel and greater concentration on her sketching and drawing. But when her daughter Lauré and John went away to boarding school, she felt deprived and anxious. She wrote of missing them, was often concerned about John's health, and awaited their holiday visits with considerable anticipation.

The older mother and child grew, the less attention women's magazines paid to them. Only Mabel Armstrong [nee Ross] and Una Falkiner continued their diaries while their children were growing up, and neither provides much insight into how she adjusted to the changes. For many women, the entry of their children into the workforce heralded a period of greater financial security and greater freedom, depending, of course, on their class and employment status. Mabel Lincoln, however, found herself assuming the responsibility for mothering her daughter's ex-nuptial child, a girl only eight years younger than her own youngest, Harold. Thus at 55 she still carried the responsibilities generally portrayed as falling to women half her age. Meanwhile, her daughter Rosie continued her life as a single woman, running the successful Lincoln's General Store.

For a married woman, her reproductive years were marked by changing pressures and needs. Marriage, pregnancy, childbirth and childrearing all imposed different physical and emotional demands. Both the domestic science and infant welfare 'experts' were purportedly equipping women to manage their homes and children better. Yet by making a 'science' out of domesticity and motherhood they located the source of knowledge of these things outside a woman's immediate experience and network. Housework and maternity were seen as true expressions of a woman's femininity, but apparently women needed to be trained in both: femininity remained a constantly elusive and unattainable quality. Mae Murphy took to heart directives on mothering, or at least her diary suggests she did. Other women allowed their diaries to reflect the tension and conflicts their responsibilities as wives, mothers and domestic managers created for them. From Dorris Duncan's diary we gain a sense of the physical and emotional exhaustion she lived with and the despair that attended the prospect of another child. Una Falkiner took considerable delight in her children and they appear to have given her a sense of purpose. Her diary is an affirmation of her mothering and a record of the children's growth and development. It also tells of the sense of vulnerability children could awaken, and the desolation their deaths could bring about.

While the early years of a woman's mothering, and indeed of her children's lives, received considerable public attention, the later years of constant work received little acknowledgment. But for many women these years made up the greater part of their life. Some, such as Mabel Lincoln, moved almost imperceptibly from the responsibilities of motherhood to the new demands of being a grandmother. For others, the departure of their children for marriage or work meant a lightening of the household work load, although their responsibilities as wives were largely

82

unchanged. Unlike married women, as single women grew older their work loads and economic situations changed little. Indeed, by the time their children left home, many mothers, particularly middle-class ones, were better off in terms of spare time, freedom and financial security than single women, who had to go on working to earn enough money to live. Whether married or single, however, as women grew older their lives were curtailed by the physical and emotional effects of ageing.

5
Relating women I: Relationships with men

'A good many ups and downs'

Fanny Barbour regularly commented on the passing of another year of her marriage. She and her husband, Jer (Jeremiah) had moved to the small country town of Mulgrave, 30 kilometres east of Melbourne, in about 1917. In 1927 they moved to Berwick. Fanny's diary-keeping was sporadic, and not all her diaries survive. However, from those available to us, we can glean some idea of the dynamics of her relationship with Jer, particularly because she was given to noting their wedding anniversary in her diary, occasionally with a comment. In 1922 she was unusually reflective.

> Jers and my 32nd wedding aniverary [sic]—It is had [sic] a good many ups & downs but on the whole it has been happy—& we are both fond of each other still— . . .
> Unfortunately Jer spoiled the day in the evening. (22 July 1922)

Fanny's words are telling, and her confused grammar reveals much about her feelings. The 'ups & downs' were a feature of the present relationship as much as of the past, a point poignantly illustrated by her concluding comment. Though Fanny's meaning is obscure, its explanation lies at the heart of her diary, and of her reasons for keeping it.

Fanny Barbour was married to an alcoholic. This knowledge illuminates the diary entry: 'ups & downs' largely referred to Jer's periods of drinking, which Fanny euphemistically noted with such phrases as 'Jer sick again'. With characteristic obliqueness, she hinted that he was drunk even on their wedding night, and

84

throughout their marriage his alcoholism clearly caused her considerable upset and pain. It is little wonder that her thirty-second anniversary caused her to reflect in such a brief, but telling, fashion.

Married women rarely wrote in detail about their relationships with their husbands. However, the little information we can glean from their diaries is generally enough to enable us to form an idea of the fabric of their marriages and the strengths and tensions within them. With the exception of Fanny Barbour, the married diarists were economically dependent on their husbands. This had many implications. Marriage has not traditionally been a contract entered into between two equal individuals, but one that secures the legal and social subjection of wife to husband. Marriage, and with it the family, serve important economic and social functions, including the regulation of reproduction and sexuality. But while we know much about the history of marriage as an institution, we know very little about the history of women's relationships with men. Aside from diaries, the primary sources of information about women's emotional lives in the interwar period are women's novels, and autobiographies written at a later date. The diaries of two single women, Norma Bull and Kathleen Hughes, reveal very different views of themselves in relation to their partners. Both women placed themselves at the centre of their narrative, an act which shifted the gender imbalance and portrayed the relationship on their own terms. For married women such as Una Falkiner and Fanny Barbour, the emotional fabric of their relationships was inextricably linked to the dynamics of power and economic dependence. It was also affected by contemporary understandings of marriage, sexuality and motherhood, yet the expectations of them as wives and lovers did not go unchallenged.

One of the central concerns of Norma Bull's diary is her exploration of sexuality and the development of her relationship with her lover, Theon. Norma portrayed her discovery of passion, love and sex on three different levels: emotional, physical and intellectual. Issues such as birth control and the conflicts between marriage and work provoked direct intellectual engagement, while her portrayal of her emotional and physical involvement with Theon is constructed around 'set pieces' which she drafted before writing them in her diary. They are literary explorations of passions which we begin to wonder whether Norma ever actually experienced. In sharp contrast, the diary of Kathleen Hughes deals with similar themes, but the immediacy of her writing leaves no doubt about her emotional involvement in the relationship, the passion she felt, or the central place it held in both her life and diary.

Norma Bull was an artist working in Melbourne in the 1930s. She had completed a Bachelor of Arts at Melbourne University and done three years of training at the National Gallery School, graduating in 1933. When her diary opens, in 1937, Norma was 31, and attempting to make a living from painting, especially portrait painting. Her patrons were mainly friends of her mother, but it is not clear whether she was completely supporting herself from her earnings. She lived with her mother and brother at Medlow, their home in Surry Hills, a well-to-do suburb in Melbourne's east.[1] Some time before 1937, Norma had been engaged to Mark, whom she usually referred to as 'M'. Her diaries, which she kept on quarto note pads, give little information about Theon, her partner at the time. But Theon was not Norma's main interest.

It was in the 'set pieces' of her diary that she engaged most directly with questions of sexuality, love and romance. She gave florid descriptions of encounters with her lover under such titles as 'Autobiography of a Couch', 'L'amour' and 'The Invitation of the Moon'. Her 1937 diary opens with herself strongly in focus. She portrayed herself as a sensual, sexual woman, playing with the trappings of romance. Her first set piece is titled in the margin, 'Romance treads Softly'. Norma provided no context for this entry, but we can assume that she had spent the evening with Theon, who had presumably greeted her with roses:

> Reluctantly I abandoned the long, clinging, black satin shirt & scarlet geranium at the neck, the cool dressing which had seen happy hours of the evening, & slid into flowing night attire preparatory to sliding into a crib on the star-lit balcony. Then, my fingers came on a fragrant bouquet of roses which perfumed my pillow in the half light with such intoxicating sweetness that my first urge was to sleep with their cool petals brushing my cheek & to wake with perfumed thoughts, serene as the lily & inspired as the garden of a thousand flowers . . . (21 March 1937)

Norma placed herself squarely at the centre of the action. She was experimenting with images of romance and sexual desire, indulging her fantasies and providing her readers and herself with a visual impression of the unfolding scene, as if we were watching a film. The details she highlighted evoke mood and lighting: the rich visual appeal of clinging black satin, the starlit balcony and the half light. The slow pacing of this entry conveys her reluctance to undo the sartorial impression she had created. The writing plays with the senses: we can feel the smoothness of the satin shirt as she abandons it, see it as it falls discarded, to be replaced by equally seductive attire. Her movement towards the bed is slow, sliding, as smooth as the satin shirt and the 'flowing night attire'. The entry continues for two more paragraphs, during which Norma takes pity on the flowers and the fate they would suffer on her pillow.

Norma's diary is a complex mixture of spontaneous jottings and thoughts, and more structured pieces, which appear frequently. In these set pieces her feelings for the men she was involved with were not at the centre of her agonies, which arose more from the conflicts she perceived between romance, marriage and her work. With the same care and attention to detail as she practised in her work, Norma portrayed herself as a character, an observer of herself and of the action. Consider her description of an evening spent with Theon, an entry entitled 'Ivy by Moonlight'. The sky was

> lined with little pavement clouds. Stars peeped out of the dusky blue ribs & invited us into the luring garden. Beyond the lake the moon regarded us through the ivy grown wilderness. A pine spread a dry carpet for us & hid the sky overhead. Like a great enchanting larva [sic] the ivy, with snail-like assurance (poise), engulfed the earth & verdure, & performed acrobatic feats up elm & plum & wattle trunks & out to the tips of the foliage with relentless (inevitable) march (certainty)
>
> The strangle-hold had not yet taken its death grip of the verdure. It slept meanwhile and there was nothing but beauty touched by the magic fingers of the moon & the crooning of the disembodied voices by night . . .
>
> 'What if the grey fingers of death steal across the morrow?' they seemed to sigh. No matter now, we are the voices of tonight.—We are the golden present.—We are the quickened pulse beat in the heart of Life. What more could you want? We have no death. The present is ours, take your fill of it, drink deeply its crimson wine.
>
> Cautiously we drank but little of the wine of the night,˙ but even so, it leapt in our veins like the deer in spring or the pulsating rhythm of a tropical night.
>
> Th [Theon] was grateful for being asked. 'You have saved my life' he said. 'This is too wonderful. It is a revelation. I will wait for you.' (31 March 1937)

Norma's creation of this scene reveals an artist's eye for detail and mood. With echoes of Eden, the site of the encounter is a wilderness, evoking entry into an unknown, 'luring' world, full of creeping danger and temptation. The imagery, the symbolism, and words and phrases such as 'great enchanting larva', 'pulsating rhythm', 'engulfed', and 'performed acrobatic feats' all carry explicit sexual overtones. The lovers were returning to the wilderness, to the centre of sexual desire. It was there they would feel the 'heart of life'. With their senses heightened by the night and the inevitability of what lay before them, the judgment of tomorrow cast only a fleeting shadow across the path they must walk. The 'pulsating rhythm of a tropical night' beat through their veins, resisting control. Just as the tension of the scene reaches its height, Norma cuts the action. Her self-censoring seems deliberately titillating. Norma, of course, is in focus here, not Theon. She is the object of his utterances, and the focus is on her: for her saving graces, for what she has revealed to him, and as the object of his undying devotion. She is the object of desire. The whole set piece has been about Norma's explorations, sexually and with prose, and Theon's presence is incidental to hers. We even begin to wonder if he ever existed.

Norma's set pieces were a means of asserting her control over the relationship and her emotions. She distanced herself from both, constructing a scene more like a nineteenth-century romantic painting than a real encounter. Norma appeared to live in her diary, rather than in the world. To create her self-portrait, she drew on several different notions of sexual fantasy. The scene's similarity to a painting, and herself as the centre of it, suggests her use of artistic images with which she was well acquainted. She was watching herself being looked at. In this scene she was both subject and object, the artist and the painting. She was asserting her own sense of desire, her sexuality and, ultimately, her power: 'I will wait for *you*', says Theon. Far from being the mere object of a man's desire, Norma portrayed herself as more powerful, more in control, than her lover. Her careful drafting and transcription of each piece asserted this.

Norma's exploration of passion seems more intellectual than actual, more concerned with the literary creation of desire than its lived expression. Compare that highly wrought set piece with a less contrived entry:

> Knitted and sewed yesterday & today. Helen shopped for me in the city [Melbourne]. Wonderful bargains. Beautiful black satin blouse, some linings etc, photos of Mrs Moris. Quite good for detail but harsh. Wrote to Betty Spooner, Alice (cousins) Eileen Fox etc. (20 April 1937)

There is a spontaneity here absent in Norma's set pieces, and a naturalness about the daily events in her life. 'Knitted and sewed' has an immediacy about it, while 'Wonderful bargains' carries an enthusiasm and conviction which sounds both sincere and convincing. Without the formality of the set pieces, there is a lightness about the writing, although everything, the photo, the blouse, like the sex, is aestheticised. The black satin blouse makes a reappearance and begins to be glamorised ('beautiful'), but the effect is cut by its inclusion in a regular list with less glamorous items, ('some linings etc.') She casts her artist's eyes over the photo of Mrs Moris, but her artist's hand does not control the entry.

In seeking to portray herself as a sexual being, Norma was engaging with contemporary ideas about women's sexuality, ideas about heterosexual desire and passion, the differing sexual response of men and women, and birth control. She was particularly influenced by Marie Stopes's *Married Love*. Some time after reading it, she came across *Sex Ethics*, a book she described as

> a brief, high handed, unscientific essay without any attempt at references or proofs or authorities quoted. . . .
> Typically medical in outlook, the book does not appear to acknowledge good derived from the power of self-control, & with them, sublimation seems unheard of. Whereas they probably overestimate the effects of sex-starvation as well as the beneficial results to the physical system of fulfilment. It is likely that romance & love in its most spiritual, ennobling, & sublimated forms is as rejuvenating & stimulating & beneficial to mind & system, or very nearly so than the not more idealistic form that love takes in complete physical expression. (12 July 1937)[2]

As this passage demonstrates, Norma was a not uncritical reader of sexological literature. She disputed the view of sexuality presented in *Sex Ethics*, especially its notion of a sex drive that required satisfaction. She implicitly rejected the separation of soul and body, arguing, from a position imbued with romanticism, for an expression of love that transcended mere physical union.

Norma was much more impressed by *Married Love*. When it was published in Britain, in 1918, Stope's book was an instant success, selling more than 2000 copies in a fortnight. In Australia her book and those reflecting her influence were disseminated widely, and her ideas were picked up by sex educationists such as Marion Piddington. Stopes argued that men's ignorance of women's sexuality led them to 'profoundly wound' their wives. While she believed men's sexual drive was constant and in need of stern restraint, women's followed a fortnightly cycle, a rhythm she called the 'Law of Periodicity of Recurrence of Desire'.[3] Men were to restrain their sexual drive until their wives were ready: 'The supreme law for husbands is: Remember that each act of union must be tenderly wooed for and won, and that no union should ever take place unless the woman also desires it and is made physically ready for it.'[4]

Stopes was arguing for women's right to determine their sexual pleasure, to choose when they wanted to have sex. It was this sense of female power that Norma imagined and articulated in her set pieces.

Norma also developed the habit of charting her periods of heightened sexual awareness. She made markings in the margin of her diary to record her level of desire (the greater the number of markings, the greater the desire), as well as registering the onset of her period with 'Ø'.

Norma's appreciation of Stopes was twofold: for the information and advice it provided to married couples, and to women in particular:

> All married people should study the book even if they make their own diagnoses without reference to medical advice or her clinics. Further books ought to be written to give details to enable intelligent women to understand their requirements without attempting to force them into clinics . . .
>
> The book is crammed with sensible information & confirms many instinctive opinions I had held re flora & secretions (chemical interchange not mentioned, only on the part of the woman), douches etc interfere with natural contents.
>
> But further, foreign matter I consider is offensive & ruins spontaneity particularly for the woman since nature has been unkind in forcing the precautions on her in particular. (15 July 1937)

Norma distinguished clearly between men and women's experience of sex. She protested against the injustice of laying the responsibility for preventing pregnancy on women's shoulders. She also recognised the difficulty women had in understanding their own needs. In an earlier entry, recording a conversation with Theon, she argued that social expectations placed upon women limited the expression of their sexual desire:

> He thinks that women have far less passion than men, that a man desires marriage before 35. I say what about women? They have sobering influences on them which in no way proves that many find restraint easy. For many it may be as difficult as for men but it is not 'done' for them to admit it. (9 April 1937)

Stopes's influence on Norma is visible not only in her recording of discussions but also in the language she used to describe her encounters with Theon. Compare her 'Ivy by Moonlight' with Stopes's comparison between urban and rural love-making: 'the opportunities for peaceful, romantic dalliance are less to-day in a city with its tubes and cinema than in woods and gardens where the pulling of rosemary or lavender may be the sweet excuse for the slow and profound mutual rousing of passion.'[5] Norma was certainly intent on demonstrating the possibility of 'the glow of spiritual understanding which a solitary soul could never attain alone'[6] in her descriptions of the 'spirit of true love': 'the wonder of thought transmission without words, the inspiration of perfect unity of idea, desire, vision, of the very breath of life, a new rhythm to live for, a fresh impulse to infuse into exalted existence' (16 July 1937).

Norma's endorsement of the union of souls through romantic love was not, however, a simple and straightforward one. As well as portraying herself in parts of her diary as a romantic heroine, she also set up a conflict between romance, marriage and her work. Norma had ambivalent feelings about marriage, partly because she believed marriage and a career for women were incompatible, and also because she saw romance as an inevitable casualty of marriage. She appropriated Stopes's ideas of sexuality and love while tacitly challenging the necessity of *married* love. 'Is there a way of retaining romantic love thro' marriage?' she asked (14 July 1937). And although part of her wished for marriage, she doubted its ability to 'fill one's life'.

> What if it did not and left one yearning still? We who crave for an individual life unswallowed in domesticity & motherhood, we would have one part of ourselves free from all enveloping hominess to satisfy the other cravings that must inevitably come. (9 May 1937)

Norma's questioning of the ideal of domesticity and motherhood sounded a note of defiance, perhaps toward Stopes as well. She challenged the ability of married women to retain their individuality or to satisfy any desires which might conflict with their domestic responsibilities. She recognised that through marriage women became subsumed under their husband's identity. In rejecting this option, she made a radical departure from dominant ideas about femininity and images of the 'good woman'. Norma quite legitimately questioned the extent to which marriage could satisfy her, but surely part of the reason for her doubt was her own investment in the image of romance. Marriage would have involved relinquishing her quest for romance. Retaining it enabled her to ensure an emotional distance from the men to whom she was attracted, and retain a form of power and control.

Kathleen Hughes portrayed her relationships with men in very different ways from Norma Bull. She, too, presented herself in her diary as the romantic heroine of her own life, but her regular entries construct a more familiar tale of romance, filled with suspense, drama and declarations of love. Several of the key incidents are written as if for a film, reflecting, no doubt, the growing influence of the cinema. At the end of each year Kathleen noted the number of men she had been out with and how many times she had worn particular dresses, her gold lamé frock being her favourite.

Kathleen met Stuart Robertson in 1937, at the age of 25, and her diary tells of their unfolding romance, the pinnacle of which, for Kathleen, was marriage. They met at the annual ball of Paynes. She had gone accompanied by Ron, on what she openly acknowledged was her foray into 'gold digging', a contemporary term for women who dated more with an eye to the wealth of their partner than anything else.[7] While Ron was busy getting drinks from the bar, Stuart materialised and asked her for a dance, after which they escaped to St Kilda beach. The waterfront scene set the tone of romance: 'we went out over the esplanade & down to the seafront near the archway & Stuart took me in his arms & kissed me—Stuart said he thought all his birthdays had come at once I felt rather het up myself' (10 August 1937). In this fairly explicit description of sexual desire (it appears that only after the encounter did they stop to discover each other's names), Kathleen portrayed herself as central to the drama. She was the focus of Stuart's interest, the centre of the story. But unlike Norma, she was involved in the exchange of passion, even if a certain coyness prevented her from admitting *how* involved.

Stuart and Kathleen's relationship developed quickly after this first, promising meeting. Only a month later she was pronouncing him to be 'the nearest approach to my ideal yet' (8 September 1937). After another month, declarations of love were in order. They were again at a ball and after a jealous remark from Stuart,

> a most important thing happened—Stuart told me he loved me . . . he said 'It's only because I love you'—said it three times—was so thrilled I could only say 'Oh Stuart', we didn't take any notice of anyone else—both thrilled— . . . then Stuart and I went for a walk over to the beach to 'our spot'—told me I would grow to love him—knew then that I did but didn't tell him—had our photos taken at the ball—wore my gold lamé frock—Stuart stood waiting for me at bottom of the stairway leading up to the ballroom after it was over, & as I saw him standing there with his blue overcoat and blue & grey silk scarf on, I thought how lucky I was to have him in love with me—had a marvellous night & it is one I'll always remember. (6 October 1937)

This episode is striking for Kathleen's skill in telling the story and the cinematic quality of the setting and action. Stuart made his declaration of love on the balcony of the ballroom, most likely overlooking Port Phillip Bay. Kathleen's conclusion again demonstrates her attention to the dynamics and politics of space. Although she is positioned above Stuart, looking down on him, she is the object of his desire, and both he and the camera are focused on her descent. Kathleen took considerable pleasure in the knowledge of herself as desirable. Reconstructing the scene in her diary, she watched herself being looked at, inviting her readers to look also. We sense her pleasure in Stuart's desire and while she allowed herself to admire him, she did not give away her feelings: Kathleen was in control; she was the centre of attention, not Stuart. The story of romance allowed women such indulgence:

> For a short time, during courtship, the illusion is maintained that women, by withholding themselves, are central. Women are allowed this brief period in the limelight—and it is the part of their lives most constantly and vividly enacted in a myriad of representations—to encourage the acceptance of a lifetime of marginality. And courtship itself is, as often as not, an illusion: that is the woman must entrap a man to ensure herself a centre for her life. The rest is ageing and regret.[8]

The following night it was Kathleen's turn to reveal all, although this time the setting was domestic: 'while we were on the couch I told Stuart I loved him—from now on Stuart & I belong to each other' (7 October 1937). Kathleen found in Stuart many of the elements of her ideal man, including his family. After meeting his father she noted, '& so now I have met all of Stuart's family & they are just right' (10 October 1937). Her diary conveys the impression that her ideal partner would not only fulfil certain social and family requirements but would also, in some mysterious way, make her feel complete. When Kathleen wrote at the end of the year in which she met Stuart, 'falling in love with Stuart was the most marvellous thing to happen to me—found myself at last & feel contented with life' (31 December 1937), she was reflecting an idea that women were somehow incomplete without men, and that it was through the right man that a woman would come to understand herself. She had found herself a centre.

It was to be another three and a half years before Kathleen and Stuart became engaged, although the assumption that they would do so pervades her diary. The progress of their love affair however was not quite as smooth as its conception, although their first real argument came 18 months into their romance. As regular atten-

Spaces in her day

dants at dances, usually at the ballrooms in St Kilda, both often
danced with other partners, and this sometimes sparked feelings
of jealousy and betrayal. Such incidents received almost as much
attention as their declarations of love: in the story of romance they
were almost as important, for they allowed moments of suspense,
and the chance for reconciliation and further avowals of devotion.

> Stuart & I had our first quarrel—both very upset—it happened this
> way—Doris & Bill were dancing & I went to powder my face & when
> I came back to the table Stuart was talking to some girl & they kept
> on talking, I sat at the table feeling very upset, when Doris & Bill
> returned, I told them & then went down to the ladies' room, came
> back after a while—Stuart was very sorry, he didn't introduce me, as
> he didn't know the girl's name & she kept on talking, she is a teacher.
> I was furious with Stuart & wouldn't be nice with him—when we came
> home I told Stuart we were thru etc., but he was so upset & I realised
> that I couldn't part with him, it was a shame our evening was spoilt
> as Doris & Bill were with us. I wore my gold lamé evening frock. (11
> March 1939)

In the face of Stuart's insensitivity Kathleen asserted her own
control over events, ensuring that he would feel as hurt as she
did. She was exercising her own degree of power. In contrast to
Norma Bull, however, Kathleen did this not by maintaining her
distance but by demonstrating her involvement in the relationship.
Her language is immediate, and her cinematic settings more
believable than Norma's artistic ones.

There is also a sense of direction in Kathleen's relationship with
Stuart which Norma's with Theon lacks. Kathleen was keen to
marry, and for her the institution presented none of the dilemmas
that it did for Norma. In 1937, when Stuart was accepted into a
Melbourne teacher's college, Kathleen wrote of her pleasure: 'it
means that Stuart & I'll be able to get married all the sooner' (17
December 1937). By 1939 Kathleen was saving money so as 'to buy
all my linen for my box this year' (18 February 1939), and she and
Stuart 'bought a cream & white utility set' for their kitchen,
prompting Kathleen to note that she was, 'thrilled with it—first
big thing in my box' (10 March 1939). The possible sexual
implications of this last comment appear to have escaped Kathleen. Unlike Norma, she did not consciously represent her
romance as a discovery of sexual passion, nor herself as a woman
intellectually or physically exploring her sexual desire. The focus
for her was on the emotional development of the relationship
rather than on sexual experimentation. Kathleen was by no means
unaware of her own sexual desire, as her initial response to

Stuart's first kiss makes clear, ('felt rather het up myself'). However, she was far more circumspect about this in her diary than Norma was. Young women's acknowledgment of and comfort with their desire varied considerably, and their ability or willingness to express it depended on both their personalities and their own perceptions of themselves.

Both Kathleen's and Norma's diaries contain strong elements of fantasy. With Norma this is an obvious, identifiable feature, while with Kathleen it comes more from her construction of movie-like sequences and settings, all conveying the strong theme of romance. For both women, fantasy was also a way of maintaining a balance in the power dynamic of their relationship. If fantasy had been a significant part of married women's relationships, their diaries suggest its importance had faded, to be replaced by daily encounters of a far more mundane kind and by a more explicit power dynamic. Husbands feature in the pages of women's diaries more often as a background to the drama of daily life than as central to the action. Few diarists revealed in any great detail the emotional structure of their marriage, or provided accounts of conversations, their interactions, or even their thoughts or feelings about their husbands. This is not to suggest, of course, that their husbands were unimportant to them, rather that the relationship did not require anxious deliberation.

Of all the married diarists discussed, Una Falkiner wrote the most about her husband. Una was Otway's second wife. His first, Elizabeth McLaurin, died soon after childbirth in 1909, leaving Otway with three children. Otway and Una married in November 1910, when Otway was 36 and Una 27, and Una bore their first child, Lauré, in December 1911. The first of her surviving diaries begins in Melbourne in January 1920, when her second child, John, was seventeen months old and ill with a gastric upset. John was definitely the focus of her writing at this stage (and for much of the rest of her diary); other family members, including Otway, received little attention. Although he did ring regularly to enquire about John's health, Una did not see him until mid-February, an occasion she noted with considerable coolness: 'Otway at last came down, & it was pleasant to see him, & hear all the home news' (16 February 1920). Such coolness was uncharacteristic, although the two did have periods of tension and ambivalence, and at times a few words in Una's diary conceal a power of emotion. Generally, however, Una was very circumspect about revealing her feelings, an attitude no doubt reinforced by her belief that her diary would have future readers. Una gained significant social standing from her position as Otway's wife, and mistress of the large Widgiewa station. She had a considerable amount invested in the appearance of their marriage, an investment Otway did not need to share: his social standing and power came directly from his wealth and prestige. Otway in fact actively discouraged Una from pursuing many of her own interests, and particularly from making any money from them. The prospect of her having her own income, or from spending her money as she wished, seemed to be objectionable to him. In this way, he maintained her economic dependence on him, and secured one means of controlling her and their relationship. In 1925, after winning £70 at the races through betting on a horse of her own choice, not Otway's, Una wrote, 'Hazel [her sister] & I romped away to our collectings! I hope I can do with it what I want to!' (21 February 1925). It appears Una wanted to buy 80 acres of land at Gembrook for £200. Gembrook, a beautiful area in the hills approximately 60 kilometres east of Melbourne, had strong childhood associations for Una, and she had been asking Otway about buying land there for at least two years. He had consistently refused. 1925 was no exception: 'I would like it but Otway says no!' (25 February 1925).

Perhaps most disappointing of all for Una was Otway's attitude to the trolley she had designed for women to wheel their washing to the clothesline. Una had great hopes for its success. She had the design approved by the Patents Office in 1920, and by 1925, along with another woman and a couple of men, she set up a company to make and market her invention, which she called 'wheel-yr-work'. She delighted in the prospect of her own income, but Otway was not so enchanted. In April 1926, just as the enterprise was beginning to take off, she wrote:

> Otway came in as I was finishing my breakfast & he wants me to give up active business in my precious & interesting 'wheel-yr-work', it is like giving up a baby! but these husbands must be propitiated! so Lance & Powell are going to direct its wheels across the continent. (23 April 1926)

Una's disappointment is only thinly disguised here. As one who had already known the grief of losing a child, she did not idly equate this with the relinquishment of her project. She had nurtured the idea of her invention for many years and gone to considerable lengths to establish the viability of the enterprise, including investigating the manufacturing methods and the requirements for setting up a company. The project was indeed 'precious' to Una, an area of her own interest. Giving it up was a cause for grief and disappointment. It was also an occasion for her to overtly reveal the way Otway could exercise power in their relationship. She did not willingly accept his power over her, yet while she could challenge his decisions she could not contravene his wishes.

Being allowed to exercise her talents and earn her own money, or to own land in a place of her desire, would have given Una an interest away from the Falkiner property and would thus have provided a divergence from her role as Otway's wife. Otway appears to have found this prospect too threatening; no doubt he realised that with success Una would also gain financial security and a degree of emotional independence. The trolley later became widely used by Australian women but, unlike the much better known Hills Hoist, knowledge of Una's technological creativity was buried.

Otway's decision was not only final in financial matters: 'I was all ready to go out riding with Madge & Lauré & [had] the horses up but Otway would not let me go, thought it too rough for me. I was *so* disappointed as I am longing to go poking about the creeks & pretty places' (13 July 1926). But her husband did accede to some activities Una loved. One of her favourite pastimes was drawing, and she could pursue this to her heart's content. Later in her life she illustrated a children's book, *The Spider's Telephone Wire*, and she wrote many short stories, usually for children, all unpublished. Perhaps Otway viewed these activities as appropriately feminine, while the skill and strength entailed in riding or inventing were not. Una was also very active in the Country Women's Association (CWA). She was president of the local Urana branch and one of the vice presidents of the federal executive of the CWA in 1932. Otway's support of the CWA's activities was so enthusiastic that in 1924 he bought a house for the Urana CWA to use for meetings, accommodation and functions. At the meeting at which his gift was announced, the members were understandably 'wild with delight' (26 June 1924). Una's involvement in the CWA enhanced Otway's status in the rural community, and kept his wife close to home. The CWA was a strong supporter of women as wives and homemakers: Una's active participation in it threatened neither conventional ideas about women's role nor Otway's economic or ideological authority. His gesture was a reminder to her fellow members of *his* power and wealth and maybe a suggestion that Una could not stand alone.

Perhaps fortunately for Una, Otway was often not around to interfere with her activities. The *Australian Dictionary of Biography* describes Otway Falkiner as a 'playboy and a strange mixture of authoritarianism, gruffness, crudity and kindness'.[9] The comment sheds some light on Una's relationship with him, and his treatment of her. While he was free to do as he pleased, she was not. He would often go off to Sydney or travelling on business, leaving Una with little or no idea of when he would return. Just how much Una knew of his 'playboy' activities, we can only speculate, but perhaps she suspected that some of his absences involved more than work. One of the most painful for her occurred at the Christmas following Diana's death. The family gathered at Macedon and were awaiting Otway's arrival on Christmas Eve when he wired from Sydney to say he wasn't coming. By 28 December he still had not phoned. The disappointment was too much for Una: 'Everybody is very kind walking up to see us, Vera & Ivy & Nina, but I am too sad Otway never came. In bed & ill, still pains on the left side of my head' (28 December 1923). Una was not given to disclosing her emotions in her diary, so these few words probably represent considerable anguish, while her state of health no doubt reflected her grief. For Una, nothing could excuse his unexplained presence in Sydney.

It would be misrepresenting Una to suggest that feelings of distress dominated her diary and her relationship with Otway. She unquestionably felt genuine affection for him, which no doubt only increased her pain at his thoughtlessness and authoritarianism. Una's expressions of unhappiness usually came when Otway was away and she was at Widgiewa by herself: 'I feel so down in the dumps when Otway is away' (30 March 1920), she wrote on one of his many trips to Sydney. And another departure prompted her to note, 'I hate him going away, even tho' we can hear his voice every evening' (15 June 1921). When he was around she was usually grateful for his presence, especially on stormy nights: 'I was so glad Otway came, as it was a blowy dismal night & he is so comforting' (28 March 1920). This was the closest Una came in her diary to any suggestion of physical intimacy between them. This reticence is in marked contrast to the relative frankness of younger diarists, for whom contemporary attitudes to sexuality were so important. Una appears to have had her own bed, if not her own room, and her depiction of her marriage was redolent of upper-class respectability. For his part, Otway—who was obviously capable of demonstrating sexual passion towards other women—gave Una impressive gifts: a racehorse valued at £2600, or a diamond brooch, for example—all of which he could, of course, afford. Such public displays of generosity served not only to please Una but to identify her as his wife, the recipient of his largesse. She carried his autograph upon her.

Una had a variety of names for Otway which suggest a combination of endearment and comic irony. She frequently referred to him as 'The Boss', a title the station workmen probably used as well, and no doubt one which reflected his role in their relationship. She sometimes opted for 'dear lamb', a phrase quite at odds with all our pictures and descriptions of Otway. 'Old man' perhaps came closer to the truth and also highlighted the age difference between them. Una could use these various titles to throw into relief the roles they played:

> Had a talk with Otway about the rose arches going up. I had such *lovely* high ones, 10 ft high, but my lord wants them waist high, so I agreed in a nice wifely way, & then we walked around the garden with the new gardener & he thinks Otway a lamb, as Otway kept appealing to him, telling him things & saying 'isn't that your experience gardener' Of course it was his experience! In the afternoon we sat out in the sun on the verandah, & wasn't it delicious! Old Chips, the Carpenter came up blowing his nose, & I called out it was quite right of him to cry about his arches. I felt like it too. (8 July 1920)

Una's ironical diction here—'my lord', 'a nice wifely way', '[the gardener] thinks Otway a lamb'—only thinly disguised her annoyance. While Otway established his superiority with the new gardener, she quietly raged, weeping silently for her lost arches.

In Una's diary the garden assumed a symbolic status as the site of conflicts and power struggles. As both a public and domestic space, midway between the house and the property, the garden carried different meanings for Una and Otway. The battles they fought over it were for authority and control, played out not only over what went into the garden, but over who would tend it.

> I was also worried about losing my gardener, who understands his job & has the garden looking beautiful. but Otway doesn't like him & says he is no good on the electric light & engine for pumping. The new man I can see only understands engines. (12 October 1920)

If Otway appointed the gardeners, then the garden would be subject to his rule; Una resisted ceding him this power. She envisaged the garden as a retreat, a place of beauty and joy, a buffer zone between the house and the world of sheep, horses, manure and making money. For Otway, the garden differed little from the paddocks beyond its fence: it should be a useful place, neat and functional. The clash of views was crystallised in the comments of an ex-gardener which Una recorded in her diary. Tom had been one of her favourite gardeners: she thought him one of 'nature's gentlemen' and very humorous company. Otway, however, did not like him. Tom turned up one day wanting his job back.

> 'Yes, Mrs F. I have been all round your garden & by gum! it needs old Tom's touch! You like a garden I know! & the Boss, with all due respect to him! he don't know nothink about 'em!
>
> Of course you wouldn't expect him to!
>
> All he wants is a bloomin' neat foot path! & as long as 'e 'as that! the gardin' is all right!! to improve matters, he might like to see a ewe or a ram tied to a rose bush!
>
> Well, I'll come around in the morning & you see what you can do. Yes! We two has a good respect for each other! all right. (18 July 1927)

Una sought to make allies of her workmen, practised a little insubordination, and attempted to establish the garden as her own. In her diary she presented herself as the partner who knew and understood gardens, she fought to maintain her control over it, a demonstration of her influence on the Falkiner estate. Una may have shared many of Otway's conservative political views, but she did not always share his views on gender relations. She challenged his exercise of power in several areas, even if she was invariably thwarted in her attempts to subvert it.

The ambivalent status of a garden, at once public and domestic, made it a ready site for marital conflict. Otway resisted all Una's other attempts to create a more public and independent life for herself. If she were allowed to have her way when it came to the garden, his efforts would be set at nought. The garden would not only display Una's talents in public, but would stand as separate from the surrounding paddocks, connected more intimately to the house than to the property. Otway wished Una to remain as bound to the domestic sphere as he could keep her, and he resisted her intrusion into more public spaces. Una, however, remained defiant. Through her regular comments on the beauty of the Widgiewa garden and her delight in it, she implicitly asserted the power she exercised there, allowing her diary to reflect the small pockets of control she was able to retain within their relationship.

Una wrote more freely of her disagreements with Otway over the garden than she did of any other marital conflicts. She obviously felt confident that such battles would not be interpreted as endangering the harmony of their marriage, and that her readers would sympathise with her view. Una invested an enormous amount in the outcome of these disputes, but she portrayed them as less threatening to the relationship than those concerning her income-earning schemes or their children's education. In the latter cases there was no garden or gardener to mediate, and the stakes were more directly personal and immediate than the height of rose arches. That other aspects of the relationship disturbed or upset Una is certain, and she obviously found a sympathetic ear in some of her friends: 'I went to lunch with Ethel Falkiner [Otway's sister-in-law] & Lady Barraclough & we had a most illuminating talk on husbands after!' (2 June 1928). But Una rarely turned to her diary as an outlet for relationship frustrations or anxieties. Her consciousness of a future audience restricted her hand: the reve-lation of too many flaws in their marriage would threaten to unravel the picture she had spent so much time and energy creating. When a visiting American commented that he did 'not know *one* happily married couple' (12 October 1925), Una did not volunteer her own as a model.

Fanny Barbour also recoiled from expressing how she felt about her marriage, revealing most through her comments on Jer's behaviour. In 1915 the couple were in England, awaiting transport home. Fanny noted, 'J looks awfully bad. I am in misery—& they are all service here—poor man' (5 February 1915). She was to describe Jer as a 'poor man' quite frequently, a comment which both reveals her recognition of his lack of control over his problem and hints at her own desperation at its continuing effect on her life. Six months later they were back in Melbourne, staying in a hotel in the bayside suburb of St Kilda. Fanny wrote, 'I went with Mrs McKillop to see Muriel Star in the Law of the Land. A little disappointed in her. When I got home I found Jer very bad. Oh Lord I am so sick of it' (19 August 1915). Fanny did not seek to explain what she was so sick of, and although she hid to the reader the nature of the problem, she could not prevent others from seeing it. 'Otto and his wife came up from Colac and they and Nellie came over to see us. Had to tell Nellie and Otto that things were going badly. Couldn't hide it' (20 August 1915). Things were going badly it seems, not just for Jer but for their relationship as well. It was another two days before Fanny revealed, for the first and only time in her diary, the reason for her despair: 'Not a nice day. Otto came up in the morning to see me privately about Jer. I am afraid there is nothing to be done—He wont stop drinking & I am so tired of it—poor man. I feel so sorry for him, but it is too much' (23 August 1915). Fanny had spent years trying to cope with the problem and her patience had run out. She no longer had the energy to deal with Jer's 'old sins'.[10] She appears unsure what to do, knowing only that she could not continue to live with her husband. The solution she, and perhaps her friend Otto, arrived at, was to send Jer to what sounds like a rehabilitation institution. Fanny was pessimistic about the good it would do: 'Poor Jer. I wonder if it will be any good—I fear not' (4 September 1915). He returned three months later and although Fanny did not remark on the state of his health, he was by no means 'cured'. During Jer's subsequent periods of drinking Fanny opted for the euphemism 'Jer sick again'. It appears, too, that she often only wrote in her diary when 'things were going badly'. Significantly, it was on her wedding anniversary in 1915, the year in which she revealed that he was an alcoholic that Fanny recorded the contract of her marriage: 'J.S. Hutchinson to F.H. Barbour July 22nd 1890 / Silver wedding day'. The state of Fanny's relationship with Jer was a constant but usually silent presence in her diary.

Fanny Barbour married Jeremiah Hutchinson in 1890. She came from a wealthy farming family in Queensland and, judging from details recorded in her diary, she appears to have been financially independent. Her diary for 1915 notes a National Bank fixed deposit of £1500, and other assets worth over £6500. She appears to have managed these assets herself, and was adept with financial matters generally. As Fanny was childless, she did not share the responsibilities of parenthood with Jer either.

Fanny could be very critical of Jer in her diary, yet even there she was circumspect, unable to articulate fully, even to herself, the difficulties of their relationship—or perhaps too conscious of her readers' judgment. His alcoholism made him a trying companion and caused Fanny considerable anxiety. Once Jer's drinking bouts had begun, they usually continued for some weeks, occasionally longer. One such period was in 1922, the year of Fanny's reflections on her 32nd wedding anniversary. A typically oblique comment suggested things were out of place: 'Miserable day—Jer very silly, poor thing makes me so anxious' (13 July 1922). Eleven days later Fanny had to stay for a few days in town: 'Nervous about leaving Jer but he promised he'd be alright—(which he didn't keep —)' (24 July 1922). Writing this entry after the date, she knew what was ahead. On her return, her fears were confirmed:

> 'No one to meet me at Oakleigh—guessed things had gone crooked— tried to get a taxi but couldn't—& no luck with the coach. Had just engaged a cab when Jer turned up—looking awful. A dreary drive home in a strong S.E. wind' (27 July 1922).

'Dreary' was a reflection as much on her own feelings of resignation and concern as on the weather. Fanny did not take up her diary again until October, but instead summarised the days, which to her seemed all the same: 'Friday—Sat—Sunday & Monday 31st All dreary. Monday just writing to the Dr in Dandenong he has a very bad foot to [sic]. Neuritis I think.' The month of August received even briefer notation: 'Telephoned Dr Langley . . . he came out & found Jer's leg was broken at the ankle. Came back in the afternoon with a nurse & they set his legs in splints, attending to his other trouble also'. Fanny was again circumspect, declining to name Jer's 'trouble'. Her reticence and allusiveness helped her retain control of the situation, as if naming it would force her to take action, as had happened on the only occasion on which she did articulate his problem. Perhaps they also allowed her the power of pity over him—hence the refrain 'poor Jer'. Fanny's euphemisms protected Fanny, too, by allowing her to postpone confronting the issue. The diary became both a retreat and a mechanism to help her through the day. The price she paid was high, for her suffering never seemed to end: 'I wish Jer would get better it just goes on & on' (10 January 1933). 'Jer looks miserable—hope he is not going to be ill again' (3 April 1933).

The dynamics of Fanny's marriage were more complex than issues of economic dependence. Analyses of family violence have revealed the complex networks of factors which prevent women from leaving destructive relationships even today, when divorce is much more common than it was the 1920s and 1930s. Among the factors which may have been relevant in Fanny's case are emotional dependence, the hope that her husband's drinking would stop, the contrast between his behaviour when drinking and in periods of sobriety, the belief that theirs was an isolated problem, a private concern whose exposure would bring shame upon their relationship and upon her. She may even have felt that her own behaviour sparked his drinking bouts, but her diary does not elaborate. It would be misleading, however, to reconstruct Fanny's marriage only in negative terms: as she noted, they were still fond of each other after 32 years of marriage, and companionship and shared interests seem to have sustained them for many years.

Fanny and Jer were regular attendants at their local Church of England, and Jer was for a time treasurer of the church vestry. We can presume that they both conceived of their marriage as blessed by God, and that, as the church did not approve of divorce, they would not have endorsed it themselves. Aside from this, women could initiate divorce only on the grounds of their husband's adultery. If Fanny had ever been able to divorce on such grounds, she would have had to live with the social stigma of being a divorced woman. Despite her economic independence, she still lived in a society which legally and politically sanctioned male dominance. Conceivably she could have simply separated from Jer. It is possible she entertained this idea in 1915, when she declared his behaviour 'too much'. But even a separation would have exposed her to a considerable amount of shame and social isolation. It would also have involved making Jer's alcoholism public, something she would have been most reluctant to do. Jer might then have been seen more widely as a 'poor man', and Fanny as the guilty party. Legally and socially she had little choice but to stay with Jer. It appears she accepted and reconciled herself to this, and used her diary to sustain her through the most difficult times.

Fanny seldom wrote about the happier aspects of her relationship. Seven years after Jer's death she commented on her loneliness and the generosity of friends in understanding it.[11] Whatever his faults, he was a companion of whom she was fond and with whom she had shared many happy times. But these are not the concern of her diary. That was reserved as the place where, unlike Una Falkiner, she was able to admit (however euphemistically) to the difficulties.

The diarists' descriptions of their relationships with their male partners reveal their struggles to establish and maintain control and power over their lives. For Norma Bull and Kathleen Hughes, the task was relatively easy. Through the language of romance and sexual desire, they were able to present themselves as desiring subjects as well as objects of desire—subjects who were in control and exercised some power. The diaries of Una and Fanny suggest that romance had left their relationships. They were then left without immediate access to a language which would allow them to construct themselves as equal partners. Marriage was not an equal arrangement and their diaries reveal their experience of this. Nevertheless, they did find places where they could attempt to redress the imbalance of power, if not always successfully. For Una the garden became her symbolic site of contestation. For Fanny it was her diary itself. As the only diarist to regularly record her wedding anniversary, she was perhaps the one most surprised to discover each 22nd of July, that her marriage had survived another year.

6
Relating women II: Relationships with family

'A chronicle of family doings'

In December 1931, Ida Dawson received a letter from one of her favourite brothers, Oswald, asking her to travel to Japoonvale in Northern Queensland to care for his three children following the death of his wife. Ida, aged 53 and living in Sydney, had herself been 'nearly dead with asthma' over the previous months, and was also waiting to hear whether she would need an operation for a bone cavity. 'I will make every endeavour to go', she wrote, but her departure was delayed owing to ill health. When she returned from a few days rest at a Wahroonga farm on the outskirts of Sydney, another letter 'was awaiting me from Oswald which made me realise I should go to him at once. So this morning [Friday] I went to town, got a berth on the "Orungal" sailing next Tuesday' (15 January 1932). She found the family well, though Oswald was 'nervy' and the children were 'not at their best, naturally' (31 January 1932), and felt reassured that she had made the right decision. Ida had been with Oswald four months when news came of her father's ill health:

> A telegram came on Friday saying 'Father not so well, gone hospital, can you spare Ida'. Of course that means the end of poor old Dad. I could not face the train journey, & could not get to Sydney before next Thursday, travelling night & day; apart from the unaffordable expense. Father has been a wonderful man, 79, and Friday night was his first ill, in hospital.[sic] (1 May 1932)

The request from Ida's siblings in Sydney was characteristic. They

Spaces in her day

looked to her for both their own support and that of their father,
but their request suggests a lack of consciousness of Ida's position:
assuming that she would be willing to make the journey, they saw
the issue as being whether or not Oswald could spare her. Practical
reasons determined her decision: she could not afford the expense,
nor would she have reached Sydney in time to see her father
before he died. The decision not to go no doubt caused her
considerable emotional pain, although she did not mention it. She
had similarly been absent in Argentina, looking after her brother
Guy's children, when her mother died. She received details of each
parent's demise through letters from her siblings and friends,
noting of attendants at her father's funeral, 'Marjory mentioned
all the names one could wish for' (15 May 1932). Except, of course,
her own.

Ida's readiness to attend to Oswald's children cost her dearly.
Her return to Sydney at the end of May was delayed when Oswald
fell ill with malaria and a poisoned arm. She finally left in July,
exhausted and in need of a holiday, which she took. She then
decided to return to Japoonvale, falling ill en route.

> Well, I have had no luck, except bad luck, & for the first time in my
> life feel Fate is unkind. Left Kuranda for Japoon on Thursday last, &
> at Cairns felt so ill that I went to the doctor, and he put me straight
> into hospital where I stayed until yesterday . . . Can not afford the
> expense, and other expenses which seemed to pick me out, & I see
> my hope of a rest gone for good. They looked after me well in hospital
> though it was lonely. Mrs Feddon came to see me on Friday, but no
> messages from Japoon [Oswald]. (16 August 1932)

Ida's despair was exacerbated by Oswald's failure to send even a
word of sympathy. Worried by her lack of money—which was
obviously not relieved in any way by her family—and yet feeling
compelled to carry out her family duty, she returned to Japoonvale
and to Oswald and his children. Four months later she again fell
seriously ill:

> On the 12th I developed a temp of 103°; & as it persisted I went into
> hospital on 15th, & came out yesterday [23rd]. The dr said 'coastal
> fever', & rheumatoid arthritis, & seems very grave about my back,
> which has troubled me for a long time; & apparently I must give up
> active work. (24 December 1932)

Ida's year in Japoonvale was a difficult and exhausting one. On
the eve of the New Year, she summed it up in the most powerful
expression of emotion her diary contains: 'I am glad this year is
ended, and only hope next will be a better one for us all. It has

been the worst year I have ever spent, & I can only look back on every month of it with loathing and sadness' (31 December 1932). We do not know all the factors contributing to Ida's unhappiness: she was circumspect about such things in her diary and rarely reflected any bitterness or anger towards friends or members of her family. The impression we do get, however, is of a woman weighed down with responsibilities beyond her physical capacity, and of a family which looked to her in every crisis, benefited from her talents as a teacher, housekeeper and nurse, yet often failed to appreciate the emotional and financial price she paid for her (however willing) service.

In Ida's readiness to go to Oswald's help, in the work she did at Japoonvale and the hardship she endured there, we can see the tensions many women experienced in the context of their family relationships. Families could provide both economic and emotional support and a sense of identity: a secure place from which they could venture and explore, yet a constant rein pulling them home and restricting their horizons.

The family is an economic and emotional unit that is in no way limited to a household.[1] This is not to imply that the family is a unified group of individuals who share common ideas about their collective well-being. As the stories of two single women—Ida Dawson and Dorothy Kendall—illustrate, the family can be a place of intense conflict, in which interests cannot be assumed to be unified and relationships can be affected by divisions of age and gender. Beverly Kingston has argued that the family had particular importance for Australian single women, who relied on their fathers or brothers for economic support and on other family members for emotional support (or not, as the case may be).[2] The following discussion reveals a more complex situation. The family was central to the lives of both Ida and Dorothy, but they also played an important role in securing its economic and emotional stability. Family relationships were characterised by affection, respect, willing sacrifice and at times great tension and resentment. As women, these diarists were charged with caring for ageing parents and often for their younger siblings as well, responsibilities they bore with little complaint but with obvious consequences for their health, financial independence and freedom of movement. A complex web of sentiment, emotion and economic interdependence bound these women to their families and influenced their decisions in ways not noticeable among their brothers.

Ida Dawson's trip to Japoonvale was the second she had made to care for a brother's children. At the end of 1919 ill health forced her to leave the small school where she had been teaching in Bombala for the warmer climate of Goulburn. She left hoping the coming year would bring better fortune, but she had no prospects nor, it seems, ideas about what job she might do. Thus she returned to her parent's home without work and once again dependent on them for shelter and support. Economic imperatives as well as sentiment and emotional ties bound her to her family. It was not a situation Ida felt happy with: when a cable from South America arrived searching for an Ida Dawson so that a sum of money might be paid into her account, Ida could barely contain her excitement: 'of course it is from Guy [her brother], but I invented all sorts of romances that Bill Hay or Mr Wilkinson (my butterfly man) had left me all their money' (17 March 1920). When £150 arrived in her account two days later, Ida could only guess at its purpose: 'I can hardly believe it. But of course Guy intends me to use it for the family' (19 March 1920). Guy's intentions were not quite so selfless. Eighteen days later Ida wrote: 'Great excitement! . . . a registered [letter] from Guy, asking me to go over as governess, & offering a splendid salary, & fare both ways, & giving all directions etc. That is what the money is for' (6 April 1920). Ida never seemed to question whether or not she would go. Guy had pre-empted her decision. In her diary the trip began to take on the qualities of a rite of passage and Ida herself suggested as much: 'Cousin Fanny came up this afternoon to see my "trousseau"' (20 April 1920). When she left Sydney on May 17, Ida began another diary in a small, unprinted notebook. Her *passage* had begun and she marked it accordingly.

The three years Ida spent as governess to Guy's family were not without difficulties and conflicts. Guy managed an *estancia* (station) in southern Patagonia, initially on the tablelands and later in a valley in the Andes. Ida loved travel and her visit to Argentina offered her a remarkable opportunity to discover a part of the world she would never have ventured to without Guy's enticement, despite her love of adventure. Once there, however, she was more taken up with the daily round of household affairs than with the 'exotic' location. Her 'duties' were not confined to teaching Guy's children: as a family member, household responsibilities also fell her way and when Guy and his wife, Prima, were away she ran the household. It was always their house, however, and she had no influence over decisions made in the running of it. Strained relations with Prima added to her unhappiness with her position and she felt excluded by both her brother and her sister-in-law: after three years with them she wrote, 'Prima & Guy took me for a nice ride!! The *first* time I have been with them alone' (1 April 1923).[3] Ida's exclamation and emphasis reveal the extent of her surprise and hint at an underlying resentment. In later years she recalled the terrible loneliness and isolation she experienced during her stay. Physical proximity was no guarantee of emotional intimacy and Ida discovered a side to her relatives she did not admire. When Guy and Prima's children were sent off to boarding school, it was time for her to find another 'billet', a task she approached without relish. This later experience she found even more isolating, and it was to her Australian family that her thoughts turned: 'Feel very lonely sometimes, & long for the family' (29 January 1924). Her diary became her confidant and her connection to her distant family, to whom she felt closer than she did to those around her. She yearned for news of their daily activities, as if being able to visualise what they were doing would ground her memories of them and comfort her. 'I am beginning to long for the home letters, it seems a long time since they wrote. I do want to know what Ella and Ethel are doing' (25 January 1924).

Ida left South America in March 1925. Her mother had died in her absence. For a while after her return she lived with relatives in Goulburn, working as a governess, and then moved from job to job until her spirit of adventure again enticed her away, this time to Java. Ida showed a remarkable degree of independence and initiative in her job-hunting. Few women in Australia during the 1920s would have travelled as extensively as she did, particularly to countries such as Java or Argentina: England and Europe were far more common destinations for those able to raise the fare. Yet Ida welcomed the opportunity to combine work and travel. She spent two years in Java, working first as a governess and later as a companion to a Mr Houwen in a mountainous part of the island. She enjoyed this job immensely, noting early in her stay, 'The days pass pleasantly though it is quiet all day while "Suchadear" [the cook's name for Mr Houwen] is in the fields. We are congenial, & I think my luck is in this time. Am getting more and more interested in the garden, & I eat & sleep like a two-year-old. There are some very good roses here' (14 December 1927). Literally and metaphorically, Ida was putting down roots, leaving her mark on her environment. She returned to Australia in 1929 at the behest of her sister: 'Ella's news is that Ethel has gone into hospital again: her heart is in a serious condition; circulation wrong, something the matter with the kidneys Ella asks me to come home so I have written to Mrs Beerstecher to get me a passage on the "Nienw [sic] Holland", Jan 24th' (31 December 1928). Again Ida responded immediately to a request from her family. When she arrived home in February, ill with a severe attack of asthma—a condition which frequently seemed to be induced by family pressures—she noted, 'Ethel is much better than I expected, though a bundle of nerves' (8 February 1929). Ida commenced a new diary in March 1929, and wrote inside the front cover: 'A chronicle of family doings. I feel as though nothing out of the way will happen.' She was not anticipating more overseas travel, or indeed movement far from home. Her focus was completely on her family. And it would be her family that would again call her away from home. Between 1929 and 1932, Ida worked at numerous short-term jobs, and secured one position, which she loved, as governess to a family at Bullagreen on the NSW–Queensland border. Then in 1932, after the death of Oswald's wife, she again set off to care for a brother's children.

Three recurring and related themes emerge in Ida's diary: the enormous significance the family held in her life, her readiness to respond to family members in times of need and crisis, and the cost to herself of doing so. The diary reveals a constant tension between the opportunities her family gave to her, especially for travel; the responsibilities it bestowed upon her and the sense of significance and identity she derived from this; and the restriction, limitations and self-sacrifice demanded of her. This tension was already inherent in her desire, expressed when she was only 20, 'to be independent and a helper besides'. The satisfaction Ida gained from helping her family came at the cost of her own autonomy.

When still a young woman, and very self-conscious of her diary writing, Ida noted, 'I never seem to put much about others of the family in this, but then it is My Diary' (12 May 1899). Her later diaries more than redressed the imbalance. Indeed keeping a record of the disparate activities of family members became one of its main functions. With one brother in Argentina, one in Fiji and later in far north Queensland, another in western Queensland, one for a time in Scotland, a sister in a convent in Maitland NSW, and herself moving around from job to job as governess, Ida had her work cut out keeping track of all their movements. She recorded letters received and sent, and their news; comments from family members on each other's well-being or activities; and her own observations on the health and movements of her family. When her nieces and nephews became independent, she noted their doings as well. It is as if through her regular and diligent record-keeping she was affirming the family unit, somehow holding it together despite its scattered nature. She was also affirming and ordering the family's relationships, conveying a sense of its internal power dynamics. As the eldest, her opinion carried considerable weight, yet she would still defer to her brothers' wishes: gender carried more authority than age. Ida translated the intangible emotional bonds of the family into a material reality: their relationships were made explicit, charted and affirmed, on the pages of her diary. Presumably, much of the information Ida gathered was passed onto other family members in letters. Thus the diary also functioned as an archive that kept the whole family informed about itself.

The prominence of Ida's family in her diary suggests other aspects of her family relationships. As a single woman, without permanent work or professional training, she looked to the family for support and a sense of identity. It may also have been an avenue to power of a *sotto voce* sort. She assumed a great degree of responsibility for the welfare of her siblings and for many years, while in her late forties and early fifties, lived with one or other of her sisters in Sydney. It seems that other family members were not always keen on Ida expressing her independent nature. When living by herself for a few days she noted, 'I am to be alone till Sat. much to everyone's horror! Ha! Ha!' (21 October 1926). She delighted in the solitude and uninterrupted time, which she devoted to housework, writing letters, and reading, noting, 'It is a long time since I have had time to read a book' (23 October 1926). Ida was usually working so hard for her family that she had little time for herself.

Single and with flexible employment, Ida was free to move as her health permitted or her family required. The housekeeping skills she had learned so well, her experience with children—first with her younger brothers and sisters, and later with those she taught—and her concern for her parents, made her the obvious choice when a nanny, teacher, nurse or housekeeper was needed. Thus the skills that might have secured her independence also worked against it: in a culture which perceived women as 'naturally' more nurturing and caring, Ida's proficiency in these skills trapped her into a role she found difficult to escape from. The periods when she was most free from family responsibilities were those when she travelled far from them: to Fiji (during the First World War), to Java, or to the country as governess. Another expression of her independence, and one of her great loves, was her writing. It was also a means by which she supplemented her

111

small income, but as was the case for many other women writers of the period, family demands and the struggle for financial survival meant that she could not devote nearly as much time to it as she would have liked. There is no indication in her diary that her family considered her writing important. Ida's primary expression of autonomy and independence was unrecognised by those closest to her.

As the eldest, Ida seemed to assume responsibility for the welfare of her family. She was not the only sister free to respond in the hour of need, as none of her four sisters married, but they were not called upon to help in far-flung crises. Admittedly, Ida appears to have been the most adventurous of the sisters, a quality she shared with her brothers, and she genuinely liked the variety and interest visiting them brought to her life. During her youth, Oswald was perhaps her favourite brother. He returned from the Great War in 1919, having spent six months in a hospital, perhaps with shell shock, and desperately ill with malaria. He was 'nervy' and 'delicate' on his return, but Ida spent a 'heavenly' two days with him in Bombala, visiting old friends and relatives (30 July 1919). Ida's concern for her family was not only reflected in her readiness to go to their aid in times of need. In 1926 the four sisters were left £3000 between them by a cousin. In a reversal of what is generally viewed as the norm of single women's economic dependence on male family members, Ida and two of her sisters used some of this money to help their brothers Oswald and Roy: 'Went over to Roy's for tea, Oswald & family there; we talked business; if Ethel will come in we can put up a bond for Rob [Roy] & Oswald to go into something in Q [Queensland]. It seems our only chance, as things are' (6 August 1926). The 'only chance' was perhaps that of ensuring the brothers' prosperity and thus the security of the extended family. Ida kept a concerned eye on her brothers' prospects. The well-being of the family was of paramount importance to her and her involvement in her siblings' lives was unusually strong and enduring. In the energy she expended in the service of her family, however, in particular Oswald's family, we can also see the ways Ida's work maintained its economic stability. Her work was both physical and emotional, supporting Oswald and his children in their need and enabling him to continue in paid employment. The public economic system to which Oswald contributed was dependent on the hidden labour of women.

Ida Dawson spent a considerable period of her adult life caring for one or other member of her family, at times at great cost to herself, as we have seen. More than once she was called on to be her relatives' domestic servant, and she responded readily to their diverse and competing demands. And yet Ida's diary refutes a simple reconstruction of her life as one of self-sacrifice. Her readiness to serve others brought her personal rewards—influence as well as responsibility, a sense of being needed as well as limitations on her freedom. When she finally did leave Japoonvale in February 1933, she wrote, 'Made my farewells; & Messrs Clark, Joy, & Wilson came to say good-bye to me. Everybody in Japoonvale has been very nice to me, & I don't know a place I have more regretted leaving' (26 February 1933). The entry is in marked contrast to her earlier, 'I can only look back on every month of [the year] with loathing and sadness' (31 December 1932). Understanding Ida's position in her family and her readiness to respond to their requests, requires understanding her subjectivity, gaining a sense of the needs it met and the security and identity with which it provided her. The restrictions her service to her family placed upon her did not mitigate the support she derived from it. After leaving Japoonvale, Ida went and stayed with another brother Rob, a bachelor, who was gold-mining near Warwick, near the Queensland–NSW border. There she began mending his clothes, cooking meals, and generally looking after him, noting with satisfaction that, after a week of her care, 'Rob is looking better' (7 March 1933). Inscribing all these details in her diary affirmed and legitimised the central place she held within her family. Ida achieved a sense of satisfaction in her nurturing skills.

The most difficult problem for Ida seems to have been balancing care of her own health with that of others. After her time in Queensland she returned to Sydney, to Willoughby, and was immediately sent to bed for a fortnight with a badly strained back and a hernia. Sydney, in her absence, had grown 'noisy, & *blatent* [sic]' (12 August 1933), and she felt too weak to cope with it. She spent the year of her return from Japoonvale plagued by ill health, especially pleurisy and arthritis, and her doctor advised her against active work for three months, a message he repeated two months later. The emotional and physical strain had left her exhausted. Ida had overextended herself and, at 55, she was paying the price. At some stage during the preceding years Ida would also have gone through menopause, or she may have been in the middle of it during this time. She made no mention of it in her diary, reflecting a general public silence on the topic and her own characteristic circumspection, but menopause could only have added to her fatigue and to the sense of despair that pervades her diary during these years.

It was in 1935 and 1936 that Ida's readiness to sacrifice her own health for another's was most graphically illustrated. Her sister Ella, the closest to her in age, was dying. Ida's diary throughout 1934, 1935 and 1936 tells of Ella's constant ill health and of her own rheumatism and lack of energy. Although Ella was living with another sister, Ethel, the responsibility for her care often fell to Ida, at least that is the way she seems to have constructed the situation. When Ella's condition deteriorated rapidly in June 1935 following a stroke, it was Ida whom the doctors advised to notify her brothers. When Ella recovered enough to leave hospital, she went to live with Ida. After months of nursing her, Ida was too enervated to cope on her own: 'Have had to get a maid to help me; as the strain has been very severe' (12 September 1935). Eventually, in March 1936, Ida took Ella to a rest home, initially for a week. The relief this provided was clear: 'Ella is doing all right, wish I could leave her there for 6 months' (26 March 1936). Again it was Ida who assumed the responsibility for her sister's care and made the necessary decisions. The financial value of her ministrations only became apparent when someone else was paid to perform them. Ella's deterioration was long and drawn out, and obviously painful to watch. The family gathered round, with brothers Roy and Fin travelling from Queensland: 'Ella just lies quiet, knows us all' (22 May 1936). When Ella finally died, it was her brother Fin who provided Ida with the most help and support: 'Fin was wonderful, seemed to be everywhere at once' (13 June 1936). The months of waiting had finally ended: Ida's chronicle of them had served her well, helping her to contain the emotions which threatened to disrupt her life and her health. The stress of Ella's protracted illness, however, took its toll on Ida. Two weeks after her death Ida fell ill herself—and had to pay for her own nursing: 'Have had a bout of asthma & broncitis [sic]: in bed since Friday night.—Dr & Nurse. Will never be able to save at this rate' (Monday, 29 June 1936).

Ida's diary spanning the years 1929 to 1936 carries a tone of resignation and weariness. Comments such as 'It is about time I received some pleasant news' (11 May 1931) reflect her general feeling of depression, a state she of course shared with the failing Australian economy. Her diary and her life begin to mirror the state of the country, and comments on employment opportunities reveal how closely connected they could be: 'Unfortunately there is little or no work offering for women at present, even less than

Dorris and Tom Duncan on their wedding day, Glenroy
Church of England, 1 March 1921.

Dorris Duncan with her daughters, Myra and Dulcie, 1927.

Mae Murphy with her daughter Marie, c. 1945.

Mabel Lincoln with her granddaughter, Mabel, 1932.

Fanny MacCarthy
O'Leary, n.d.
LaTrobe Library
Collection, State
Library of Victoria.

A page from Mabel Lincoln's 1930 diary.

Cecily Rowe in her room, reading and surrounded by
photographs of her family. LaTrobe Library Collection, State
Library of Victoria.

for men' (1 November 1934). Her sister lost money when the Commonwealth Bank foreclosed, her brothers were hit badly by drought and the general lack of work in rural Queensland, and she lost some government bonds. In her own life Ida perceived the hand of fate: 'suppose my bad luck of the last few years will stick to me' (1 November 1934). Her bad luck included not just her own suffering but that of various family members, and the deaths of several relatives and close friends. Ida's fortunes were inseparable from those of her family and found reflection in those of society at large. For her, public and private worlds meshed.

The reconstruction of Ida's family relationships is pieced together through the brief and unexpansive references she made to them throughout her long diary. Not given to direct revelation of her emotions, nor to critical comment on family members, it is only through her allusion, silences and routine recording of events and family activities that we can re-create her family life and glimpse the nature of her emotional involvement. In marked contrast to Ida, Dorothy Kendall wrote in considerable detail about her family relationships. And although the two women were subjected to similar family expectations, Dorothy resisted those placed upon her and articulated her resentment of them. In Ida's and Dorothy's different responses, we can perceive differences not only in personality, but also in age and historical circumstances. Ida reached maturity at a time when work opportunities for middle-class women were very limited and when those who did not marry were generally expected to stay with their parents and care for them in old age. Ida's degree of independence, then, was relatively unusual and her service to her family not uncommon. By the interwar period, opportunities for women to work had expanded dramatically and single women were expected to work for their support and independence. While this did not relieve them of domestic responsibilities, it opened up alternative possibilities, leading Dorothy Kendall, at least, to imagine, and eventually work toward, other horizons.

Dorothy was working in the city and living with both parents when her diary opens. She was the second of four children—in order, Marge, Dorothy, Nance and Jack (also called John). The years covered by her diary, 1932 to 1939, were ones of considerable change and upheaval in the Kendall family: illness, death, marriage and moving house all placed strain on family members and tested their patience and resilience. Dorothy chronicled all the transitions: it is through her eyes that we know of her parents and siblings, and it is her voice which describes the family dynamics.

Dorothy's relationship with her mother was far from smooth and harmonious. Mrs Kendall appears to have been a nervous woman, often ill and irritable. Dorothy found her difficult, dependent, moody and at times manipulative. Yet she still confided in her, sought her opinion, and was intensely sensitive to her moods. The relationship between Dorothy's parents also seems to have been strained. Her father was a veterinary surgeon and had served in that capacity during the First World War. His practice must have suffered during the Depression, for money was scarce in the early years of her diary, and Dorothy recorded pawning her mother's jewellery, 'the price of gold being so high and she being so hard-up' (22 March 1932). When her mother's birthday came around three months later, she received mainly money, even from 'Pop', provoking Dorothy to comment: 'Pop gave her £1. Poor Pop' (13 August 1932). Money was obviously another of her mother's worries, and Pop a ready target of complaints. Maintaining the trappings of middle-class respectability in the face of increasing financial distress was a strain felt keenly by many women who saw it as part of their duty to keep up appearances. Dorothy arrived home from work one Saturday to find her 'Mother worrying over everything she can find, tiring herself out and picking Pop to pieces' (14 May 1932).

The constant ill health and fragility of Dorothy's mother led to rather fraught relations in the Kendall household, between parents, between siblings, and across generations. Mrs Kendall could not be left alone at night because she worried too much, and as Pop was frequently out at the Masonic Lodge, one of the children had to be home to stay with her. Inevitably Dorothy felt that the responsibility was too often left to her. Marge, who worked as a gym instructor, seemed to escape lightly. However, the children did try to negotiate around their mother. They took turns at rising earlier in the morning to make her a cup of tea, but even this new routine did not go uncontested: 'there was a row because I said to leave Marge out of that, Nance said she gets out of everything. Most cheerful day' (8 May 1932). Irony was a tactic Dorothy occasionally used to dissipate tension at times of great stress. Although she often felt frustrated by the difficulties of living with her mother, they still shared moments of intimacy, during which Dorothy was forced to acknowledge her mother's side of the story (which unfortunately she did not elaborate on in her diary). 'Everyone was out at night so Mother and I had a good yarn. I lay on the bed with her. It's about time she had a break. None of us has ever realised what she's gone through' (5 September 1932).

Dorothy's mother may well have been exhausted by the effort of raising her family, of struggling to keep them financially secure, of coping while her husband and brother were away at the war, and of remaining in a far from happy marriage. Soon after this tête-à-tête she was admitted to hospital for three weeks complete rest. Responsibility for housekeeping in her absence fell to Dorothy, who took it on with the comment 'It'll be hard but I'll do my best' (16 September 1932). Her mother had doubts regarding whom her hospitalisation was designed to benefit. She was very depressed, and '[q]uite sure we were glad to get rid of her. We are, but not the way she means' (20 September 1932). Having their mother in someone else's care for a while gave Dorothy and her brother and sisters a reprieve from the constant demands of caring for her and her consequent domination of the house. They could move more freely in her absence.

Dorothy's mother's ill health and 'nerves' caused considerable tension in the family and her moods permeated the household. When one of the children upset her, they all suffered: when she discovered that Nance smoked 'on the sly', Mother 'was in a fearful stew'. As 1933 progressed and her mother's condition became worse, Dorothy recorded several occasions when the slightest upset induced tears. She sought release by shutting herself in the piano room and playing long and hard; this was by no means a private form of relaxation. A further tension in the Kendall family arose from the power struggle between Dorothy's father and her brother, John. Inevitably this too affected her mother: 'Mother not at all well. Sometimes I think it can only end one way, and that she's just holding out by sheer will-power to do what she set out to do—live till Jack turned 21 and was his own Master' (17 October 1933). Dorothy's assessment was an astute one. John turned 21 in November 1933, and her mother was admitted to hospital in April of the following year. She died three weeks later. Her deterioration had been slow, and during it, the dynamics between Dorothy and her mother had changed significantly. As her mother became weaker and more irritable, Dorothy confided in her less. The more dependent her mother became, the more Dorothy was forced to assume responsibility for the management of the household and her mother's care. Significantly, Dorothy did not write in her diary for the first few months of 1934 but resumed doing so on the day her mother was admitted to hospital. Given the domestic burden she was carrying, it is possible that she simply did not have the time to write, but perhaps, too, the emotional impact of her mother's illness left her too enervated for the daily task of inscribing. Chronicling the long decline may have proved too depressing.

The death of Dorothy's mother caused many changes in the Kendall family. Most notable was the alliance between the siblings against their father. This first becomes apparent in the discussion of the will. Its settlement took considerable time, and emotions ran high, a situation not helped by the fact that her father was one of the executors, along with her mother's brother, Phonno, who lived in Adelaide. Dorothy was quite clear in her assessment of her father: 'Pop and I being alone, had a discussion of what we were going to do about selling "Netley" [their house] and our future, when we leave here. He's out to do the best he can for himself all right. Fortunately I can see through him' (2 October 1935). The prospect of selling the house, the symbol of their unity (and disharmony) as a family, sparked intense controversy. When the family finally gathered to settle matters, tensions rose:

> The famous family pow-wow . . . We wasted so much time on prelim-inaries that I thought we'd never get anywhere. We finally got Pop down to facts and drew up a rough agreement. Fur flew in all directions on· several occasions when we disagreed with Pop's suggestions. His ideas on how we'll manage in a new house are preposterous but Phonno can't help us in that—we'll have to fix that up ourselves when the time comes. (3 December 1935)

Dorothy's account of negotiations over the will reveals Pop in a very unfavourable light. It appears he was so used to Dorothy and her sisters managing household affairs that he had no idea how much it cost to maintain a home and family. Dorothy perceived him as self-centred and concerned chiefly with his own financial well-being: they struggled for power and control. Phonno, it seems, was on the children's side, for Dorothy commented a few days later, 'wish Phonno were going to be here a little longer to keep Pop up to the mark' (5 December 1935). During these negotiations her diary-keeping became a kind of catharsis, a way of venting her frustration and anger yet containing it within the space allotted to each day's entry. Dorothy did not disclose the final details of the settlement, but the typing of it fell to her, provoking the comment, 'It's a rotten job as far as typing is concerned' (5 December 1935). She was understandably nervous when the day came to take it to the solicitors and have it finalised.

Economic considerations were at least as important as emotional ties in the Kendall family. When Dorothy's mother was alive, the income of the children was needed to maintain the household. After her death it appears that relations with Mr Kendall were based more on economic than emotional considerations, while those between Dorothy and her brother and sisters carried a mixture of both. As Dorothy began to find Pop more and more difficult and obstreperous, her patience with him dwindled. Having decided to sell Netley, Dorothy and Nance began looking for a place to rent, for themselves and Pop. He, however, was very uncooperative:

> One minute I think that I'll dare everything and see on what terms the lady in Hotham St. will take Nance and me, and leave it to Pop to make his own plans, and then I decide that perhaps things are not as bad as all that, and so long as he can and is prepared to support us we might as well get along as well as we can. (17 September 1936)

Pop's place in Dorothy's life seems to have been reduced by this time to a financial one: she resigned herself to putting up with his idiosyncrasies in return for his economic support. However, he became more difficult as the months passed. His mind seemed to deteriorate and his demands on his children became unreasonable. In the first flat they rented in Dandenong Road, Pop's room was upstairs. He was literally and metaphorically removed to the back of the house, but he still attempted to exert his influence and succeeded in making his presence felt: 'Outburst from Pop at tea-time about being neglected—I forgot to give him his apple for afternoon tea. Surely he could have walked to the kitchen and helped himself' (20 June 1937). Dorothy had no time for his antics, although was forced at points to accede to his demands. Containing her outbursts within the pages of her diary helped her maintain outward calm in the face of Pop's explosiveness. When they were forced to leave this flat in September 1937, a preoccupying concern for Dorothy was what would be done with Pop—there was obviously no question of his moving with them. The solution the children arrived at was to install him in a rest home. A subsequent visit prompted Dorothy to write: 'it is pitiful to think what he has come to' (11 April 1938). There was no longer any need for daily interaction with Pop and thus for coping with his moods and tempers. As had happened with her mother, the children's initial position of dependency had been completely reversed. Any regard Dorothy still had for Pop was a vestige of filial loyalty: her respect for him had long since evaporated.

The death of Dorothy's mother and the demise of her father left the Kendall children with only each other as immediate family. Because Dorothy's diary-writing dwindled soon after their second move, the dynamics of relations between herself, Nance and John are not recorded. During her mother's lifetime, however, Dorothy

119

did write of her relationships with her siblings, and of the competition and jealousy which infused them. These, of course, were exacerbated by the strain of caring for their mother, but, particularly with her younger sister, other factors came into play: she felt jealous of the attention Nance received, especially from her own friend Sheilagh: 'if she can hold Nance's hand and leave me alone well I'm fed up' (10 February 1933). With her other sister, Marge, Dorothy seemed to take a far more practical role. When Marge was saving for her wedding in 1935, Dorothy gave her financial advice:

> Marge and I had a heart to heart pow-wow about ways and means regarding the wedding. I made her work out on paper how much she owes and how much she will earn till the end of first term, and so get an idea of how much she can save. The result made her realise how carefully she will have to go. (23 January 1935)

Dorothy's continued to play the role of financial consultant with Marge, and also with other family members. Obviously her training as a clerk gave her skills which others were keen to utilise. Five months after Marge was married, Dorothy was again discussing money matters with her. She chose a time when the two sisters would be alone, their intimacy unthreatened by the presence of men: 'While Stan [Marge's husband] was at Church managed to have a few words to Marge about their finances. Its [sic] all mostly bad luck, but apparently Stan didn't have enough money to get married on. I've been wondering what was at the back of it all' (17 November 1935). When Dorothy, Nance and John were sharing a flat, all financial arrangements fell to Dorothy, and she and John took on the responsibility of claiming money owing to their father's accounts. In this way Dorothy exerted considerable influence over family affairs.

Dorothy appears to have become a surrogate mother of the family. The news that John was moving to Sydney, which came while her mother was still very ill, left her despairing, for both financial and emotional reasons. 'Goodness knows how we'll manage, because I'm pretty sure Nance wont give up any more and Marge wont. Oh dear, if I didn't hold on to the hope that things must get better soon, I'd go mad' (15 December 1933). She took it upon herself to maintain both the emotional and financial stability in the family, and her relationship with Marge, especially after Marge's marriage, seemed to move between that of confidante, counsellor, mother and nurse. For her part, Dorothy learnt through listening: 'Went over to [Marge and Stan's] flat at night . . . Being married isn't all a bed of roses, and a man's company all the time is not always satisfying. Had a great yarn' (5 September 1935). Whatever the popular image of romance, women kept on discovering for themselves another reality, and sharing this knowledge with those close to them. The shine had worn off rather quickly for Marge, and she was obviously missing female companionship. Reasons for the tension between Marge and Stan are not made clear in Dorothy's diary: they seem to relate to financial pressures and a certain degree of naivety on Marge's part, perhaps about sex. Dorothy wrote of 'a confidence chat' she and Marge had 'about the problems of marriage'. She commented wryly, 'I've had such experience and know so much about it all? I certainly know as much as Marge about some things' (5 January 1936). As well as looking to Dorothy for advice and consolation, Marge called on her to nurse her when she was sick: Stan was obviously unwilling or incapable of looking after her. On one such occasion, Dorothy washed all Marge's underclothes, noting that they were 'in a terrible state' (8 August 1936). Dorothy, the responsible and sensible sister, reprimanded Marge on her conduct over intimate matters. She assumed a role towards Marge similar to that she had adopted towards her mother, and Marge began to show character traits similar to her mother's, especially 'nerves'. Marge's nerves could drive Dorothy to exasperation, even when they were no longer living together: 'Her nerves are in a shocking state—no control at all—I could scream at her sometimes' (18 November 1936). Dorothy's diary became an aid to, perhaps even a means of, self-control. It was also a place where she could assert her control over other members of her family. This function is more apparent in Dorothy's diary than in Ida's, perhaps because the relationships themselves, and the power balance within the family, appear to have been more contested.

The significance of the family in the lives of single women is readily apparent in Ida's and Dorothy's diaries. Both women worked hard at maintaining their relationships with their parents and siblings, even, in Ida's case, when they were far away. Their emotional work helped secure the family's survival as a unit and as a network. The intricacies of family dynamics defy any simple categorisation of the family as either an oppressive unit or a place of security and retreat. The family could be a source of diverse and at times competing demands as well as rewards, as Ida found when, on the death of her father, she was wanted by both Oswald in North Queensland and the other siblings in Sydney. Ida seemed to derive pleasure and comfort from her ministering role, despite its toll on her health and freedom. As with Dorothy, her experience of family was in many ways contradictory—at the same time restrictive and supportive, rewarding and debilitating. Both women contributed a great deal to the economic viability of their family and worked hard to ensure its emotional stability, a tall order in Dorothy's case. Neither at any point explicitly questioned her responsibility to her family, or expressed any desire to separate herself from it. And although their diaries differ considerably in both form and content, both women used them to reinforce the significance of their family relationships and of the family itself: Ida through her continuous inscribing, Dorothy as an outlet for emotions which could threaten the fragile truce she sought to maintain.

7

Relating women III: Relationships with women

'A world apart'

Among Winifred Tait's diaries is an envelope containing letters from her close friend Jean Lloyd, who had embarked on an overseas trip with her husband in 1925. Jean wrote weekly to Winifred, who awaited the arrival of her letters with considerable anticipation, frequently expressing delight in their contents. She was the 'dear one' to whom Jean wrote after attending an international conference of women in The Hague:

> I felt you would have been very happy with it all. And with all these wonderful and famous women I realised that the spirit of love and understanding is even more important than intellectual prowess.
> Together we'll do great things for the women of the world—for the world altogether—& our own friendship makes it possible to believe in friendship & on that foundation to build up more & greater things—I don't want to stop but I must. My heart is very full. Good-bye, dear one—
>
> Lovingly Jean Lloyd

Jean's letter is a heartfelt testament to the depth of the relationship she and Winifred shared, and confirmation of the power she felt lay in the community of women. In 1925 women had limited means of advancing their collective cause, but Jean's expression of hope and of love carried the suggestion that women's contribution would come through both emotional and intellectual insights. She affirmed the importance of friendship in women's lives and declared her belief that individual friendships could form the basis for 'great things'. Jean knew that the particular love she and Winifred shared spoke of larger things, and indeed her letter alerts us to the ways in which the specific and particular provide an entry point into broader themes in women's lives and in history.[1]

Since 1975 when Carroll Smith-Rosenberg published her pathbreaking essay, 'The Female World of Love and Ritual: Relations Between Women in Nineteenth Century America',[2] the study of relationships between women has become a field of considerable discussion and debate, one which has relied heavily on women's letters and diaries, sources which tell, often beautifully, if falteringly, of the passion, love and richness women found in relationships with each other. Much of this interchange has attempted to assess the impact of sexologists' classification of women's intense friendships as 'unnatural' on women passionately involved with other women. The diaries examined in this book reveal the range and diversity of emotions women expressed towards their friends, and underline the difficulties of labelling and classifying the often intense feelings aroused through such relationships.[3]

In 1929 Virginia Woolf described the fictional depiction of relationships between women as

> that vast chamber where nobody has been. It is all half lights and profound shadows where one goes with a candle peering up and down, not knowing where one is stepping.[4]

Her apprehensions remain pertinent. We do not have immediate access to the language and meanings women used to write about their intimate friendships. In our own historical context, sexuality is understood to be integral to identity. If we assume, however, that desire means only sexual desire, we will blind ourselves to the range and intensity of emotions women have expressed towards both women and men. In my discussion here I move away from a focus on roles or on romantic friendship and look instead at the different ways two women—Kathleen Hughes and Dorothy Kendall—interpreted their intense relationships with women friends. As Martha Vicinus argues, women in the past have been able to categorise and thus view their relationships with other women in many different ways.[5] We have access to these differences through women's words: we can see in diaries and letters the interactive nature of relationships and the meanings women give them. This was a dynamic process. Women's love for other women, like Dorothy's for her friend Sheilagh, frequently defies simple categorisation and while their diaries point to the signifi-

cance of language in generating understandings of women's relationships, they also suggest the fluidity of meanings women were
able to derive from public discourse and thus the multiplicity of
ways they could interpret their emotions. At times those meanings
will remain illusive to a later reader and open to a variety of
interpretations.

In several of the diaries in this study, men are almost entirely
absent from their pages: women predominate. Toward women
who shared their class and status, diarists often expressed a degree
of solidarity, while towards the likes of their servants, their trou-
blesome deeds were usually recorded while their years of faithful
service went unacknowledged. An exception to this was an entry
of Una Falkiner concerning a previous cook who came to conva-
lesce on the Falkiner property after a severe operation. 'Poor girl,
for the second time she married the wrong man, a drunkard that
Otway warned her against, & from being madly in love with her
& promising her everything, he turned against her & treated her
awfully. She is the best cook ever too, & was with us for three
years when we were thoroughly spoiled' (2 August 1920). Significantly Una's concern for her previous servant arose through the
ill-treatment she received from men. Expressions of sympathy and
solidarity occurred most frequently in the diaries of married
women when they reflected on the treatment of their friends at
the hands of a husband. Una Falkiner's comment about the husband of one friend reveals not only her sympathy for her plight,
but also indicates shared confidences: 'Spent most of the day with
Mrs Lee Steer, glad I'm not married to him, should have killed
him long ago! He left her at the Cup, then was furious because
she went to see it and had a good day' (30 March 1921). Una's
comment was also implicitly a reflection on her own marriage,
and the quality of treatment she received from Otway. However
much he may at times have shown a striking lack of consideration
for her needs, she never expressed the outrage she obviously felt
about Mr Lee Steer's treatment of his wife.

Mabel Lincoln commented quite frequently on the treatment
some women received from their husbands and did not restrict
her remarks to women she knew well. Her reflections conveyed
her recognition of the economic difficulties faced by women who
could not rely on their husbands for financial security, while the
backdrop of the Depression adds a greater poignancy to her
words. One such woman was the wife of a customer who had
cashed a cheque with Rosie (her daughter) at her shop. The cheque
bounced: 'told me he had a job with the Victorian Producers &

125

told Rosie The Gippsland & Northern & that he has a wife and daughter, well I am sorry for the poor thing God knows where her dinners will come from unless she has someone to look after her' (11 October 1930). Economic security, Mabel realised, was one thing marriage could offer women, although at times they paid a high price for it. She wrote of a local woman named Mary who had 'gone back to her husband being tired of keeping or trying to keep herself. I must say she looked better when she came up here than when she went away, whatever hubby's faults' (12 March 1930). Mabel dismissed any idea that children were always wanted, and recognised the unrelenting strain pregnancy and childbirth could place on women: 'Mrs Tommy Williams is in hospital with another baby, I am sure', she added ironically, 'she needed it very much' (20 May 1930). Mabel was not unequivocal in her support for women, however: 'Rosie tells me Mrs O'Connors [sic] baby has been dead a fortnight, & Mrs O'Connor has not been back . . . well she will show some sense if she stays away, but I know these women, the men have nothing on them' (28 October 1932). The meaning of Mabel's last comment remains obscure, but the suggestion appears to be that the blame for the breakdown of a relationship did not only lie with the husband. Mabel's overall support for women was neither sentimental nor polemical.

In the diaries of married women, it is their families who feature most prominently. Other women move in and out of the pages, their friendships important but not portrayed as central to the writer's life. For most single women, however, female friends provide their main support networks, their social circles and their intimate relationships. Margaret Strongman liked 'chinwagging' with women and described an enjoyable dinner spent with female friends as a 'thoroughly feminine evening' (23 November 1938). Her friend Lexie, with whom she had travelled to Australia, faced a possible transfer to Sydney soon after they settled in Melbourne, prompting Margaret to reflect, 'the roots had begun to penetrate & our regrets will be deeper when we pull them out' (29 June 1938). For other young women, girlfriends provided companionship on social occasions, advice on clothes and make-up, and shared confidences about men. Often these friendships appeared relatively uncomplicated and enjoyable, although even they could cause pain and upset. Kathleen Hughes's closest friend was Glad. Sometimes she would stay the night at Glad's (who lived by herself), usually sleeping in the same bed. 'At Gladdies—We lay in bed all morning reading & listening to the radio which Glad had moved into her bedroom, after lunch we spent the afternoon playing tennis on courts belonging to a big guest house' (27 August 1937). But Kathleen's friendship with Glad had its moments of tension. When Kathleen began going out with Stuart, Glad became 'bored & had nothing else to do' except date a boy she wasn't interested in (1 November 1937). Months later they had a falling-out when Kathleen felt slighted by Glad's treatment of her: 'saw Glad [at a dance], but didn't go over to her, as I was feeling annoyed with her for not bothering to let me know about the ball—first time I had seen her since July 19th—didn't bother to ring me either—passed her on the floor & gave her a stiff smile' (13 August 1938). The incident led to a month of estrangement, until Kathleen received a letter from Glad, written from Adelaide:

> our friendship is still in 'the air'. I haven't spoken to Glad since Aug 15th, when Glad rang, & asked me why I had snubbed her at the Palais on the previous Saturday night, & I told her that I was peeved with her . . . answered it [the letter] 8 pages but Glad just puzzles me. I do wish she were not so mysterious. (7 September 1938)

It was to be another six weeks, however, before the friendship between Kathleen and Glad was restored to a more even footing. When Glad returned from Adelaide, she called on Kathleen, staying from '10 past 10', 'till 10 past 12':

> she thought I was still 'off' her. I told Glad that I couldn't make her out—told me she had gone for a holiday & paid for herself. I was very pleased to see Glad again, & we decided to 'make things up', it is so long since we have seen each other—she went to Adelaide on Sep 2nd & we were not friendly for sometime before that. Glad annoys me at times with her 'mystery', but I can't help liking her. (22 October 1938)

Kathleen provides no further insight into what she terms Glad's 'mystery' but it perhaps held the key to Kathleen's feelings toward her friend: Glad's aloofness, even off-handedness, both perplexed and intrigued her. She was interested in her, and, given that the central focus of Kathleen's diary is her friendships with men, the importance she placed on this friendship is significant.

The more involved with Stuart Kathleen became, the greater the difficulties which rose in her friendship with Glad. In telling the story of their friendship, Kathleen carefully noted all the details of time and place. The account has its own narrative, a sub-plot to her main story of romance. Her entries reflect a rare consciousness of the language she was using to describe her feelings and decisions, and she drew attention to this through the use of inverted commas around phrases which read to us, and presumably to her, as clichés. They are also phrases which identify the two women as a couple: things were 'in the air', they 'made things up'. She used similar language when describing her conversations and arguments with men, but in these cases never used quotation marks. Kathleen's self-consciousness arose from her use, for a female friendship, of language otherwise reserved for heterosexual behaviour. It suggests that she perceived her language, if not her emotions, to be somehow inappropriate when used in reference to other women.

Kathleen's friendship with Glad affords us some insight into the tensions which could arise in friendships between young women. A great deal more complex was Dorothy Kendall's relationship with her friend Sheilagh. Dorothy kept her diary in a small, thin, pocket-sized book, and filled each entry with tiny writing. When the allotted space ran out, she attached pieces of paper to the pages, filling them with her thoughts and emotions about Sheilagh. Her first entry for 1932 began 'Sheilagh & I have cleared up a little of the fog. She seemed to think I leave it to her to come to me. I thought it was the other way. Just two different points of view' (1 January 1932). Dorothy was to arrive at this conclusion many times during the following four years of almost daily interaction, which were broken only by Sheilagh's move to Sydney and the start of a lifetime of letter writing.

Dorothy was 22 when she began writing her diary in 1932. It is not clear how long she had known Sheilagh, who was a similar age, nor the circumstances of their meeting. Throughout the years of their friendship, both young women were living with their parents. Sheilagh resided in a seemingly contented home, although her mother was not married to the man with whom she lived, a fact which caused Sheilagh some embarrassment. Dorothy's home was far from happy. As previously discussed, her mother was a highly strung, nervous woman, who did not like to be left alone in the house and who was often found bursting into tears or taking to her bed. It was against this background that Dorothy and Sheilagh rode the ebb and flow of their somewhat tempestuous friendship. Dorothy's diary was her confidant through it all.

Dorothy and Sheilagh had apparently established a stable pattern to their relationship by 1932. Typically, Dorothy would become upset by some action or comment of Sheilagh's, brood on it and then confront Sheilagh with her feelings. Sheilagh would explain or justify herself, pacifying Dorothy but often leaving her feeling inadequate. One of the difficulties Dorothy faced was in trying to convey to Sheilagh the way she felt:

> She keeps saying how cold I am, but I am so clumsy when I give in to my affectionate impulses, that I feel its better to keep cool I know its [sic] lonely without all the little things but my education in that direction was sadly neglected. I can only hope for the best and that I'll improve with practice. (25 January 1932)

It was to her diary that Dorothy could most easily convey her emotions and she frequently wrote about her hurts and anxieties before talking them over with Sheilagh. Her diary both recorded the friendship and anticipated its developing patterns. Sometimes she would store up her grievances and then let them out all at once, shocking Sheilagh with the intensity of her emotions. Dorothy, it appears, tended to focus on Sheilagh's negative points, perhaps as a way of lessening her own feelings of inadequacy and insecurity. 'She asked me to tell her things and then when she doesn't like them she gets peeved. Of course I generally do find something wrong its about time I found something right for a change' (25 February 1932). Dorothy recognised the destructiveness of her patterns of behaviour, and felt hampered by her inexperience in such relationships. Her feeling that she was not the easiest friend to be with did nothing for her self-confidence.

> Walked up to Orrong Rd with her and had a bit of a talk. I think I'm pretty hard on her, I bother too much about her faults and don't appreciate her good points . . . We'd get on much better if I could only talk things over and get them off my chest like she has. She's either got a double dose of intuition or else she's studied me until she knows me as well as any one ever will. Makes me realise what I've missed through not having anyone like her before. Especially at school.
> Gosh—if she likes me as much as she seems to, its rather terrifying. I'm not used to it. (7 February 1932)

Dorothy was clearly not used to being well liked, nor to showing affection. Instead she resisted her loving emotions and focused on Sheilagh's faults, while constantly seeking her company. Her insecurity in the relationship, and the vulnerability she felt, caused her constant emotional conflict. She resented Sheilagh paying attention to other friends and expressed her envy. After discovering Sheilagh had lunched with a friend, Dorothy wrote 'I try not to be jealous but she never seems to get off to meet me. I can't help not being as bright as Joan' (17 February 1932). Her jealousy was not only confined to Sheilagh's friends. Dorothy also resented the attention she paid to her sister Nance.

Sheilagh said something about me quarrelling with Nance, and that we'd quarrel more if she wasn't the asking sort. I suppose I didn't quite get what she meant anyway I got nasty. If I keep this up it won't be long before she gets tired of it and then I'll wake up when I'm in the soup . . . I told her to go home and leave me alone, it was nothing. It would have served me right if she'd taken me at my word . . . I don't know whether its [sic] just imagination apparently it is, because she explained it all, but I suppose when other people keep rubbing it in that she seems to think more of Nance I just couldn't help thinking likewise . . . I was rather nasty and said I thought she revelled in these explanations. Fortunately she didn't take it in the wrong way and get offended. What I meant was that she has a wonderful way of putting things clearly and explaining them. I could be full of the best intentions in the world and go blundering in saying the wrong thing. Felt better but still think I should have made the extra effort and slept on it then waited till I could think it out reasonably. However it was bound to come out some day. She's a brick and I don't deserve her. (28 February 1932)

Dorothy portrayed herself in relation to Sheilagh as an unreasonable, demanding friend, restricted by her inability to express herself clearly. Yet at the same time as she accepted much of the blame for her difficulties with Sheilagh, she also conveyed a sense of herself as a victim: of Sheilagh's amiability and articulateness, of her willingness to suffer Dorothy's outbursts and to reason with her jealousy, and of her own awkwardness and insecurity. Dorothy was constantly wracked by remorse in the way she handled these exchanges with Sheilagh. She was terrified lest she lose Sheilagh's friendship, and her jealousy drove her to anger and accusations: her fear became an almost self-fulfilling prophecy and Sheilagh's understanding and tenacity only perpetuated her sense of inadequacy. Her acute sensitivity to Sheilagh's behaviour distorted her perceptions and left her emotions in a highly volatile state. Frequently they erupted over events which were not the cause of the problem:

I got wild with Sheilagh at Girls Club. She always improves the shining hour by attending to her nails. Its [sic] most irritating and in my opinion bad manners!! She didn't like it when after trying to keep it in, I told her I thought there was a time and a place for everything. (13 March 1932)

The day before this incident, Dorothy had been angry with Sheilagh for inviting Nance to the cricket and not her. Dorothy had very clear ideas about behaviour suitable for public places, just as she did about issues which were only to be discussed in 'private'.

It was not only their interactions with each other which concerned Dorothy; she also desired to regulate their interactions with other people:

> Sheilagh and I will have to come to some sort of understanding regarding our behaviour towards other people when the other is present. She was in her most annoying as far as I was concerned mood. I hate her when she does anything to keep herself the centre of attention. (4 December 1932)

Dorothy's insecurities in the relationship, and her feelings of social inadequacy were most exacerbated when other people were around, and when Sheilagh was not paying as much attention to Dorothy as she desired. Clarifying the rules of social behaviour was a way for Dorothy to assert some authority, an attempt to shift the balance of power in her direction. For Dorothy, it was events which happened in the presence of other people, or which involved other people, that caused so much anxiety in their relationship, revealing its points of stress and strain. The distress she felt reflected the vulnerability she experienced in the friendship, and the importance she placed on it. Her desire to observe certain conventions of behaviour in public places may suggest her wish to avoid any public suggestion of the intimacy of their friendship.

Inevitably, Dorothy's outbursts and her insecurity worked to destabilise the relationship, and Sheilagh soon felt the strain:

> she said she thought we weren't loving enough and we'd better part. I couldn't say anything except All right, goodbye foolishly, which she did not take seriously, but sometimes I really think that we're not a good pair. I blame myself but it doesn't matter how hard I try somethings [*sic*] always wrong. (18 March 1932)

Dorothy's language suggests she saw herself and Sheilagh as a couple whose relationship was being destroyed by conflict. Sheilagh's comment reflects a notion of an alternate friendship, one in which love was freely expressed, not battled over. As seen with Kathleen Hughes, such language was not the prerogative of heterosexual partnerships. We might speculate that Kathleen's later and more self-conscious use of couple imagery six years later reflects rapid changes in the social understanding and construction of women's sexuality. For while the tradition of deep friendships between young girls remained strong,[6] the suggestion that women's love for each other was in fact sexual and 'inverted' had by then forever changed the perception and understanding of women's friendships.[7]

These examples all come from Dorothy's 1932 diary, the year

she turned 23. The tensions between herself and Sheilagh did not ease during 1933, leading Dorothy to observe in July, 'Oh dear, we're always in some sort of mess' (13 July 1933). She did become more confronting with Sheilagh, however, as she recognised the danger of harbouring resentments. In a comment suggestive of the psychological discourses gaining credence at the time,[8] she noted, 'I had things out with her. I've learned by experience that if you hug small misunderstandings to yourself your imagination magnifies them out of all proportion' (22 May 1933). Dorothy's new tactic, however, did not prevent rows erupting, nor did it ease her feelings of jealousy and inadequacy. 'As long as she's got the limelight she's happy, I think she's a callous little wretch and told her so which was not very tactful of me' (18 August 1933).

Dorothy recorded in her diary not only her intense, often ambivalent feelings towards Sheilagh, but also the time lapses between their interactions, the number of days which passed without Sheilagh ringing her. When Sheilagh failed to ring following a bridge party she had been to with her new boyfriend, Dorothy was very annoyed: 'She's got funny ideas of how to treat her friends' (23 July 1933), she wrote. The next day she had still had no word from Sheilagh: 'I almost made up my mind to wait and see how long she'd go without ringing me but there's no point looking for trouble and I really don't want to bust things up permanently' (24 July 1933). Dorothy decided to let things 'blow over', hoping that the upset would prove temporary and soon be forgotten. She was acutely conscious of the power of her emotions, and the ways they infused other aspects of her life. It was partly this which heightened her awareness of time: emotional time could increase her awareness of linear time, seeming to slow the passage of hours as she waited for Sheilagh to ring and became angrier, more anxious, more impatient. In this instance, the issues did not blow over, prompting Dorothy to record the following day 'I really have got the miseries over this business with Sheilagh' (25 July 1933). The diary served as a record of it all, a means of both noting the passage of time and testing the validity of her concerns: as time passed, the more legitimate the concerns appeared. Rather than providing a space for working through her emotions and understanding them more clearly, Dorothy's diary writing reiterated and magnified her anxieties.

Dorothy expressed her feelings toward Sheilagh, as she did most things she recorded in her diary, in an intense, passionate style. An extremely sensitive young woman, she felt many things very keenly, although it was invariably her negative emotions that she noted in her diary. She rarely revealed her positive emotions in relation to her friend, nor did she mask her personal desires with religious vocabulary as had many women before her. Nowhere in her diary, however, is there any hint of desire for physical intimacy or even of what we might readily identify as repressed sexual feelings, such as those which have been detected between women in the late nineteenth and early twentieth century.[9] Dorothy's concentration on the negative emotions she felt towards her friend, however, may disguise such feelings. It is possible that the very intensity of her emotions, the extent of her jealousy, the height of her anger and depth of her despair when things between them were difficult, came from a source of passion she could not herself identify. In the absence of a language which allowed her to express the range of emotions and desires she may have been feeling, the love and need Dorothy obviously felt for Sheilagh but could not express as such, became displaced into complaint and criticism.

Although Sheilagh dominated Dorothy's emotions to a degree which left no time or energy for other intense relationships, Dorothy continued throughout her diary to construct herself within what we might call the dominant discourses of heterosexuality. She did everything the magazine advertisements promised her would bring romance to her life: 'Spent most of my money on a new pink pique frock, gloves and sandals and think I will get a boy. I need one badly enough' (2 December 1932). It is possible, however, that Dorothy herself wondered about the intensity of her feeling towards Sheilagh, commenting, 'Tried to explain my peculiar attitude lately. [Sheilagh] can't understand what I mean by unnatural and I'm afraid I left her more puzzled than ever' (18 December 1932). We can only surmise what Dorothy meant by 'unnatural', for she did not elaborate, nor is it clear what she was referring to in her phrase, 'peculiar attitude'. Whether she felt that the intensity of the relationship set it apart from other friendships, or whether the endless emotional rollercoaster they seemed to be on was the cause of her unease, is unclear. 'Unnatural' was one of the terms used by contemporary sexologists in their construction of the heterosexual relationships as normal, and homosexuality as inverted, perverted or unnatural.[10] Dorothy's discomfort with the word is apparent in the difficulty she had explaining to Sheilagh what she meant. Sheilagh apparently perceived nothing 'unnatural' in her feelings towards Dorothy. But Dorothy had reason to feel uneasy. In its intensity, its exclusion of others—especially, for Dorothy, men—and its near total absorption of Dorothy's emotional commitment, her relationship with

Sheilagh seemed to conform to contemporary definitions of an 'unacceptable' female friendship. Dorothy appears uneasy with the idea that her feelings for Sheilagh may have been considered in any way 'unnatural', that is, sexual. Her consciousness of such a possibility threw into doubt her behaviour and unsettled her understanding of the relationship.

Dorothy's diary provides us with considerable insight into her relationship with Sheilagh and the conflicts it evoked for her. The regularity with which she wrote about the friendship suggests how important her diary was in providing a safe outlet for her emotions, while her habit of attaching extra pieces of paper to the diary, space she filled with detailed prescriptions of her interactions with Sheilagh, indicates her almost obsessive desire to capture the nuances of their meetings and the subtle shifts in their intimacy. Dorothy's diaries, however, also leave many things unexplained, reminding us again that diaries can conceal as much as they disclose.

Reconstructing the relationships of diarists involves speculation and conjecture. Dorothy did not clearly articulate the terms on which she understood her intimate friendship, but it is clear that at times she felt distressed and concerned about the nature of her feelings. Perhaps even more important than identifying repressed sexual desire or possible physical intimacy, however, is recognising the strength and support women drew from their friends. In a society where marriage was represented as the path to a woman's fulfilment, and single women were marginalised, some women were able to challenge dominant constructions of womanhood and actively explore their own paths to emotional and intellectual satisfaction.

8
Life cycles III: Ageing and death

'Growing old is difficult'

When Winifred Tait observed her elder sister's unhappiness, she commented in her diary on the difficulty of growing old. Her reflection was not a distant observation: at 76 Winifred also knew what it was like to grow old, indeed she had been anticipating her own death for years and would go on doing so into her nineties, an ever-diligent diary keeper. The framework within which she contemplated death was a deeply religious one. Just as there was a purpose for her life, so the timing of her death was planned, and held a reason. In 1944, aged 67, Winifred seemed particularly preoccupied with thoughts of death. The war made it even more visible than usual, and Winifred felt her own advancing years and those of her sisters and friends. Her prayers, her Bible reading and her notes about world events suggest a particular interest in the subject of death. When a close friend died, she noted that they were all growing older. Death could come at any time: Winifred's sense of her own ageing helped her acknowledge death's inevability. Winifred did not believe she had many more years to live, but she wanted to use them productively. On her 67th birthday she reflected on how richly blessed she was with friends and much more. Winifred used her diary as a place of prayer and dialogue with God. In anticipating her own death, she resigned herself to God's will—but not to an old age of inactivity. Rather, she sought to see God's hand in the mysteries of both death and life.

Not all diarists were so well prepared for death, or at least not in ways discernible in their diaries. Many, however, had witnessed death at close quarters and, watching loved ones die, contemplated their own mortality. Some grew old alone and in dread, afraid of the indignities age might bring. They had few models to help them approach ageing and death in positive ways: old age, particularly for women, was portrayed as a time of decay and decline. The ageing body was a failing one, and contemporary views of ageing as a medical and social problem throw its changes into relief. Diarists, however, sought and found alternative ways of constructing their later years. Often the diary itself became a mechanism of control, a reflection on the meanings of the ageing process, a dialogue between the writer's past and her present.

Feminist historians have been surprisingly neglectful of the lives of older women. Aside from biographers, who are forced to deal with the psychological effects of ageing on the individual, feminist writers have generally focused on women in their reproductive years. Only recently, as feminists of the late 1960s and early 1970s have themselves grown older, has any attention been paid to experiences such as menopause and ageing.[1] During the interwar years, the meanings and rituals surrounding ageing and death were changing. The ageing process was increasingly resisted, while the moment of death became both prolonged and more hidden. The process of ageing ran counter to the principles of modernity: the ageing body was declining, not progressing, its functions no longer amenable to rational management and tight control. Implicit in the representation of old age was a conflict between biological and industrial time: between the natural conclusion of the life cycle and modern attempts to reduce the experience of time to a mechanical measurement. While for the diarists death was always a traumatic event, especially when those who died were younger than those left behind, their representations of themselves as older women are far more positive than contemporary attitudes to ageing might lead us to expect. In their own ways, these diarists were challenging the modern representation of time.

Marjorie Barnard's short story 'The Wrong Hat' is one of the few pieces of fiction by Australian women between the wars that deal with the subject of women and ageing. It tells of a woman who, after six years of widowhood and wearing a 'dowdy hat of a dingy woman', is taken by her children to buy a new hat. It is to mark the end of her mourning, a second spring. She goes with her daughter to a very flash hat shop, the sort of place where no one asks the price. A particular hat catches her eye—a shiny black straw hat, 'the gayest, smartest hat she ha[s] ever seen'. The attendant, however, smiles and observes it is 'not quite madam's style'. Madam is not so easily deterred, and while no one else is looking, she tries on the hat.

> Carefully, she pressed the front of the brim against her forehead and fitted the ribbon bandeau over the back of her head as she had seen the assistant do. Unconsciously she imitated her most caressing gesture. She looked in the mirror. Horrified, she peered closer. A pain, sharper than she had known for years, twisted her heart, a despair more sudden and complete than she believed possible, engulfed her. The hat was jaunty and young, but the face beneath it was old and tired. The hat jeered. It threw into pitiless relief every wrinkle and blemish. It marked the collision of two worlds . . .
>
> She sat down again, staring blankly before her. She had seen the image of her own death, and in this one moment it struck more closely home than anything that had ever happened to her . . . The six years of her widowhood had been quite safe. She hadn't challenged time.[2]

'The Wrong Hat' eloquently conveys the prevailing attitude to age during the interwar years: as a negative contrast to youth, as a state of bodily decline, as an admission of defeat by time, and as a harbinger of death. It was a 'condition' modern medicine was attempting to 'cure'. Ageing was portrayed as more detrimental for women than for men, for it took away their looks, their femininity, their sexuality and their desirability to men. For men, age was linked more closely to a declining capacity for work, rather than a changed appearance. Because masculinity was identified with neither youth nor mere sexual attractiveness, it was far more possible for an older man to be sexually desirable than it was for a woman. And while men's bodies also underwent physical changes, they retained virility and power. The meanings of gender were reproduced on the ageing body. The older woman's body was asexual, unproductive, powerless.

By 1933, 14.8 per cent of the population was considered 'aged', a term which appears to mean 'more than 60 years old'. Old-age pensions were introduced in Australia in 1903. By the interwar years the number of 'aged' people was growing, as was the recognition that families could not be relied upon to support and provide for older relatives. While life expectancy was rising, older women were three times more likely to find themselves incarcerated in mental hospitals than they had been in 1880.[3] Some of the reasons for this may lie in contemporary attitudes to femininity, sexuality, childrearing and motherhood. Older women did not conform to the ideal of the modern, feminine woman, and their social and economic marginalisation must have put many under considerable mental strain.[4]

According to magazine advertisements of the interwar period, middle age fell between the ages of 35 and 45; one advertisement called it 'a woman's most difficult time', presumably because by then her children had grown up and she was headed for menopause. Advertisements, intent on creating and securing markets, portrayed age as women's enemy. To keep their youthful appearance, they would need lotion to soften rough hands, bras to firm sagging breasts, cream to prevent wrinkles. There were Kruschen salts for a supple body and J.D.K.Z Gin for depression (presumably when all other products failed). Thus the emphasis was not on accepting one's age, but rather on seeking to look younger, to hide and disguise the effects of age upon the body. previously Kathleen Court advertised its beauty products as helping women to 'keep youth and defy age', which the ads construed as a masculine enemy:

> Age cunningly creeps upon you unawares. His first approaches seem to be fairly innocent—tiny laughter lines around eyes and mouth; a faint tracery on forehead, throat and neck; slight droopings at the chin! Tragedy comes suddenly, when, in the one tired morning you find the tiny lines are wrinkles, the chin droop is a sag.[5]

Not only advertisements encouraged women to stay young-looking. Beauty advisers urged women of 50 and over to improve their figures and faces so that they would look 'years younger'. There was no room for the maturity or potential gracefulness of age in a discourse which defined youth as the site of sexual attractiveness and desirability. Older women had no access to the predominant standards of femininity.

Women's magazines focused on the physical deterioration associated with age, the unwelcome changes it brought to the body. Women were warned 'never to permit the development of unwanted flesh about the waist, about the hips and back'.[6] Young women were perceived to have figures like a peg-top: wide at the chest and narrow at the abdomen, while older women became narrow at the chest and wide at the abdomen, 'like a hanging pear'.[7] Single, childless women were doubly condemned as they grew older: they had failed to attract a man and to reproduce, and had therefore failed as women. The language with which age was written about was that of decay and decline and women were admonished to halt and resist the ageing process by maintaining or asserting control over their bodies. Just as the youthful body had to be fit and streamlined, so the ageing body was subject to self-monitoring and self-discipline.

The popular preoccupation with age and decline reflected wider concerns. Australia's population was ageing, and the fear of national decline pervaded discussions on the economy, health, eugenics and population growth. Youth was regarded as a time of vigour and hope. For those in their forties, youth was also associated with the years before the First World War, a golden age in comparison to the chaotic present. The youthful body itself was seen as more ordered and predictable, while the ageing one was a reminder of entropy and dissolution. Frederick Thwaites, one of the most popular Australian novelists of the period, suggested the danger of women succumbing to disorder. He wrote of a 'ghastly procession of crumbling females, with dishevelled looks and wild features'.[8] We can read in this linkage of disorder and ageing, cultural anxieties about the need for control, regularity and order. Even in old age, or perhaps especially then, when reproduction could no longer claim women's time and energy, women's sexuality and power needed to be contained. Women were particularly susceptible to the equation of age with decay and decline. For them, menopause was an inevitable concomitant of ageing, an event which could not be postponed and yet which heralded significant changes. There was considerable discussion about menopause in the pages of the *Medical Journal of Australia* in the early 1930s. It portrayed menopause largely in terms of a failing body. According to one writer, between the ages of 40 and 50 women underwent 'a permanent ebbing of the ovarian tide'. One of the 'symptoms' he associated with menopause was the middle-aged spread: '[t]his adiposity, bringing with it a certain dullness, apathy and lack of energy, still further harnesses the woman's mental state'.[9] Bodies could be disruptive. A more sympathetic commentator discussed the impact of social ideas about sexuality and reproduction on the menopausal woman. The association of reproduction with heterosexual attractiveness made menopause a difficult time during which women needed sympathy and understanding from their doctor.[10] The growing medicalisation of menopause reflects the increasing medical control of women's bodies generally, particularly during pregnancy.

Popular admonishments to women to resist ageing contained an inherent contradiction. While they stressed that the effects of ageing must be hidden and denied, they implicitly acknowledged both that there were older women in the community and that ageing happened: it was an irreversible process. A woman could not halt the onset of menopause, a change which rendered her infertile and implicitly excluded her from the category of 'good woman'. Thus even if she managed to look younger than her years, if she had undergone the 'change' her age negated the effort. Time and her body had defied her.

In women's diaries, there is very little comment or discussion about the visible effects of ageing: it is the internal physical changes and psychological strain that they comment upon. The experience of age was mediated by more than just physical condition: the marital status of women could determine their financial security, the presence of children or grandchildren could reinforce the passing of time as well as add interest and activity to a woman's life, and ageing parents, relatives or siblings could impose significant demands and responsibilities. One's age was always relative to that of the people one was closest to. Ida Dawson was 53 when her 79-year-old father died, and although Ida herself felt the effects of failing health, she was still young by comparison.

Ida anticipated ageing with dread. Even during her forties she had been plagued by rheumatism and asthma, but she noted at 50, 'am afraid the day is not far distant when I shall not be able to do much' (15 May 1930). After her stint in northern Queensland looking after her brother and his children, she returned home with a 'badly strained back & a hernia' (26 July 1933). After three months of enforced rest, she again became very ill, acknowledging her doctor's prescription that she 'must live a "quiet life"!' (16 October 1933). Ida reflected his perception of her as an older woman with a failing body. It was a difficult lesson to learn: she was more used to caring for others than for herself. She resented the increasing restrictions her advancing years placed upon her, in particular her bouts of ill health: 'I spent yesterday in bed, (heart attack), am better today, but shakey; suppose I must accustom myself to these spasms' (26 June 1938). She saw the several illnesses which befell her during the war years as the result of 'over doing things', and wrote, at the age of 63, of her need to 'realise [her] limitations' (7 October 1942). Ida both reflected and resisted prevailing attitudes to ageing. Her diaries convey the image of a body in deterioration, a process she attempted to deny and yet was forced to acknowledge. The changes were not positive ones, however: age was her enemy—as with the woman with the hat, it was a recognition of the girl she no longer was. A single woman, Ida had no children to look after her, a reminder that she had not fulfilled a central requirement of the 'good woman'. Perhaps as compensation, she had acted as surrogate mother to her siblings and their children. But her advancing years denied her even this consolation. As she grew older, the scope of her world contracted. Distances she had once seen as manageable were no longer so, and her body constricted her movements. Women's magazines may have portrayed the tragedy of ageing for women as lying in their loss of youthful allure and sexual desirability. Diarists were more concerned with other physical changes, but they wrote of them in similar ways: as a lack of control over the body, as decline and inevitably as loss. Ida Dawson resisted the changes by continuing to be active and defying her doctor's advice. She kept discovering, however, that her capacities were limited.

Ageing was about learning to live not only with physical restrictions but with the inevitability of death. As Ida entered old age, people she had known all her life were ageing and dying. As they did so, her links with her past became more tenuous, surviving more in her memory than in the fabric of her daily life. Her diary now became a central link with the world of her past, providing a sense of continuity when other connections were broken. When her Aunt Nellie died in 1936, Ida wrote, 'She was in her 83rd year, birthday in Nov. & was the eldest daughter of Wm Leonard Dawson (who came out here with Gov. Gipps)—Father's father, so she is a link with the early days. It is a break for me, we were great mates' (22 June 1937). In recording her aunt's death, Ida both registered Nellie's passing and reviewed her own position in the family and in the history of white settlement. Only a few days later, she lost another friend, Ethel Cummins: 'Poor Ethel, one of my best & oldest friends; she had a marvellous spirit' (3 July 1937), Ida's reflections on other older women were positive and affirming. She recognised the contributions they had made, their significance in the family structure, and their importance as individual friends. In writing of other older women in such a way, Ida implicitly allowed for a similarly positive construction of her own life. The diary was a means through which women could deal with the psychological impact of old age. It was proof that their years had been full and active, and it served as both a reminder of the past and an aid in preparation for the future:

> Yesterday Mary Jasper came to see me! She, & her two younger brothers were the pupils at the first position I had as governess, at Bullagreen, 45 years ago!! We had much to talk about, & recall; I had got out my old Bullagreen diary. (22 November 1947)

As a countermeasure to the loss she felt as friends died, Ida sought out old acquaintances. In conjunction with her diary, her friends brought a sense of unity and cohesion to her life. Ida was also bringing together other threads:

> I have been making a start to put my various articles in book form; have had encouraging letters from 'Bulletin' & 'Mirror', & the B'tin will write the foreword. What a compliment. But what a time I have chosen! So I fear will not have much luck. (12 July 1947)

Ida's sense of bad timing stemmed from her belief that under the Chifley government the nation was in 'bad hands', especially given the current coal strike. This did not seem to deter her, however. Four weeks later she took a manuscript of her 'book' to Angus & Robertson, noting after a couple of months, 'Angus and Robertson returned my MSS (as of course expected) but with a very nice & encouraging criticism & if possible I will try again' (5 October 1947). If Ida did 'try again', there is no record of it in her diary, nor has any collection of her writings survived. Perhaps she lacked the confidence to endure further rejection letters, or simply could not summon the energy or commitment for the task. Whatever the reason, the body of Ida's writing is lost.

There is a strong sense in Ida's diary that she herself believed her life was drawing to its close, and that her days were numbered. We can observe this in her actions, and also in her reflections. In 1947, aged 67 and in the same year as she wrote of her manuscript and reread her old diaries, she began to reflect on what the world would be like when she was no longer alive to watch and record it: 'The whole world is in a state of upset—mild word—morally & economically—don't suppose I will ever see it settle down another war seems looming' (18 July 1947). Ida, who lived a further eleven years, saw the battle lines of the Cold War drawn, but by then she had ceased to comment regularly on world events and was focusing more than ever on her family.

Ida kept her diary less regularly in the last years of her life, which saw the first notable lapses since she had begun in 1894. She wrote in 1955, at the age of 75, 'Am sorry I gave up the diary, as really the most interesting periods of our lives have been during the missed periods; so I'll make a new beginning' (8 February 1955). For the first time she was writing with a ballpoint pen, her hand was shaky, and time was playing tricks with her usually astute eye for detail: one entry, written in 1953, she had dated 1853; she only realised her mistake when she resumed the diary in 1955. No record remains of the last three years of Ida's life. She ceased writing just before being admitted to hospital for a small operation. Her nephew Allan was to take her to the hospital, and her friend of 63 years, Ilma, brought her a bedjacket for her stay. Ida was at last receiving the kind of care she had for so long given to other people. Her last entry suggests that her mind was as alert and engaged as ever:

> Ethel forwarded Rob's letter: most interesting he can tell more in a few lines than any writer I know of: am sending a copy to Ethel Symmons [an English friend]. Nothing exciting to note,—some of the papers seem to have gone quite mad about Pr Margaret's engagement. (13 March 1955)

The entry is written on the last page of the diary. Ida did not begin a new diary, perhaps feeling that she would not live long enough to make it worthwhile. The energy which had characterised her life's chronicling was no doubt waning. At some point in her last years, however, she read through her diaries, especially those written during her time in Argentina, and excised paragraphs and sentences. Her surviving South American diaries have passages cleanly cut from the page. Most often these appear to be related to either Guy and Prima or a Mr Nicholson, who lived on the *estancia* and with whom Ida formed a close and enduring friendship. The anticipation of an audience prompted Ida to reshape aspects of her life, ensuring that knowledge of some things would die with her.

The resistance which characterised Ida's early years of failing health diminished with time, a reflection of her acceptance of the inevitable and, perhaps, the growing public acceptance of elderly people. She settled into her older years. The increasing life expectancy of both men and women forced a greater recognition of the contribution older people made to the community and thus no doubt eased the special difficulties older women experienced. The last years of Ida's diary suggest a state of contentment with both her present and her past. She died in 1958.

Fanny Barbour spent the last years of her life alone, noting each year the anniversary of her husband's death and her fears for the future. The diary is a record and reminder of the past, and time—linear, biological and individual—hangs very heavily in it. As with Ida Dawson's diary, notes of other people's deaths occur more regularly, and those of close friends brought particular sadness. They were a regular reminder of her own mortality. As she grew older, the celebration of her birthday became increasingly elaborate. This probably reflected both a genuine celebration and acknowledgment of her years and a ritualised performance which grew more assertive as her hold on life became more tenuous. Age changed her relationship with time: as the years passed, the future shortened and the past grew longer and weightier. The aspect of old age Fanny found most difficult to deal with was loneliness. Generally she filled her days with Red Cross and CWA meetings, and activities involved with the church. This provided her with a network of friends, although it did not always alleviate the long days and nights she spent alone. After an invitation from a friend for tea, Fanny noted, 'Nice of her to take pity on my lonliness [sic]' (6 April 1941). Details such as the weather could make an enormous difference to the way Fanny spent her days and to her state of mind: 'A very miserable cold day stayed in Jer's 'Little Room' by the fire all day did tapestry work & read & was very bored—' (23 March 1943). Her state of health did not help matters: 'had breakfast in bed, feeling miserable with rheumatism' (30 July 1943). At 78 she portrayed herself as a rather pathetic figure, valued not for herself but as an object to be pitied. In January 1944 Fanny was prompted to record a visit to church: 'Rev W. Veal preached he is 91—I hope if I live that long—I can keep my faculties like that but I think I wont [do] either—' (2 January 1944). As she grew older, her diary began to reflect the slower pace of her life and her contracting world. The relentless progression of time had slowed down, and her body was faltering with it. It took her longer to do less, and outings or trips to town assumed greater significance. When a visit to her eye specialist revealed that her eyes 'were in a serious state', her comment 'oh it will be awful if I go blind' (14 February 1940) evokes years of limited activity stretching slowly before her. Her body had lost its youthful vigour and was failing.

We can see reflected in the pages of Fanny's diary popular ideas about age as a time of decay and of loss of control over one's body. But despite this, and despite her age and rheumatism, at 78 Fanny was elected president of the local CWA, and she continued to be involved in the church and Red Cross. Her life, then, was far from inactive, her mind far from senile and her body not about to give up. The organisations she was involved in would have given her access to women who would have shared and endorsed her experience of ageing. Yet women such as Fanny were not to be found in magazines. Pictures of women over 40 only ever appeared in *Woman's World* in the 'What women are talking about' feature: generally they showed women who were notable for their relationship to famous men, or were single and in unusual occupations. There were no pictures of grandmothers representing the wisdom of experience, and the contribution older women made to their communities was rarely recognised: modernity celebrated the new and had no time for the old. However, while Fanny appeared to have great difficulty coping with some aspects of it, ageing for her does not emerge as a predominantly negative experience. While her physical deterioration, illness and loneliness were depressing and painful, she also derived considerable satisfaction from her involvement in local organisations. She wrote of her first day as president of the local CWA with a lack of confidence but a sense of achievement nevertheless: 'think I got on alright—Mrs Sewell thought I did—Mrs Farnham is a great help' (16 December 1943). Fanny's diary confirms that the realities of older women's lives were very different from the images portrayed in (or omitted from) public discourses. Old age held no fixed meaning.

For Winifred Tait age provoked the contemplation of death. It did not, however, reduce the mystery of death, nor of illness. While her close friend Jean suffered from a disease which left her severely incapacitated, Winifred sought to understand the meaning of illness and wondered at the mysteriousness of death. Winifred thought in 1944 that she did not have long to live, in fact she lived until 1968, dying at the age of 91. The most enriching experience of her last 25 years was her relationship with Grace, whose sudden death from a heart attack in 1966 left Winifred grief-stricken and confused. Overwhelmed, she was unable to understand why Grace, so much younger than herself, should have died first. As Winifred continued to await her own death, the years stretched on long past her expectations.

For Winifred, the tragedy of Grace's death lay not just in the loss of her dearest friend but in its untimely nature. It seemed a travesty of natural justice. The death of loved ones younger than themselves caused most diarists unusual grief. And while a preoccupation with death and dying was not exclusive to old age, as Una Falkiner learned on the death of her daughter Diana, the untimely loss of loved ones often appeared to make women feel suddenly years older. After receiving news of John's death, Una Falkiner wrote, 'The day seemed 100 years I felt 100! but I know he is safe in his Father's Home' (14 September 1942).

The diaries of Cecil [Cecily] Rowe and her sister Fanny MacCarthy O'Leary for the years 1919 and 1920 are preoccupied with illness and death. As close relatives died one by one their diaries suggest exhaustion with life: it had gone on long enough. Cecil Rowe kept her diary while living with the widowed Fanny and her daughter, Amy, in the Melbourne suburb of Hawthorn.

Cecil had never married. Both she and Fanny kept diaries, although Cecil's is the more detailed and expansive of the two. It gives us considerable insight into the rituals surrounding illness and death, and the place of women at the bedsides of the dying. The Rowe family were gentry impoverished by misfortune and bad management, and Fanny in particular felt her life had been touched by sadness beyond bearing. The years 1919 and 1920 were to confirm her belief.

The two dominant characters in Cecil's diary are Amy and Cecil's other sister Janey. In March 1919, Amy became very sick. Cecil and Fanny cared for her until Fanny's son-in-law, a physician, advised them to call a doctor. She was diagnosed as suffering from bronchial pneumonia. For weeks Cecil's diary provides daily accounts of Amy's state of health, including details such as her temperature and the quality of her night's sleep. In the midst of this, Cecil was also very concerned about Janey, who was mentally disturbed and required constant nursing. Cecil made regular visits to her sister, who lived with her husband, Alex, in the town of Bayswater on Melbourne's eastern fringe. Cecil always referred to her as 'poor Janey': 'Went to Boonong [the Bayswater house] 8.52 train—Alex to meet me—Poor Janey more mental than ever— Nurses going on quietly—I came back by 3.27 train' (11 April 1919). Keeping nurses to attend to Janey was a constant battle, and a responsibility Cecil assumed. Although she never revealed precisely what was wrong with her, it appears Janey was a difficult patient: 'Poor Janey *very* wild. I helped Nurse Abbit to dress Janey—and stayed with her all afternoon' (24 May 1919). The health of her sister and niece was the central theme of Cecil's diary, in which sickness and health formed a pervasive dichotomy. Even when Janey was well, Cecil wrote of it with resignation and regret: 'I went to Boonong by early train, Alex met me. Poor Janey looking well, but cried much when I spoke to her. Alex came down with me by 3.37 train' (14 October 1919).

Janey was soon to die. Cecil wrote on 22 December 1919:

> Mrs Kennedy came down for me by 1st train & we went by 8.52—she said Janey was very low & that Alex wanted me at once—alas! my dear little sister had gone before Mrs K got to Bayswater she didn't tell me till I got close to the house—I found poor Alex beside himself with grief—dear Janey had died with his arm round her at 6.32 in the morning Dr Craig arrived & we asked him to make all arrangements for the funeral which is to take place tomorrow afternoon they brought the coffin in the aft. & we sat with it & watched in turns all night.

There were rituals to be observed in the event of death. The news had to be broken gently: Mrs Kennedy did not tell Cecil until she had nearly reached Janey's bedside. The precise time and manner of death had to be recorded. Janey's death was witnessed only by Alex. In death, as in life, Janey was thus excluded from the larger family.[11] But she died consoled by her husband, and with no sign of the torment which had marked her later years. The image of her death is a peaceful one; torment was for those left behind. Alex was 'beside himself with grief'; Cecil joined him in his despair. In their mourning, Cecil and Alex turned to their Catholic faith. Religious rituals and understandings of death offered solace. The body was to be blessed and prayers offered for the release of her soul from purgatory. After an all-night vigil, at noon the following day the priest came and, with the rosary and the blessing, concluded the sacred 'hour of death'.

> Our darling was taken away about 2 o'clock, they carried the coffin through the garden, & poor Alex was alone at the Funeral—she was buried at Box Hill—dear little Doanni [identity unknown] & Alex being the only 2 people there. Alex took Doanni back to Box Hill—& then came to Ringwood—he walked home from there—it is terribly sad, we feel broken hearted—. (23 December 1919)

Only Alex and 'little Doanni' publicly mourned her death, funerals still being a site for male grief and there being few other men to mourn. The privacy of Janey's death was broken as the funeral moved out of the house, through the garden and then on to the cemetery.[12] But the isolation of her life was echoed in the lack of mourners at her graveside.

Denied a public expression of her grief, or a place at the dying woman's bedside, Cecil continued her mourning within the privacy of the house and the pages of her diary. Christmas Day, just two days after Janey's death, Cecil recorded as 'The saddest I have ever spent' (25 December 1919), and New Year's Eve could bring only more sorrow: 'The last day of a very sad year—I was determined not to see the New Year in—' (31 December 1919). Cecil's diary became an expression of her devotion to her sister, an affirmation of her significance in the family. She remained at Bayswater long enough to clear away Janey's things, pack up her belongings and remove the more incidental evidence of her life from the house.

The New Year itself brought yet more sadness for Cecil and Fanny. Amy remained very ill, with only occasional respites. Cecil herself fell ill with bronchitis and pleurisy: 'it is terrible for me to give Fanny this extra trouble & yet I am helpless as they would'nt [sic] hear of a Nurse—what a position I am in!' (29 May 1920).

Cecil's position was that of a single woman dependent on the goodwill of her family to provide shelter and care. She felt its indignities keenly, and no doubt sought to compensate through the care and attention she offered so freely to Fanny and her children. In this way she could, in a sense, 'earn her keep', and her diary was a witness to her worth. Cecil's pivotal role in Fanny's family became obvious when Fanny's daughter Florence died suddenly while Fanny and Amy were staying at Bayswater. Florence had been taken to hospital and had had an operation.

> Alas! Tom & Nurse Boucher arrived at a quarter to 7 in the morning to say our darling Florence had died at one o'clock this morning. God rest her dear soul—it is impossible to realise it—I rang up Charlie—he arranged to take us up to Boonong by car & bring Fanny down—he came at 10 Alex & Dolores & I went with him—& told Fanny that Florence was very ill & had to have an operation so she went off at once with Charlie & Dolores—they had to tell her when she got home. I stayed with dear Amy & told her Florence was gravely ill—it was a terrible day for me, but, God helped me. (1 September 1920)

The news of Florence's death, as of Janey's, had to be broken gently to those most closely touched by it. The responsibility of arranging to inform Fanny and of telling Amy fell to Cecil, who played her part with a solemn heart. She remained with Amy and broke the news to her the following day: 'God only knows what it was to me—she was convulsed with grief—I was afraid she would die in her agony—poor darling!' (2 September 1920) Fanny was in Melbourne, 'stunned and heart broken' (1 September 1920). She gave only the barest details of the funeral: 'We all went to Mass My darling Florence's coffin before the altar the funeral to Box hill [sic] & Tom [Florence's husband] went again in the afternoon' (2 September 1920). Unlike Janey's meagre funeral procession, Florence's left from the church.[13] Fanny did not join the procession but visited the cemetery the following day: 'went to see my darlings [sic] grave alas! it is too awful' (3 September 1920). Fanny and Cecil reacted to Florence's death with a sense of shock and disbelief not present when Janey died. Their faith was their only consolation. Now Amy, too, was dying, but at least the task of nursing her gave the two sisters a role at her bedside.

The treatment of Amy fell largely to male doctors. They came regularly to prescribe drugs and assess her condition. When she continued to decline, however, Fanny in desperation resorted to her own forms of healing. Cecil noted, 'Amy in terrible agony this morning Fanny put leeches on & she was easier but still suffering. The doctor came' (16 November 1920). Fanny thus attempted to combine the advice of the medical experts with more traditional female remedies:

> Amy had very bad night—Fanny & I up with her most of the night putting on hot compresses etc. A nurse came from Miss Lorrie's home, but would'nt [sic] stay as it is a lung case. Dr James came—a bit annoyed about the Nurse rang for another—said Amy was just the same —. (25 November 1920)

Again, Cecil's diary affirmed her role at the dying woman's bedside, while her daily descriptions of Amy's state served as a means of ordering the days and nights and provided an account of her final hours. By December of 1920 Amy was delirious and the Rowe sisters turned to God:

> Amy terribly ill all day—not speaking at all—we asked Father Chaffey to come, he did & gave her Holy Communion & anointed her. Please God! she will be better after it. Lenore [Amy's sister] spent the afternoon here—very sad & distressed . . . God help us. (20 December 1920)

Perhaps mercifully, Amy only had another three days to live:

> Dear Amy left us at 8.30, R.I.P.—Oh what a sad sad Xmas Eve: she looked so lovely. We had to have the funeral at 4 this aft as tomorrow is Xmas Day & on Sunday they don't have funerals. Father O'Keefe came to bless her dear body—Charlie Murphy. Edward Ryan M^r M^cC[?] & Tom went to the grave Dear Lenore has been here all day—We are all heart broken God help dear Fanny. (24 December 1920)

Though she had been ill for nearly two years and near death for months, Amy died at a time that made detailed funeral preparations impossible. This only added to the despair of those left behind. The rushed funeral allowed only those closest to Amy to attend, and while it had been the women who watched over her during her illness and at the hour of her death, the men of the family were again the ones charged with the public expression of grief. Cecil, Fanny and Dolores made their pilgrimage to the cemetery on Boxing Day, but found little consolation there: 'our dear Amy's grave was so unfinished it gave us a shock, however we put lovely white flowers on it & came away' (26 December 1920). Cecil found herself unable to take an interest in anything, concluding the year—which had seen the deaths of three of her closest relatives—with a simple plea: 'what a sad old year could anything be worse.—God give us Peace & resignation' (31 December 1920). Cecil did not even ask for acceptance, hoping only for quietude. The New Year could hold no greater tragedies.

Cecil did not continue her diary after 1920. The state of Amy's health had been pivotal in the diary and the house for two years.

When she died, Cecil fell silent. Her diary had helped her to give words to feelings, to order the almost unspeakable events which had dominated her life, to express the questions and fears which plagued her. It thus helped her make sense of the incomprehensible, providing a consoling ritual in the face of desolation. Cecil was devoted almost entirely to the care of others. Unlike Winifred or Una Falkiner, in the face of the deaths of loved ones younger than herself she did not mention her own sense of mortality, but after Janey's death she made her will, preparing for the inevitable.

Cecil died on 8 August 1925. She had returned ill from an outing and taken to her bed. Two days later she seemed to have recovered enough to sit by the fire and knit, but it was a temporary respite. Fanny recorded her death: 'My dear Cecil died suddenly at 4.15 Dr James came I was in terrible trouble no one at home until Nurse & Charley' (8 August 1925). Though her death came as a shock to Fanny, Cecil herself seems to have anticipated it. Two months before, she had written her sister a letter and sealed it in an envelope marked: 'Mrs Fanny MacCarthy O'Leary/to be read when I am dead.' Inside was a list of her possessions and to whom they were to go:

> To my dear sister Fanny to be read when I am gone. I have made my will, it is in Gaven Duffy King & Company's hand. In it I have said that I will leave you my written wishes as & [sic] the disposal of my personal possessions. Now that dear Amy has gone & also dear Florence, I find it very difficult to divide my little articles of jewelry [sic] as there are so few, if any now, who love me, & would like to have them because they belonged to me . . . [14]

Cecil's sadness permeates this letter. Single, aged 71 and still living in her sister's house, she had lost nearly all those she cared for most. The timing of the letter, its content, and Cecil's death soon after writing it suggest she was preparing to die. It took only a brief illness, which did not appear serious, to end her life. Fanny, now so familiar with death and grief, appears this time to have attended the funeral: 'it was dreadful to see the last of my beloved sister' (10 August 1925). It would indeed have been a 'cold bleak' Melbourne day for Fanny, who herself lived until 1941, when she was 95.[15]

As Cecil's and Fanny's diaries show, death was not confined to the elderly. Without antibiotics or sophisticated medical knowledge, common illnesses could easily result in death. Death was also an event that commonly took place at home. During the interwar period, however, the death rate began to decline, and the ill were increasingly nursed in hospital rather than at home. As death and dying became less and less a part of everyday life, popular anxiety about them grew, and they were pushed more and more into the background and away from public view.[16] The movement of death away from the home, and the concomitant professionalisation of health care shifted responsibility for the care of the sick and dying to a (male) medical profession. Just as women's knowledge of and expertise in midwifery were being eroded, so their intimate knowledge of the processes of death and their role as attendants of the dying were gradually being lost. The result was a general disempowering of women as healers, a denigration of both their service and their knowledge.

For many Australian women, the Second World War both brought death to their door and, paradoxically, ended their involvement in it. Una Falkiner's beloved son John was killed in a flying accident during the war, at the age of 24. Her record of the days after she learned the news appears to have been made some time later; she used it as a place to balance both her grief and her hopes:

> When John was a little boy he always said he would make his name to shine! & he has!
> Life has stopped for me today! & hence forth I shall go through my time left with the blinds drawn down.
> The sun & radience [sic] have ceased to sparkle— . . .
> The day seemed 100 years I felt 100! but I know he is safe in his Father's Home. Safe, safe, at last! The Harbour past! (24 September 1942)

Una made no attempt to hide her anguish, using her diary to give John the glory she felt he deserved. Death played havoc with her sense of time: eternity hung in the hour, the present obliterated by a future heavy with the past. In a far less exalted style, and the day after she heard the news, Una wrote simply, 'Otway and I went out driving. I felt 100' (25 September 1942). She captured the desolation she felt, the weight of her grief and her pain in bearing it. The entry has a simplicity more in keeping with an immediate response to death than does the text which followed it:

> All night, all night! & in the day too, I always pray that our gallant son will be safe & in His Father's keeping
> & I know when he goes up over John's hand is in God's & he will be guided by His divine wisdom
> & suddenly! to find he will not have to 'go up over' any more on stormy nights, & in the cold & darkness!
> It is wonderful for him! & to be in the glory unspeakable 'eye hath

not seen, nor ear heard the glory that God had prepared for those that love him.'

But one cannot help being so disappointed, bitterly, that he could not have been left here to be an inspiration to those he met in his path of life—He stood like a rock for good! & all that was beautiful . . . (25 September 1942)

As Una struggled to make sense of John's death, she drew on images both religious and military. As he had been killed while training in England, Una could not even find solace in the knowledge that he had died in battle, defending his country. Her use of heroic and military images is thus even more poignant. To add to her despair, Otway had to leave Widgiewa two days after they heard the news of John's death to attend to the sale of some property. He returned in time for a memorial service held for John in their local church, but left again soon afterwards. Una was alone in her grief.

One month after John's death, she wrote, 'My darling has been in glory for one month now', noting at the top of the entry, 'It feels like a lifetime' (23 October 1942). She did not wish to recover from John's death. To do so would somehow have been a travesty. Rather, she would live the remaining years—few, she hoped—with the 'blinds drawn down'. 'Oh! if only I could go to [sic]' (14 December 1942), she noted, echoing a year later, 'Of course nothing can happen anymore! I feel we are all waiting to leave this sphere'; she later added: 'which has gone mad' (11 October 1943).

During the years left to her, Una coped with her own increasing age and loss in various ways. She sought solace in her strong religious convictions, became increasingly interested in spiritualism, and tried to contact John through a medium. As her health deteriorated she began reading her diaries, perhaps to help her deal with her present. She would have found in them a reflection of her former life, and affirmations of herself as a mother, a wife, and the successful mistress of the Falkiner property. She would also have gained a perspective on her life, a sense of its patterns and rhythms. Una began writing summaries of each year's events, using her diaries as repositories of memory,[17] but as another year became condensed into a few pages, we can see her mind becoming lost in the past, the task of reconstruction too demanding for her. As she wrote these summaries, she also added comments to her original diary. The most telling of these is the addition she made to her entry for the day of Diana's death. The entry had read simply, 'At a quarter to four this morning the angel came. I left for Macedon before seven and Otway came later' (30 January

1922). To it Una now added: 'All the birds were singing a chorus of song heralding the new dawn. Something had gone from my life never to be replaced. My lovely baby Diana gone home.'

Una also commented on the art of diary-writing, adding to an entry in February 1926, 'Poor Lauré sternly sent back to school/Some people always leave out the juicy bits of news yet they think they can write a diary!!' (9 February 1926) Una obviously believed herself to be a good diary-writer, an assessment she was forced to re-evaluate in the later years of her life. Her diary became a literal dialogue between her past and present: a history.

Una died at home in November 1948. Her final illness received only scant mention in her diary, the missed entries explained by her bedridden state. A calmness pervades her writing, and she made no mention of the gravity of her condition. Just as she had been silent about many things in her diary, so she was silent about her approaching death. She remained in character to the last.

As the diarists grew older, we can see in their writing some of the ways in which they came to terms with their increasing years, the different meanings age held for them, and the significance of their diaries in shaping their lives and forming a bridge between present and past. As they had done throughout their writing lives, they took the time to write, made space for themselves, transformed the fleeting moments of their days into a permanent chronicle. The concluding years of their lives were generally a time of reflection, of looking back on dreams realised, hopes fulfilled, and pain and hardship endured. It was a time when their diaries served them well, reminding them of details of events and feelings faded or obliterated by time. And as they read through their volumes, they became characters in their own plays, members of their own audience, directors adding the final touches to dramas others would rehearse.

Notes

Introduction

1 When Virginia Woolf read over the early years of her diary, she reflected on its limitations, 'The rough and random style of it, so often ungrammatical, & crying for a word altered'. Virginia Woolf, April 20, 1919.

2 Dure Jo Gillikin, 'A lost diary found', in Leonore Hoffman & Margo Culley (eds) *Women's Personal Narratives: Essays in Criticism and Pedagogy*. New York, Modern Language Association of America, 1985, p. 132.

3 ibid. p. 126.

4 Dale Spender, 'Journal on a journal' in *Women's Studies International Forum*, vol. 10, no. 1, 1987, p. 3.

5 Thomas Mallon, *A Book of One's Own*. London, Picador (1984), 1985, p. xvii.

6 Margo Culley (ed.) *A Day at a Time: The Diary Literature of American Women from 1784 to the Present*. New York, The Feminist Press, 1985, pp. 10–12.

7 Harriet Blodgett, *Centuries of Female Days: Englishwomen's Private Diaries*. London, Allan Sutton (1988) 1989. p. 5.

8 Estelle Jelinek (ed.) *Women's Autobiography: Essays in Criticism*. Bloomington, Indiana University Press, 1980, p. 19; Suzanne Juhasz, 'Towards a Theory of Form in Feminist Autobiography: Kate Millet's *Flying* and *Sita*; Maxine Hong Kingston's *The Woman Warrior*', in Jelinek, E. (ed.) *Women's Autobiography*, pp. 223–4

9 Blodgett, *Centuries of Female Days*, p. 5.

10 See Culley, *A Day at a Time*; Elizabeth Hampsten, *Read This Only to Yourself: the private writings of Midwestern Women, 1880–1910*. Bloomington, Indiana University Press, 1982, p. 6.

11 Linda Anderson, 'At the threshold of the self: Women and autobiography', in Moira Montreith (ed.) *Women's Writing: A Challenge to Theory.* Brighton, Harvester Press, 1986. pp. 60, 63.
12 Anne Martin-Fugier 'Bourgeois Rituals' in Michelle Perrot (ed.) *The History of Private Life IV: From the Fires of Revolution to the Great War,* Cambridge, Mass., Harvard University Press, 1990, p. 265.
13 ibid.
14 David Landes, *Revolution in Time: Clocks and the Making of the Modern World,* Cambridge, Mass., Harvard University Press, 1983, p. 15.
15 E. P. Thomson, 'Time, work-discipline and industrial capitalism', *Past and Present,* 1967, p. 93. For further discussion of historians and time, see Katie Holmes 'Making Time: Representing temporality in Australian Women's Diaries of the 1920s and 1930s' *Australian Historical Studies,* vol. 26, no. 102, 1994, pp. 1–18.
16 Graeme Davison, *The Unforgiving Minute: How Australians Learned to Tell the Time.* Melbourne, Oxford University Press (OUP), 1993.
17 Richard Whipp, '"A time to every purpose": An essay on time and work', in Patrick Joyce (ed.) *The Historical Meaning of Work.* Cambridge, Cambridge University Press (CUP), 1987, pp. 211, 214.
18 See, Frieda Johles Forman (ed.) *Taking Our Time: Feminist Perspectives on Temporality.* Toronto, Pergamon Press, 1989.
19 Margaret Conrad, '"Sundays always make me think of home": Time and place in Canadian women's history', in Veronica Strong-Boag and Anita Clair Fellman (eds) *Rethinking Canada: The promise of women's history.* Toronto, c1986, p. 79.
20 Judy Nolte Lensink, 'Expanding the boundaries of criticism: The diary as female autobiography', *Women's Studies,* vol. 14, 1987, p. 42.
21 Linda Kerber, 'Separate Spheres, Female Worlds, Women's Place: The Rhetoric of Women's History', *Journal of American History,* 75:1, p. 37. See also Leonore Davidoff and Catherine Hall, *Family Fortunes: Men and Women of the English Middle Class, 1780–1850,* London, Century Hutchinson, 1987.
22 Quoted in Humphrey McQueen, *Black Swan of Trespass: The emergence of modernist painting in Australia to 1944,* Sydney, Alternative Publishing Cooperative, 1979, p. 102.
23 Drusilla Modjeska, *Poppy,* Melbourne, McPhee Gribble, 1990, p. 90.

1 Youth

1 *Woman's World,* 1 June 1928.
2 See Joseph Fraser, *Husbands: How to Select Them, How to Manage Them, How to Keep Them,* Melbourne, 188?; *Australian Etiquette,* Sydney & Melbourne, 1885.
3 See Judith Allen, '"Our deeply degraded sex", and "The animal in man": Rose Scott, feminism and sexuality 1890–1925', *Australian Feminist Studies,* nos. 7 & 8, Summer 1988, pp. 65–94.
4 *Home,* 1 August 1925.

5   *Everylady's Journal*, 1 February 1925.
6   *Home*, 1 December 1925.
7   *New Idea*, advertisements for lipsticks, 15 March 1935; 15 May 1936.
8   Marilyn Lake, 'Female desires: The meaning of World War II', *Australian Historical Studies*, vol. 24, no. 95, October 1990, p. 273.
9   See Sally Alexander, 'Becoming a woman in London in the 1920s and 1930s' in David Feldman and Gareth Stedman Jones (eds), *Metropolis London: Histories and Representations Since 1800*, London, Routledge, 1989, p. 248.
10 *New Idea*, 19 February 1930, p. 42. The comment bears a striking resemblance to sexologists' discussions of lesbians.
11 ibid. 15 February 1935, p. 9.
12 Or perhaps the question of masculinity was simply evaded: as Judith Allen's account of postwar Australia suggests, men, in particular returned soldiers, were having considerable psychological difficulty adjusting to life in peacetime. (Judith Allen, *Sex and Secrets*, Melbourne, OUP, 1990, ch. 6, 'Heroes at Home'.)
13 *New Idea*, 9 July 1937, p. 15.
14 ibid. 23 June 1933, p. 5.
15 ibid. 30 June 1933, p. 9.
16 Jill Matthews, 'They had Such a Lot of Fun: Women's League of Health and Beauty', *History Workshop Journal*, no. 30, Autumn 1990, p. 37.
17 See Jill Matthews, 'They had Such a Lot of Fun', (p. 37) for her list of the fears and desires the Women's League of Health and Beauty answered for women, some of which I have adapted here.
18 Alison Light, '"Returning to Manderley"—romance, fiction, female sexuality and class', *Feminist Review*, no. 16, Summer 1984, p. 22.
19 Jill Matthews, 'Building the Body Beautiful', *Australian Feminist Studies*, no. 5, Summer 1987, p. 31.
20 *New Idea*, 6 January 1933, p. 9.
21 Marie Stopes, *Married Love*, London, 1918. See also Carol Bacchi, 'Feminism and the "eroticisation" of the middle-class woman: the intersection of class and gender attitudes', *Women's Studies International Forum*, vol. 11, no. 1, 1988, pp. 46–7.
22 Susan Bordo, 'Reading the slender body', in Mary Jacobus, Evelyn Fox Keller & Sally Shuttleworth (eds), *Body/Politics: Women and the Discourses of Science*, New York, Routledge, 1990, pp. 89, 103.
23 *New Idea*, 8 May 1931. Original emphasis.
24 Advertisement for Myzone tablets, *New Idea*, 22 May 1931.
25 *Everylady's Journal*, 3 July 1919.
26 *Home*, 1 March 1926.
27 *New Idea*, 24 March 1933, p. 39.
28 ibid. 6 May 1937, p. 73.

2 Paid work

1 *Bulletin*, 13 November 1919.
2 ibid. 20 May 1920, p. 42.
3 Drusilla Modjeska, *Exiles at Home: Australian Women Writers, 1925–1945*. Melbourne, Sirius Books, 1981, p. 16, p. 20.
4 *Bulletin*, 16 July 1925.
5 Virginia Woolf, *A Room of One's Own* (1929) London, Grafton, 1988, p. 46.
6 Rev. David Millar, *The Spider's Telephone Wire*, London, Allenson, 1930.
7 Quoted in Marilyn Lake & Farley Kelly, *Double Time: Women in Victoria, 150 Years*, Penguin, Melbourne, 1985, p. 325.

3 Domestic work

1 I am indebted to Liz Brydon, Mabel's sister-in-law, for this information.
2 For a detailed study of the interwar home, see Peter Cuffley, *Australian Houses of the 1920s and '30s*, Melbourne, Five Mile Press, 1989. See also Robin Boyd, *Australia's Home: Its Origins, Builders and Occupiers*, Melbourne, 1952.
3 *Woman's World*, 1 December 1921, p. 33.
4 ibid. 1 June 1923, p. 312.
5 *Home*, 1 December 1920.
6 *Woman's World*, 1 June 1937, p. 24.
7 13 October 1943, quoted in Marilyn Lake, 'Historical homes', in John Rickard & Peter Spearritt (eds), *Packaging the Past? Public Histories*, Melbourne, Melbourne University Press/Australian Historical Studies, 1991, p. 53.
8 *Woman's World*, 1 February 1932, pp. 39, 42.
9 ibid. 1 November 1927, p. 661.
10 My thoughts in this section draw on some of the ideas discussed by Anne Hoban, 'Anne Drysdale: A sense of place'. Unpublished Honours thesis, Department of History, LaTrobe University, 1987.
11 Susan Hosking, '"I 'ad to 'ave me Garden": A perspective on Australian women gardeners', *Meanjin*, vol. 47, no. 3, Spring 1988, p. 444.
12 Cuffley, *Australian Houses*, p. 150.
13 ibid. pp. 151–2; Chris McConville, 'At Home with Sandy Stone: conserving Camberwell' in Rickard & Spearritt, *Packaging the Past*, pp. 88–101.
14 John Foster, 'Brunning's Australian Gardener', *Meanjin*, vol. 47, no. 3, Spring 1988, p. 416.
15 Cuffley, *Australian Houses*, pp. 154–5.
16 Una Falkiner, under 'Notes from 1922' in the 1923 diary.
17 *Woman's World*, 1 December 1921.

18 Electricity did not reach Mary Bicknall's area until after the Second World War.

4 Marriage to motherhood

1 Beverly Kingston, (ed.) *The World Moves Slowly: A Documentary History of Australian Women.* Sydney, Cassell, 1977, p. 58. Under the NSW Divorce Extension Amendment of 1892, cruelty was instituted as a sole ground for divorce.
2 Jill Matthews, *Good and Mad Women: The Historical Construction of Femininity in Twentieth Century Australia.* Sydney, Allen & Unwin, 1984, pp. 86–88 & ch. 9.
3 Notable exceptions to this include, Martha Vicinus, *Independent Women: Women, Work and Community for Single Women, 1850–1920.* London, Virago, 1985; Lee Virginia Chambers-Schiller, *Liberty, a Better Husband. Single Women in America: The Generations of 1780–1840,* New Haven, Yale University Press, 1984.
4 Carolyn Heilbrun, *Writing a Woman's Life,* London, The Woman's Press, 1989, p. 31. For a discussion on the meanings of the single woman in Australia in the interwar years, see Catriona Elder 'The question of being single in Australia in the 1920s and 1930s', *Australian Feminist Studies,* no. 18, 1993, pp. 151-75 and '" It was hard for us to marry Aboriginal": Some meanings of singleness for Aboriginal women in Australia in the 1930s', *Lilith,* no. 8, Summer 1993, pp. 114-35.
5 *Everylady's Journal,* 6 December 1919, p. 478.
6 *Woman's World,* 1 January 1924, p. 16.
7 *Woman's World,* 1 October 1929, p. 692.
8 *New Idea,* 31 August 1934, p. 36.
9 ibid. 6 May 1938, p. 14.
10 ibid. 22 October 1937, pp. 14–15.
11 Quoted in Kay Daniels and Mary Murnane (eds), *Uphill All the Way: A Documentary History of Women in Australia,* University of Queensland Press, Brisbane, 1980, p. 135.
12 *Woman's World,* 1 January 1924, p. 103.
13 *Woman's World,* 1 July 1929, p. 493.
14 *New Idea,* 28 February 1930, p. 38.
15 Clipping in Winifred's diaries on the occasion of her 90th birthday.
16 Meredith Foley, 'The Women's Movement in NSW and Victoria, 1918–1930', Unpublished PhD thesis, Department of History, University of Sydney, 1985, p. 5.
17 Kerreen Reiger, *The Disenchantment of the Home,* Melbourne, OUP, 1984, p. 161.
18 *Woman's World,* 1 October 1935, p. 19.
19 ibid. 1 December 1937, p. 19.
20 *New Idea,* 20 January 1930, p. 16.

5 Relationships with men

1 I am very grateful to Margaret Piesse for discussing with me her work on Norma Bull and her thoughts on Norma's diaries.
2 My attempts to discover the authors and the content of *Sex Ethics* have proved unfruitful.
3 Marie Stopes, *Married Love*, G.P. Putnam's Sons, London, 1918, pp. 8–38.
4 ibid. p. 45.
5 ibid. pp. 12–13.
6 ibid. p. 6.
7 Kathleen's decision to be a 'gold digger' came after the end of her rather unhappy relationship with Edgar: 'now that Edgar has broken his promise everything is changed for me—no one is going to hurt me anymore—made up my mind to be a 1937 gold digger' (27 July 1937).
8 Carolyn Heilbrun, *Writing a Woman's Life*, London, The Woman's Press, 1989, p. 21.
9 John Atchinson, in *Australian Dictionary of Biography*, vol. 8: 1891–1939, Melbourne, Melbourne University Press, 1981, p. 465.
10 Fanny had commented in her diary a month before this entry: 'cross with him [Jer]. old sins' (13 July 1915).
11 Fanny's diary for the year of Jer's death is not held in the LaTrobe Library, and it is unclear whether she was keeping it at this point.

6 Relationships with family

1 The very understanding of the family was changing during the inter-war period, as it has done throughout Australia's history. For discussions of the twentieth century family, see Lake, *The Limits of Hope*; Matthews, *Good and Mad Women*; Reiger, *Disenchantment of the Home*; Michael Gilding, *The Making and Breaking of the Australian Family*, Sydney, Allen & Unwin, 1991. On the family as an economic unit, see Desley Deacon, *Managing Gender: The State, the Workers and the New Middle Class*, Sydney, Allen & Unwin, 1989; Kerreen Reiger, *Family Economy*, McPhee Gribble, Melbourne, 1991.
2 Beverly Kingston, *My Wife, My Daughter and Poor Mary Ann: Women and Work in Australia*. Melbourne, Nelson, 1975, p. 120.
3 Nine months earlier Ida had noted, 'Guy and Prima went for a ride—they go two or three times a week, but have never once asked me to go with them all the time I have been here. I wonder why.' (22 June 1922)

7 Relationships with women

I am indebted to Martha Vicinus for her thoughts and comments on this chapter.

1 . Due to restrictions placed on the publication of Winifred Tait's diaries, I am unable to discuss this relationship any further. See Holmes, K. 'Relating Women: Ausralian women diarists and their relationships' *Lilith*, no. 7, 1991; see also, 'Spaces in Her Day: Australian Women's Diaries 1919–1945' PhD thesis, University of Melbourhe, 1992.
2 Reprinted in her *Disorderly Conduct: Visions of Gender in Victorian America*, Oxford University Press, New York, 1985.
3 Attempts to define and describe women's relationships have provoked considerable discussion amongst historians. For a summary of these debates, see Martha Vicinus, '"They wonder to which sex I belong": The historical roots of the modern lesbian identity', *Feminist Studies* 18, no. 3, Fall 1992, pp. 468–73.
4 Virginia Woolf, *A Room of One's Own* (1929) Grafton, London, 1988, p. 80.
5 Martha Vicinus, 'They wonder to which sex I belong', pp. 473–7.
6 Martha Vicinus, 'Distance and Desire: English Boarding School Friendships, 1870–1920' reprinted in M.B. Duberman et al., *Hidden from History: Reclaiming the Gay and Lesbian Past* (1989) London, Penguin, 1991, p. 228.
7 For a discussion of the impact of sexologists' work on the relationships of American women, see Carroll Smith-Rosenberg, 'The New Woman as Androgyne: Social Disorder and Gender Crisis, 1870–1936' in *Disorderly Conduct*, pp. 270 ff. More recent work on the dissemination of ideas about homosexuality and homosexual types, suggests that the sexologists were themselves picking up on existing perceptions and stereotypes. See Lisa Duggan 'The Trials of Alice Mitchell: Sensationalism, Sexology, and the Lesbian Subject in Turn-of-the-Century America', *Signs*, vol. 18, no. 4, 1993, pp. 791–814. In the Australian context, see Sylvia Martin 'Rethinking Passionate Friendships: the writings of Mary Fullerton' *Women's History Review* vol. 2, no. 3, 1993 pp. 395–406; and Ruth Ford, 'Lady Friends and Sexual Deviationists: Lesbians and the Law in Australia 1920s–1950s', in Diane Kirby (ed) *Sex, Power and Justice: Historical Perspectives on the Law in Australia 1788–1990*, Oxford University Press, 1995 (forthcoming)
8 See Reiger, *The Disenchantment of the Home*, ch. 7 for a discussion of the new psychological discourses, especially in relation to childrearing. Such ideas were widely disseminated through the pages of women's magazines, as discussed in Life Cycles II. See also Gail Reekie, 'Impulsive women, predictable men: Psychological constructions of sexual difference in sales literature to 1930', *Australian Historical Studies*, vol. 24, no. 97, October 1991, pp. 359–63.
9 See, for example, Martha Vicinus, *Independent Women: Women, Work*

and Community for Single Women, 1850–1920, London, Virago, 1985, esp. chs 4 & 5.
10 Carroll Smith Rosenberg, 'The New Woman . . .', pp. 275–8.

8 Ageing and death

My thanks to Pat Thane for her comments on this chapter.

1 Germaine Greer's most recent book *The Change*, is an example of this. An exception is Simone de Beauvoir's *Old Age* (*La Vieillesse*, 1970), London, Penguin, 1977. Other feminists are beginning to explore the gendered nature of ageing in contemporary society, eg: Cherry Russell, 'Ageing as a feminist issue', *Women's Studies International Forum*, vol. 10, no. 2, 1987, pp. 125–132; Anne Deveson, *Coming of Age*, Melbourne, Scribe Publications, 1994; Betty Friedan, *The Fountain of Age*, New York, Simon & Schuster, 1993.
2 Marjorie Barnard, 'The Wrong Hat', in *The Persimmon Tree and Other Stories* (1943), London, Virago, 1985, p. 65.
3 Stephen Garton, *Medicine and Madness: A Social History of Insanity in NSW, 1880–1940*, Sydney, NSW University Press, 1987, p. 103.
4 ibid, p. 154; see also, Matthews, *Good and Mad Women*.
5 *New Idea*, 5 October 1934, p. 54.
6 *Woman's World*, 1 May 1932, p. 22
7 *New Idea*, 12 June 1936, p. 29
8 David Walker, 'Mind and Body', in B. Gammage & P. Spearitt (eds) *Australians 1938*. Sydney, Fairfax, Syme & Co, 1987, p. 228.
9 Bruce Mayes, 'The treatment of menopausal symptoms', *Medical Journal of Australia*, 6 April 1935, p. 440.
10 Dr James Buchanan, 'Disorders of Menopause', *Medical Journal of Australia*, 14 July 1934, p. 48.
11 Marion Aveling notes that by the nineteenth century, the usual circle of witnesses to a death had narrowed to the immediate family. See her 'Death and the family in nineteenth century Western Australia', in Patricia Grimshaw, C. McConville, E. McEwan (eds) *Families in Colonial Australia*. Sydney, George Allen & Unwin, 1985, p. 34.
12 See Graeme Griffin & Des Tobin, *In the Midst of Life: The Australian response to death*, Melbourne, Melbourne University Press, 1982, p. 101. The custom of funerals leaving from the house began changing in the 1920s, especially in the cities. As the interwar years progressed, funerals increasingly left from the funeral parlour, and undertakers assumed a greater role in the rituals of death. See also Ken Inglis, 'Passing Away', in *Australians, 1938*, pp. 239–43.
13 Ken Inglis notes that one in ten funerals in 1938 left from a church, while most country funerals still left from home. 'Passing Away', p. 239.
14 Letter in Rowe Family Papers, LaTrobe Library of Victoria.

15 Fanny ceased writing her diary in 1927, perhaps too overwhelmed by grief to find interest in it.
16 Griffin & Tobin (eds) *In the Midst of Life,* p. 6. For a discussion of the fears and uncertainty surrounding the dead body, see Simon Cooke, 'Death, body and soul: the cremation debate in NSW, 1863–1925', *Australian Historical Studies* vol. 24, no. 97, pp. 323–39.
17 Anne Martin-Fugier, 'Bourgeois Rituals', p. 265.

Select bibliography

Contemporary material

Unpublished papers

Barbour, Fanny (1865–1952). Diaries, 1887–88, 1913, 1920, 1933, 1940–41, 1943. MS 11302, Box 2510/7. LaTrobe Collection, State Library of Victoria.

Bicknell, Mary (1871–1956). Diaries, 1894, 1928, 1932–39, 1945. Private collection.

Bull, Norma (1906–80). Papers, 1937–40. MS 12481, Box 3369/1–7. LaTrobe Collection, State Library of Victoria.

Cameron, Mrs James (Roo) (1856–1936). Diary, 1924. MS 11593, Box 1811/6. LaTrobe Collection, State Library of Victoria.

Dawson, Ida (1879–1958). Diaries, 1894–1955. Uncatalogued MSS, Set 475. Mitchell Library Collection, State Library of NSW.

Duncan, Dorris (1891–1948). Diaries, 1918, 1926. Private collection.

Falkiner, Una (1883–1948). Diaries 1920–1948, ML MSS 423/1–113; and papers, ML MSS 4342, ML 1725/78, Boxes 1–7; sketchbooks and loose sketches PIC ACC 5715. Mitchell Library Collection, State Library of New South Wales.

Hughes, Kathleen (1912–71). Diaries, 1937–41. Private collection.

Kendall, Dorothy (1909–78). Diaries, 1932–38. Private collection.

Lincoln, Mabel (1878–1952). Diaries, 1930, 1932, 1935. MS 9748, Bay 18. LaTrobe Collection, State Library of Victoria.

MacCarthy O'Leary, Fanny (1846–1941). Rowe family papers; Diaries, 1888, 1914, 1916–26. MS 12298, Boxes 3067/2, 3068. LaTrobe Collection, State Library of Victoria.

Murphy, Mae (1913–84). Diaries, 1943–44. Private collection.

163

Spaces in her day

Ross, Mabel (1873–1957?). Diaries, 1890–1943. MS 12218, Box 2799/4. LaTrobe Collection, State Library of Victoria.
Rowe, Cecil (1854–1925). Rowe family papers. Diaries, 1905, 1907, 1909, 1914–20. MS 12298, Boxes 3067/2, 3068. LaTrobe Collection, State Library of Victoria.
Strongman, Margaret (1910–78). Diaries, 1937–44. MS 12176, Box 2753/4. LaTrobe Collection, State Library of Victoria.
Tait, Winifred (1877–1968). Diaries, 1914, 1923–65. Private collection.

Newspapers, magazines, journals

Bulletin, 1920–30, selected editions.
Everylady's Journal, 1919–38.
Herald, selected editions, 1919–42.
The Home, 1920–40.
Medical Journal of Australia, 1928–38, selected editions.
New Idea, 1900–05, 1929–40.
The Woman, 1923.
Woman's World, 1921–40.

Published works: diaries, directories, novels, autobiographies

Barnard, Marjorie. *The Persimmon Tree and Other Stories* (1943), Virago, London, 1985.
Hall, Radclyffe. *The Well of Loneliness* (1928), London, Virago, 1990.
Millar, David. *The Spider's Telephone Wire*, London, Allenson, 1930.
Thompson, Tierl (ed.) *Dear Girl: The diaries and letters of two working women, 1897–1917*, London, The Women's Press, 1987.
Stopes, Marie. *Married Love*, G.P. Putnam's Sons, London, 1918.
Underhill, Evelyn. *The Life of the Spirit and the Life of Today*, London, Methuen, 1922.
Woolf, Virginia. *The Diary of Virginia Woolf*, vols 1–5, edited by Anne Oliver Bell (first published between 1978 and 1984), London, Penguin, 1988.
Woolf, Virginia. *A Room of One's Own* (1929), London, Grafton, 1988.

Historical, literary and cultural commentaries

Books

Allen, Judith. *Sex and Secrets: Crimes involving Australian women since 1880*, Melbourne, OUP, 1990.
Aptheker, Bettina. *Tapestries of Life: Women's work, women's consciousness and the meaning of daily experience*, Amherst, University of Massachusetts Press, 1989.
Ariès, Phillippe. *The Hour of Our Death*, (1977) New York, Alfred A. Knopf, 1981.

Armstrong, Nancy & Tennenhouse, Leonard (eds). *The Ideology of Conduct: Essays on literature and the history of sexuality*, New York, Methuen, 1987.

Australian Dictionary of Biography, Melbourne, Melbourne University Press, 1981.

Benstock, Shari. *The Private Self: Theory and practice of women's autobiographical writings*, Chapel Hill, University of North Carolina Press, 1988.

Betterton, Rosemary (ed.). *Looking On: Images of femininity in the visual arts and media*, London, Pandora, 1987.

Bevage, Margaret, James, B. & Shute, C. *Worth Her Salt: Women at work in Australia*, Sydney, Hale & Iremonger, 1982.

Berger, John. *Ways of Seeing*, London, Penguin, 1973.

Blodgett, Harriet. *Centuries of Female Days: Englishwomen's private diaries*, London, Allan Sutton, 1989.

Caine, Barbara. *Destined to be Wives: The sisters of Beatrice Webb*, Oxford, OUP, 1986.

Caine, Barbara, Grosz, E. & de Lepervanche, M. *Crossing Boundaries: Feminism and the critique of knowledges*, Sydney, Allen & Unwin, 1988.

Campbell, Rosemary. *Heroes and Lovers: A question of national identity*, Sydney, Allen & Unwin, 1989.

Caplan, Pat (ed.) *The Cultural Construction of Sexuality*, London, Tavistock, 1987.

Carr, David. *Time, Narrative and History*, Bloomington, Indiana University Press, 1986.

Cartledge, Sue & Ryan, Joanna (eds). *Sex and Love: New thoughts on old contradictions*, London, Women's Press, 1983.

Chambers-Schiller, Lee Virginia. *Liberty, A Better Husband. Single women in America: the generations of 1780–1840*, New Haven, Yale University Press, 1984.

Coward, Rosalind. *Female Desire: Women's sexuality today*, London, Paladin, 1984.

Cuffley, Peter. *Australian Houses of the '20s and '30s*, Melbourne, Five Mile Press, 1989.

Culley, Margo (ed.). *A Day at a Time: The diary literature of American women from 1784 to the present*, New York, The Feminist Press, 1985.

Davidoff, Leonore & Hall, Catherine. *Family Fortunes: Men and women of the English middle class, 1780–1850*, London, Hutchinson, 1987.

Davison, Graeme. *The Unforgiving Minute: How Australia learnt to tell the time*, Melbourne, OUP, 1993.

Deacon, Deasley. *Managing Gender: The state, the new middle class and women workers 1830–1930*, Melbourne, Oxford University Press, 1989.

De Beauvoir, Simone. *Old Age (La Vieillesse, 1970)*, London, Penguin, 1977.

D'Emilio, John, & Freedman, Estelle B. *Intimate Matters: A history of sexuality in America*, New York, Harper & Row, 1988.

Duberman, Martin B, Vicinus, M. & Chauncey, G. Jr (eds.). *Hidden From History: Reclaiming the gay and lesbian past* (1989), London, Penguin, 1991.

Spaces in her day

Elshtain, Jean Bethke. *Public Man, Private Woman: Women in social and public thought*, New Jersey, Princeton University Press, 1981.
Faderman, Lillian. *Surpassing the Love of Men: Romantic friendship and love between women from the Renaissance to the present*, London, Junction Books, 1981.
Forman, Frieda Johles. *Taking Our time: Feminist perspectives on temporality*. Toronto, Pergamon Press, 1989.
Fothergill, Robert A. *Private Chronicles: A study of English diaries*, Oxford, OUP, 1974.
Foucault, Michel. *History of Sexuality* vol. 1, London, Penguin, 1976.
Game, Ann & Pringle, Rosemary. *Gender at Work*, Sydney, George Allen & Unwin, 1983.
Gammage, Bill & Spearritt, Peter (eds). *Australians 1938*. Sydney, Fairfax, Syme, & Co, 1987.
Garton, Stephen. *Medicine and Madness: A social history of insanity in NSW, 1880–1940*, Sydney, NSW University Press, 1987.
Gilding, Michael. *The Making and Breaking of the Australian Family*, Sydney, Allen & Unwin, 1991.
Griffin, Graeme & Tobin, Des. *In the Midst of Life . . . : The Australian response to death*, Melbourne, Melbourne University Press, 1982.
Grimshaw, Patricia, McConville, C. & McEwan, E. *Families in Colonial Australia*, Sydney, George Allen & Unwin, 1985.
Grimshaw, Patricia. *Paths of Duty: American missionary wives in nineteenth century Hawaii*, Honolulu, University of Hawaii Press, 1989.
Gurvitch, Georges. *The Spectrum of Social Time*. Dordrecht, D. Reidal Publishing Co., 1964.
Hampsten, Elizabeth. *Read This Only to Yourself: The private writings of Mid-western women, 1880–1910*, Bloomington, Indiana University Press, 1982.
Haraven, Tamara. *Family Time and Industrial Time: The relationship between the family and work in a New England industrial community*, New York, CUP, 1982.
Heilbrun, Carolyn. *Writing a Woman's Life*, London, The Woman's Press, 1989.
Hoffman, Leonore & Culley, Margo (eds). *Women's Personal Narratives: Essays in criticism and pedagogy*, New York, Modern Language Association of America, 1985.
Hooton, Joy. *Stories of Herself When Young: Autobiographies of childhood by Australian women*, Melbourne, Oxford University Press, 1990.
Houlbrooke, Ralph (ed.). *Death, Ritual and Bereavement*, London, Routledge, 1989.
Huff, Cynthia. *British Women's Diaries: A descriptive bibliography of selected nineteeth-century women's manuscript diaries*, New York, AMS Press, 1985.
Humphreys, S.C. *The Family, Women and Death: Comparative studies*, London, Routledge & Kegan Paul, 1983.
Jacobus, Mary, Fox Keller, Ev. & Shuttleworth, S. (eds). *Body/Politics: Women and the discourses of science*, New York, Routledge, 1990.

166

Jeffreys, Sheila. *The Spinster and Her Enemies: Feminism and sexuality, 1880–1930*, London, Pandora, 1985.

Jelinek, Estelle. *Women's Autobiography: Essays in criticism*, Bloomington, Indiana University Press, 1980.

Kern, Stephen. *The Culture of Time and Space*, Cambridge, Massachusetts, Harvard University Press, 1983.

Kingston, Beverly. *Bright, Confident Morning. Oxford History of Australia, vol. 3, 1860–1900*, Melbourne, Oxford University Press, 1988.

—— *My Wife, My Daughter and Poor Mary Ann: Women and work in Australia*, Melbourne, Nelson, 1975.

Kolodny, Annette. *The Land Before Her: Fantasy and experience of the American frontier, 1630–1860*, Chapel Hill, University of North Carolina Press, 1984.

Lake, Marilyn. *The Limits of Hope: Soldier settlement in Victoria, 1919–38*, Melbourne, OUP, 1987.

Lake, Marilyn & Kelly, Farley (eds). *Double Time: Women in Victoria—150 years*, Melbourne, Penguin, 1985.

Landes, David. *Revolution in Time: Clocks and the making of the modern world*, Cambridge Massachusetts, Harvard University Press, 1983.

Light, Alison. *Forever England: Femininity, literature and conservatism between the wars*, London, Routledge, 1991.

Lockridge, Kenneth. *The Diary, and Life, of William Byrd of Virginia*, Chapel Hill, University of North Carolina Press, 1987.

Lowe, Donald M. *History of Bourgeois Perception*, Chicago, University of Chicago Press, 1982.

Mallon, Thomas. *A Book of One's Own: People and their diaries*, London, Picador, Pan Books, 1985.

Macintyre, Stuart. *The Oxford History of Australia. Volume 4, 1901–1942*, Melbourne, Oxford University Press, 1986.

Mackinolty, Judy (ed.). *The Wasted Years?* Sydney, George Allen and Unwin, 1981.

Marcus, Andrew. *Governing Savages*, Sydney, Allen & Unwin, 1990.

Martin, Emily. *The Woman in the Body: A cultural analysis of reproduction*, Milton Keynes, Open University Press, 1987.

Matthews, Jill Julius. *Good and Mad Women: The historical construction of femininity in twentieth century Australia*, Sydney, Allen & Unwin, 1984.

McCalman, Janet. *Struggletown: Portrait of an Australian working class community, 1900–1965*, Melbourne, Melbourne University Press, 1984.

McQueen, Humphrey. *The Black Swan of Trespass: The emergence of modernist painting in Australia to 1944*, Sydney, Alternative Publishing Cooperative, 1979.

Modjeska, Drusilla. *Exiles at Home: Australian women writers 1925–1945*, Melbourne, Sirius Books, 1981.

—— *Poppy*, Melbourne, McPhee Gribble, 1990.

Montreith, Moira (ed.). *Women's Writing: A challenge to theory*, Brighton, Harvester Press, 1986.

Nassbaum, Felicity. *The Autobiographical Subject: Gender and ideology in eighteenth century England*, Baltimore, John Hopkins University Press, 1989.

Nicholson, Linda. *Gender and History: The limits of social theory in the age of the family*, New York, Columbia University Press, 1986.

Pateman, Carole. *The Sexual Contract*, Cambridge, Polity Press, 1988.

Perrot, Michelle (ed.). *The History of Private Life IV: From the fires of revolution to the Great War*, Cambridge Mass., Harvard University Press, 1990.

Personal Narratives Group. *Interpreting Women's Lives: Feminist theory and personal narratives*, Bloomington, Indiana University Press, 1989.

Ponsonby, Arthur. *English Diaries: A review of English diaries from the sixteenth century to the twentieth century with an introduction on diary writing*, London, Methuen, 1923.

Rabine, Leslie. *Reading the Romantic Heroine: Text, history, ideology*, Ann Arbor, University of Michigan Press, 1985.

Radway, Janice. *Reading the Romance: Women, patriarchy, and popular literature*, Chapel Hill, University of North Carolina Press, 1984.

Raymond, Janice. *A Passion for Friends: Towards a philosophy of female affection*, London, Women's Press, 1986.

Reiger, Kerreen. *The Disenchantment of the Home. Modernising the Australian Family*, Melbourne, OUP, 1985.

Rickard, John & Spearritt, Peter (eds). *Packaging the Past? Public Histories*, Melbourne, Melbourne University Press/Australian Historical Studies, 1991.

Rotenstreich, Nathan. *Time and Meaning in History*, Dordrecht, D. Reidal Publishing Co., 1987.

Russell, Penny. *'A Wish of Distinction': Colonial gentility and femininity*, Melbourne, MUP, 1994.

Ryan, Edna & Conlon, Anne. *Gentle Invaders: Australian women at work, 1788–1974*, Melbourne, Nelson, 1975.

Saunders, Kay & Evans, Raymond (eds). *Gender Relations in Australia: Denomination and negotiation*, Sydney, Harcourt, Brace Jovanovich, 1992.

Scott, Joan. *Gender and the Politics of History*, New York, Columbia University Press, 1988.

Smith, Sidone. *A Poetics of Women's Autobiography: Marginality and the fictions of self-representation*, Bloomington, Indiana University Press, 1987.

Smith-Rosenberg, Carroll. *Disorderly Conduct: Visions of gender in Victorian America*, New York, OUP, 1985.

Spearitt, Peter & Walker, David (eds). *Australian Popular Culture*, Sydney, George Allen & Unwin, 1979.

Tristram, Philippa. *Living Space in Fact and Fiction*, London, Routledge, 1989.

Vicinus, Martha. *Independent Women: Work and community for single women, 1850–1920*, London, Virago, 1985.

Weedon, Chris. *Feminist Practice and Poststructuralist Theory*, London, Basil Blackwell, 1987.

Weeks, Jeffrey. *Sex, Politics and Society: The regulation of sexuality since 1800*, (1981) London, Longman 1989.

—— *Sexuality and its Discontents*, London, Routledge & Kegan Paul, 1985.

Whitrow, G.J. *Time in History. The evolution of our general awareness of time and temporal perspective*, Oxford, OUP, 1988.

Windschuttle, Elizabeth. *Women, Class and History: Feminist perspectives on Australia 1788–1978*, Melbourne, Fontana/Collins, 1980.

Wolff, Janet, *Feminine Sentences: Essays on women and culture*, London, Polity Press, 1990.

Young, Iris Marion. *Throwing Like a Girl and Other Essays in Feminist Philosophy and Social Theory*, Bloomington, Indiana University Press, 1990.

Articles

Alexander, Sally, 'Becoming a woman in London in the 1920s and 1930s' in Feldman, David & Stedman Jones, Gareth, *Metropolis London: Histories and Representations since 1800*, London, Routledge & Kegan Paul, 1989.

Allen, Judith. '"Our deeply degraded sex' and 'The animal in man": Rose Scott, Feminism and Sexuality 1890–1925', *Australian Feminist Studies*, nos 7 & 8 (Summer 1988), pp. 65–94.

Bunkers, Suzanne L. '"Faithful Friend": Nineteenth century midwestern American women's unpublished diaries', *Women's Studies International Forum*, vol. 10, no. 1, 1987, pp. 7–17.

Chauncey, George Jr, 'From sexual inversion to homosexuality: Medicine and the changing conceptualisation of female deviance', *Salmagundi*, 58–59, Fall 1982–Winter 1983, pp. 114–46.

Conrad, Margaret, '"Sundays always makes me think of home": Time and place in Canadian women's history', in Strong-Boag, Veronica & Fellman, Anita Clair (eds). *Rethinking Canada: The promise of women's history*, Toronto, 1986.

Cooke, Simon. 'Death, body and soul: the cremation debate in NSW, 1863–1925', *Australian Historical Studies*, vol. 24, no. 97, pp. 323–39.

Cooper, Joanne E. 'Shaping Meaning: Women's diaries, journals, and letters—the old and the new', *Women's Studies International Forum*, vol. 10, no. 1, 1987, pp. 95–9.

Curthoys, Ann. 'Eugenics, feminism and birth control: The case of Marion Piddington', *Hecate*, vol. 15, no. 1, 1989, pp. 75–89.

Damousi, Joy. 'Socialist women and gendered space: The anti-conscription campaigns of 1914–1918', *Labour History*, no. 60, May 1991, pp. 1–15.

Davidoff, Leonore. 'Class and gender in Victorian England: The diaries of Arthur J. Munby and Hannah Cullwick', *Feminist Studies*, vol. 5, no. 1 (Spring 1979), pp. 87–141.

Davison, Graeme. 'Historic time and everyday time', *Australia 1888 Bulletin*, no. 7, 1981, pp. 3–9.

Duggan, Lisa. 'The trials of Alice Mitchell: Sensationalism, sexology and the lesbian subject in turn-of-the-century America', *SIGNS*, vol. 18, no. 4, 1993, pp. 791–814.

Ford, Ruth. 'Lady Friends and Sexual Deviationists: Lesbians and the law in Australia 1920s–1950s', in Diane Kirkby (ed.) *Sex, Power and Justice:*

Spaces in her day

Historical perspectives on the law in Australia 1788–1990, Melbourne, OUP, 1995 (forthcoming).

Foster, John. 'Brunning's Australian Gardener', *Meanjin*, vol. 47, no. 3 (Spring 1988), pp. 413–20.

Grosz, Elizabeth, 'Notes towards a corporeal feminism', *Australian Feminist Studies*, no. 5, Summer 1987, pp. 1–16.

Holmes, Katie. 'Relating women: Australian women diarists and their relationships, 1920s and 1930s', *Lilith: a feminist history journal* 7, 1991, pp. 86–99.

—— 'Making time: Representations of temporality in Australian women's diaries of the 1920s and 1930s', *Australian Historical Studies* vol. 26, no. 102, April 1994, pp. 1–18.

Hosking, Susan. '"I 'ad to 'ave me Garden": A perspective on Australian women gardeners', *Meanjin*, vol. 47, no. 3 (Spring 1988), pp. 439–453.

Hampsten, Elizabeth. 'Tell me all you know: Reading letters and diaries of rural women', in *Teaching Women's Literature from a Regional Perspective*, New York, Modern Language Association of America, 1982.

Huff, Cynthia. 'Chronicles of confinement: Reactions to childbirth in British Women's diaries', *Women's Studies International Forum*. vol. 10, no. 1, 1987, pp. 63–8.

Kerber, Linda K. 'Separate spheres, female worlds, woman's place: The rhetoric of women's history', *Journal of American History* 75:1, June 1988, pp. 9–39.

Kristeva, Julia. 'Women's time', *SIGNS*, vol. 7, no. 1, 1981, pp. 16–35.

Lake, Marilyn. 'Building themselves up with Aspros', *Hecate*, vol. 7, no. 2, 1981, pp. 7–19.

—— 'Female Desires: the meaning of World War Two', *Australian Historical Studies*, vol. 24, no. 95, October 1990, pp. 267–84.

—— 'Mission Impossible: How men gave birth to the Australian nation. Gender, nationalism and other seminal acts.' *Gender and History*, vol. 4, no. 3, 1992, pp. 305–22.

—— 'Sexuality and Feminism: Some notes on their Australian history', *Lilith: a feminist history journal*, no. 7, 1991, pp. 29–45.

Light, Alison, '"Returning to Manderley"—Romance, fiction, female sexuality and class', *Feminist Review*, no. 16, Summer 1984, pp. 7–25.

Lensink, Juldy Nolte. 'Expanding the boundaries of criticism: The diary as female autobiography', *Women's Studies*, vol. 14, 1987, pp. 39–53.

Martin, Sylvia 'Rethinking Passionate Friendships: the writings of Mary Fullerton', *Women's History Review*, vol. 2, no. 3, 1993, pp. 395–406.

Matthews, Jill Julius. 'Building the body beautiful', *Australian Feminist Studies*, no. 5, Summer 1987, pp. 17–34.

—— 'They had such a lot of fun: Women's League of Health and Beauty', *History Workshop*, no. 30, Autumn 1990, pp. 22–54.

Newton, Esther. 'The mythic mannish lesbian: Radclyffe Hall and the New Woman'. *SIGNS*, vol. 9, no 4 (Summer 1984), pp. 557–75.

Pumphrey, Martin. 'T he flapper, the housewife and the making of modernity', *Cultural Studies*, vol. 1, 1987, pp. 179–94.

Reekie, Gail. 'Impulsive women, predictable men: Psychological constructions of difference in sales literature to 1930', *Australian Historical Studies*, vol. 24, no. 97, October 1991, pp. 359–63.

Rich, Adrienne. 'Compulsory heterosexuality and lesbian existence' *SIGNS*, vol. 5, no. 4 (Summer 1980), pp. 631–60.

Rupp, Leila. '"Imagine My Surprise": Women's relationships in historical perspective', *Frontiers*, vol. 5, no. 3, 1981, pp. 61–70.

Russell, Cherry. 'Ageing as a feminist issue', *Women's Studies International Forum*, vol. 10, no. 2, 1987, pp. 125–32.

Sahli, Nancy. 'Smashing: Women's relationships before the fall', *Chrysalis*, no. 8 (1979), pp. 17–27.

Scott, Joan. 'The evidence of experience', in *Critical Inquiry*, 17 (Summer 1991), pp. 773–97.

Simmons, Christina. 'Companionate marriage and the lesbian threat', *Frontiers*, vol. iv, no. 3, 1979, pp. 54–9.

Smith-Rosenberg, Carroll. Review of Martha Vicinus's, *Independent Women* in *SIGNS*, vol. 13, no. 3 (Spring 1988), pp. 644–9.

Spender, Dale. 'Journal on a journal', *Women's Studies International Forum*, vol. 10, no. 1, 1987, pp. 1–5.

Stanley, Liz. 'Biography as microscope or kaleidoscope? The case of 'power' in Hannah Cullwick's relationship with Arthur Munby', *Women's Studies International Forum*, vol. 10, no. 1, 1987, pp. 19–31.

—— 'Moments of writing: Is there a feminist auto/biography?' *Gender and History*, vol. 2, no. 1 (Spring 1990), pp. 59–67.

Sterns, Peter. 'Old women: Some historical observations', in *Journal of Family History*, Spring 1980, pp. 44–57.

Thomas, Julian. 'Amy Johnson's triumph, Australia 1930', *Australian Historical Studies*, vol. 23, no. 90 (April 1988), pp. 72–84.

Thompson, E.P. 'Time, work-discipline and industrial capitalism', *Past and Present*, 38 (1967), pp. 56–97.

Vicinus, Martha. 'Distance and desire: English boarding-school friendships'. *SIGNS*, vol. 9, no. 4 (Summer 1984), pp. 600–22.

—— '"One life to stand beside me": Emotional conflicts in first-generation college women in England'. *Feminist Studies* 8, no. 3 (Fall 1982), pp. 602–28.

—— 'Sexuality and power: A review of current work in the history of sexuality'. *Feminist Studies* vol. 8, no. 1 (Spring 1982), pp. 133–56.

—— '"They wonder to which sex I belong": The historical roots of the modern lesbian identity', *Feminist Studies*, vol. 18, no. 3 (Fall 1992), pp. 468–73.

Whipp, Richard. '"A time to every purpose": an essay on time and work', in Patrick Joyce (ed). *The Historical Meanings of Work*, Cambridge, Cambridge University Press, 1987.

Unpublished theses

Foley, Meredith. 'The women's movement in NSW and Victoria, 1918–1938.' PhD Thesis, Department of History, University of Sydney, 1985.

Hoban, Anne. 'Anne Drysdale—A sense of place'. Unpublished Hons. Thesis, Department of History, LaTrobe University, 1987.
Hooley, Beryl Margaret. 'Domestic economy in Melbourne, 1890–1940'. Unpublished MA Thesis, Department of History, University of Melbourne, 1984.
Jones, Gwen. 'A lady in every sense of the word: A study of the governess in Australian colonial society'. Unpublished MA Thesis, Department of History, University of Melbourne, 1982.
McBurnie, Grant. 'Constructing sexuality in Victoria, 1930–1950: Sex reformers associated with the Victorian Eugenics Society'. Unpublished PhD Thesis, Department of History, Monash University, 1989.

Index

birth control, xix, 3, 5, 16, 70, 89, 90
Blodgett, Harriet, xvi–xvii
body *see* body functions; body image
body functions *see* menopause; menstruation; pregnancy and childbirth; sexuality
body image, xxii
  ageing body, xxiii, 18, 135–41
  beauty products, 2, 5–6, 10, 16–17, 20, 126, 138
  clothes, 18–19, 30, 53, 89, 92, 94, 126, 133
  dieting, x, 16–18
  exercise, 17–18, 57
  hair, 20
  influence of modernity, 16–17
  maternal v. youthful body, 18, 70, 74
  symbolism of cutting of hair, 1, 20, 78
  youthful concept of beauty, 5–6, 16–20, 138–9
Bordo, Susan, 17
Bull, Norma (1906–80), xxv, 68, 85–91, 93, 94, 95, 104
Bulletin, 35–6, 38, 142

Cameron, Mrs James (Roo) (1856–1936), 63–4
censorship *see under* diaries
childbirth *see* pregnancy and childbirth
children *see* motherhood
cinema, 5–6, 29, 91–5 *passim*
class, xiv, xvii, xxi–xxii, xxv–xxvi, 2, 7, 14–15, 24, 26, 50, 56, 57, 64, 67, 70, 83, 116, 125
clothing, 18–19, 30, 53, 89, 92, 94, 126, 133
Conrad, Margaret, xx
Country Women's Association (CWA), 34, 97, 144–5
courtship *see* romance
Culley, Margo, xvii

dailiness *see* diaries; domestic work
dances, 1, 3–4, 8, 10, 12–13, 34, 65, 92–4, 127
Dangar, Anne, xxii
Davison, Graeme, xx
Dawson, Ida (1879–1958), x, xiii–xxvi, xxviii, xxix, 3–5, 9, 16, 31–8, 39, 40, 59, 68, 74, 105–15, 140–3
death, 135–53 *passim*
  anticipation, 135, 136, 143, 145, 153
  funerals, 146–50 *passim*
  grief, 59–60, 145–51 *passim*
  hidden, 136, 151
  home deaths, 150–1
  lack of positive models, 136
  life rhythm, xxi, xxiii
  of children, x, 59–60, 75, 78–9, 82, 96, 98, 136, 145, 151–3
  of family and loved ones, xxviii, 106, 109–10, 114–15, 117–20, 135–6, 140–53
  rituals, 136, 146–50 *passim*
  role of doctors, 146–50 *passim*
  spiritual aspects, 135, 147–9, 152
  wills and legacies, xxvi, 35, 112, 118–19, 150
  see also ageing
Depression, xiii–xiv, xxi, 14–15, 26, 114–15, 116
diaries
  as confidant, ix, 128–34 *passim*
  as family chronicle, xiv, 115–16, 122
  as fiction, 66–7, 85–92
  as history, xvii, xxii, 153
  as permanent record, xvi, xviii, 62–3, 90, 110–11, 129, 132, 140, 143–4
  as protest, x, xii, xvii, 5, 53–4, 104
  as romance, 3, 6–14, 85–92, 127
  as tool for historical research, ix–xi, xii–xiii, xv–xvii, xxix, 124–5

employment *see* paid work
Everylady's Journal, 19, 68

Falkiner, Una (1883–1948), x, xiv, xv, xviii, xxv-xxvii *passim*, 38, 44, 48–50, 56–60, 62, 67, 73–4, 95–101, 104, 125, 145, 150, 151–3
family, xvii, 44, 105–22
 age and gender divisions, xxiv, 107, 118–19
 as source of identity, 107, 110, 111, 113
 conflicts, xvi, 15–16, 107, 115–20 *passim*
 deaths, xxviii, 106, 109–10, 114–15, 117–20, 135–6, 140–53
  of children, x, 59–60, 75, 78–9, 82, 96, 98, 136, 145, 151–3
  of parents, xxviii, 106, 109, 117–20, 140
 diary as record of activities, 110–11, 115–16, 122
 dynamics, 117–21
 economic dependence on male members, 112
 family duties v. independence, 2, 5, 32–3, 107–8, 110, 113
 finances, 26–7, 112, 115–16, 120
 illness, 105–10 *passim*, 112–17 *passim*, 120
 legacies, xxvi, 35, 112, 118–19, 150
 role in old age, 135, 140, 142, 144, 148
 single women's interface with family, 2, 32–3, 35, 105–22 *passim*, 141, 148
 see also marriage; motherhood
fantasy *see* romance
femininity
 alternative frameworks to new femininity, xviii, 21–2, 91
 flappers, 5
 good wife and mother, 70, 80–1
 good woman, xviii, 67, 68, 70, 91, 140, 141
 mature woman, 70
 meanings of 'woman', xiii
 modern girl, xxiii, 2, 5, 9–10, 22
 modern woman, xxiii
 see also ageing; body image; marriage; motherhood; pregnancy and childbirth; romance; sexuality; youth
feminism, xvi–xviii, 4, 69, 136
flappers, 5
friendship, 123–34
 all-women social occasions, xv, xviii, 15, 39, 101, 126
 between young women, 128–34
  appropriate public behaviour, 130–1
  class solidarity in diaries, 125
  jealousy, 120, 129–30
  tensions over men, 127–8
  tradition of deep friendships, 131
 couple imagery, 124, 128, 131–4 *passim*
 death of loved ones, 115, 135–6, 141–2, 145
 diaries and letters as research tools, 124–5
 female workmates, 23, 24, 29–30
 importance to single women, 126
 intimate female friendship, xxiv, 124, 131
 language of friendship, 124–5, 133–4
 married women's friendships, 101, 125–6
 role in old age, 135, 140, 142, 144, 148
 romantic women's friendship, xxviii, 124–5, 131
 supportive networks in pregnancy, 71–5
 see also lesbianism; marriage

gardens, xxii, xxvii–xxviii, 29, 34, 44, 54–60, 73
 and class, 56, 57

as basis for interpersonal
communication, 59
as boundary of domestic space,
55–8 *passim*, 60, 99
as domestic chore, 57
as public space, 55, 99, 100
as refuge, 59, 99
as source of grief, 59–60
as source of marital tensions,
58, 99–101, 104
as source of pleasure, 55–9, 109
design, 55–7
functions, 54–5, 58
gardeners, 57, 59, 99–101
health aspects, 57
influences, 55–7
plants, 57–9
see also houses
gender, xi, xiii, xviii–xxii, xxiv,
27–8, 43, 107, 118–19
Gillikin, Dure, xiii
Gilmore, Mary, 37
governessing, 2, 3, 32–5 *passim*,
37–40 *passim*, 108–13 *passim*, 141

health *see* ageing; body functions;
death; pregnancy and childbirth
Heilbrun, Carolyn, 68
Home, 19, 45, 47
home *see* domestic work; gardens;
houses
homosexuality *see* lesbianism
horse races, 34, 65, 98, 125
Hosking, Susan, 55
houses, 34, 35, 44–54, 77
as revealed in diaries, 43–4
design, 43–4, 49
home as refuge for men, xxii,
46, 68
kitchen
as place of hospitality, 43, 46,
49–50
as place of work, 43, 45–7
passim, 49
as site of labour relations
with domestic servants,
48–9

centrality of, 48–9
design, 49
function related to social
class, 50
laundry, 55
as female space, 50–1
equipment, 50
position, 44
see also domestic work; gardens
Hughes, Kathleen (1912–71), x,
xxv, xxviii, 3, 6, 10–14, 16, 18,
20, 21, 22, 40, 85–6, 91–5, 104,
124, 126–8, 131

International Conference of
Women (Hague), 123
isolation, 32, 33, 36, 81, 104, 111,
144; *see also* rural women

Kendall, Dorothy (1909–78), x, xi,
xiv, xxv, xxviii, 3, 6–9, 13–16
passim, 18–29 *passim*, 31, 33,
40–1, 107, 115–22 *passim*, 124,
128–34 *passim*
Kingston, Beverly, 107

labour *see* domestic work; paid
work
Lake, Marilyn, 6
language, xxii, xxiii, 21, 40, 99, 104
couple imagery for female
friendships, 124, 128, 131–4
passim
euphemistic usage in diaries,
11, 19, 52–3, 74, 84, 90, 101–4
for romance, 2, 3, 8, 9, 13, 40,
85–92 *passim*, 104, 127–8, 133
of friendship, 124–5, 133–4
of modernity, 16–19, 80–1
of old age, 138–9
of pregnant diarists, 71, 73, 74
see also advertising; cinema;
magazines
Lawson, W., 37
leisure *see* art; diary writing;
gardens; horse races; social
activities; tennis; travel; writing

Spaces in her day

calculation of arrival dates,
71–4 *passim*
decline in birth rate, 70, 79
emphasis on self-care, 70–1
experience of pregnancy, xxvii,
71, 72
home v. hospital births, 74
hysterectomy, 75
idealisation, 72, 79
influence of infant and
maternal welfare movement,
69, 73, 79, 82
labour, 72–4, 77
language, 71, 73, 74
maternal body, 18, 70, 74
medicalisation, 67–8, 71, 139
miscarriages, 53, 72, 74–5
personal supportive networks,
71, 73–5 *passim*
pregnancy advice, 70–1, 74
risks, 74, 75
silence on women's troubles, 74
women's knowledge, 71, 151
see also motherhood
public/private dichotomy, xiii,
39–40, 43, 53, 55, 62, 64, 75, 99
ideology of separate spheres,
xvii, xxi–xxii, 31, 40, 46, 68, 82

Red Cross, 144
Reiger, Kerreen, 79–80
relationships *see* family;
friendship; marriage; romance
religion, xv, xvi, xxviii–xxix, 21,
31, 38, 103, 135, 145–53 *passim*
representation *see* advertising;
body image; cinema;
femininity; magazines and
newspapers; modernity
romance, 1–22, 84–95
and marriage, 5, 6, 14–15,
17–18, 85, 87, 91, 92, 104
as discovery of sexual passion,
85–92
class indifferent, 7, 15
conflict with marriage and paid
work, 85, 87, 91

diary as romance, 3, 6–14,
85–94, 127
diary as sexual fantasy, 85–92,
95
etiquette, 7–10
falling in love, 13–14, 16, 22,
92–3
fantasies, xxviii, 6–9, 15–16, 22,
27–9 *passim*, 120
finding the right man, 14, 92, 93
flirting, 3–4, 12–13
frictions in relationships, 93–4,
127–8
influence of art, 85–92
influence of cinema, 5–6, 91–5
jealousy, 12–13, 93–4
language of romance, 2, 3, 8, 9,
13, 40, 85–92 *passim*, 104,
127–8, 133
priority over career, 10, 25, 29,
40, 85, 87, 91
relationships with men, 85–95,
101–4
social context, 14–15
stories in women's magazines,
14
unrealised dreams, x, xviii, 6–9,
13, 16, 18–20, 22, 26–7, 41
youthful liaisons, x, xxviii, 2–3,
10–14, 85–95
see also friendship; marriage;
sexuality; youth
Ross, Mabel (1873–1957?), 4, 65–6,
74, 81–2
Rowe, Cecil (1854–1925), xxv, 68,
145–50
rural women, xxvi–xxvii, 42–3,
45–6, 53–4, 61–4

servants *see* domestic servants
sexuality, xxix, 84–95
construction of self as object of
male desire, xxiii, 3, 10–14
passim, 20, 92–4 *passim*
contemporary discussions, x, 85
diary as sexual fantasy, 85–92,
95

femininity as youth and
  desirability, 5–6, 70
language for desire, 3, 9, 13,
  85–92 *passim*, 104, 133
representation of women as
  sexualised objects, 5–6
sexological literature, 17, 89–91,
  124, 133–4
see also lesbianism; romance
single women, x, xxvi, xxix,
  23–40 *passim*
and femininity, 68, 79
effect of ageing, 83
family as source of identity,
  107, 110, 113
family duties v. independence,
  2, 5, 32–3, 107–8, 110, 113
financial insecurity, 34–5, 37
ill-health, 140
importance of friendship, 126
relationship with family, 2,
  32–3, 35, 105–22 *passim*, 141,
  148
social activities, 126
supportive of family, 2, 32–3,
  105–10 *passim*, 112, 113, 115,
  116, 121, 141
work, 34, 39–40
see also youth
Smith-Rosenberg, Carroll, 124
social activities, xv, xviii, 15,
  27–30 *passim*, 34, 37, 39, 43, 46,
  49–50, 54, 60, 97, 101, 126, 132,
  143, 144–5; *see also* dances;
  leisure
space, xi–xii, xix–xxiv *passim*, 17,
  56–7; *see* also gardens; houses
spinsters *see* single women
Stock and Station Journal, 4, 35
Stopes, Marie, 17, 89–91
Strongman, Margaret (1910–78),
  xxv, 20–2, 29–31, 33, 40, 66–7,
  72–3, 126

Tait, Winifred (1877–1968), xxv,
  xxviii–xxix, 38–40, 68, 79, 123,
  135, 145

teaching, xxvi, xxix, 31–2, 34, 35,
  38–40, 107–8; *see also*
  governessing
tennis, 1, 21, 78, 127
Thomas, Mallon, xv
Thompson, E. P., xix
Thwaites, Frederick, 139
time, xix–xxxiii *passim*, 143–4
biological, xx–xxi, xxiii, 18, 43,
  52–3, 67–8, 73, 75–6, 136, 143
diary, ix, xviii–xxiv *passim*
domestic, xxi, 28, 43–4, 46–7,
  49, 51–3, 75, 79
historian's, xxii–xxiii
industrial, xix, xxi, 28, 44, 51–3,
  67–8, 75, 79, 136
linear, xix, xx, 22, 52, 73, 76,
  132, 136, 143
seasonal, 61–4
travel, x, xxvi, 21, 31–3 *passim*,
  36–8 *passim*, 105, 108–12 *passim*

Vicinus, Martha, 124

Wallace, Dr, 49
Walling, Edna, 56
war, 81, 142
death of sons, 78–9, 145, 151,
  152
social effects, xxi-xxii, 2, 14–15,
  45, 76, 112, 116
weddings *see* marriage
Woman's World, 25, 47, 49, 50–1,
  61, 68–9, 72, 80, 144
Woolf, Virginia, xi, 37, 38, 124
work *see* domestic work; paid
  work
writing, xxvi, 142
as source of income for diarist,
  111–12
autobiography, xvii, 85
children's literature, 38, 97
diaries and letters as research
  tools, 4–5, 90, 91, 109–11
  passim, 123–5 *passim*
essays and diaries on women's
  friendships, 124

ghosting, 37
letters, xvii, 109, 110, 111,
   123–5, 128, 150
literary explorations of passion,
   85–92
literary self-representation,
   xvii–xviii
on ageing, 139
sexological literature, 17, 89–91,
   124, 133–4
short stories, 32, 79, 136–7
women writers, xxiii, 2–3, 5–6,
   7, 15, 32, 35–8, 70

youth, 139
   as stage of life and as
      construct, 2
   debates on young women, 2, 5,
      9–10
   flappers, 5
   modern girl, xxiii, 2, 5, 9–10, 22
   new femininity, 1–22
   see also body image; femininity;
      friendship; paid work;
      romance; sexuality

LANGUAGE AND STYLE SERIES

General Editor: STEPHEN ULLMANN

IX

THE LANGUAGE OF TENNYSON'S

IN MEMORIAM